KEATING, Rex. Nubian rescue. Hawthorn, 1975. 269p il map bibl. 12.50. ISBN 0-8015-5469-1

Precipitated by the building of Egypt's High Dam at Aswūn, the UNESCO salvage operations in Nubia (1960–69), themselves and their findings, are discussed in an interesting and useful manner by a broadcast journalist, author of radio documentaries and articles. Keating's style combines travelogue in picturesque descriptions of the landscape with historical texts, both quoted and retold with all the imagination of a storyteller. No novice in the matters about which he writes, the author has benefited from many years of personal friendship with recognized authorities whose reputations, at least in part, have been built around their work in Nubia. More important, he has done his homework, reflected in accurate information and in a substantive bibliography that constitutes the searchings of one who is more than popularly oriented. The book, whose view is essentially from prehistoric to Christian times in Sudanese Nubia, is enhanced by a chronological table, a useful summarizing chapter, carefully selected photographs, and thoughtful line-drawings. Not written for scholars, the book is nevertheless informative and deserves a place in public and undergraduate academic libraries.

NUBIAN RESCUE

Rex Keating is a writer, broadcaster, lecturer and photographer, who has been involved with Middle Eastern archaeology, in particular Egyptology, for over thirty years. From 1936–1945 he was in charge of the European Division of Egyptian State Broadcasting and it was during this period that he arranged the world-wide broadcast of Tutankhamun's Trumpets, thereby attracting the accusation of his being responsible for the outbreak of the Second World War a few months later. After the War, during which he was a war correspondent in the Middle Eastern area, he moved to Palestine as Deputy Director of the Palestine Broadcasting Service for the last three years of the Mandate. Thereafter he joined the Near East Arab Broadcasting Station in Cyprus, leaving it after three years to set up and direct the Cyprus Broadcasting Service. After a brief spell in Independent Television News in 1955, he joined the UNESCO Secretariat in Paris where he remained until his recent retirement. In the course of his UNESCO duties he travelled widely and in 1960 became deeply involved in the Nubian Campaign by reason of his archaeological connections with the region. Over the succeeding nine years of the Campaign he wrote many radio documentaries and articles as the Campaign progressed, together with a film, *Land of Kush* and a book, *Nubian Twilight*.

Also by Rex Keating

NUBIAN TWILIGHT

Nubian Rescue

Rex Keating

ROBERT HALE & COMPANY · LONDON
HAWTHORN BOOKS, INC · NEW YORK

First Published in Great Britain and the United States 1975

ISBN 0 7091 4720 1 – British
ISBN 0 8015 5469 1 – American

Robert Hale & Company
Clerkenwell House
Clerkenwell Green
London EC1R 0HT

Hawthorn Books, Inc.
260 Madison Avenue
New York, N.Y. 10016

Computer Typeset by
Print Origination, Bootle, Merseyside
and printed and bound in Great Britain by
Redwood Burn Limited, Trowbridge & Esher

CONTENTS

ILLUSTRATIONS

PHOTOGRAPHIC CREDITS

The following photographs were taken by the author: Plates 1, 3, 4, 5, 8, 9, 10, 11, 12, 15, 16, 20, 21, 22, 25, 28, 32, 33, 34, 35, 36, 37, 38, 39, 40, 46, 47, 48, 49, 50, 53, 54, 55, 56, 57, 58.
The remaining photographs were supplied by the following: Cairo Museum (Plate 30); French Archaeological Mission (Plates 18, 19, 23, 24, 26, 29, 41, 42, 51, 52); *Illustrated London News* (Plate 31); Nördstrom (Plate 7); Scandinavian Joint Expedition (Plates 6, 13, 14, 43, 44, 45); UNESCO/Nonadovic (Plate 2) and UNESCO/Sudan Government Aerial Survey (Plates 17, 27).

FIGURES IN THE TEXT

TO LIZ

ACKNOWLEDGEMENTS

I am indebted to Professor W. Y. Adams, Professor T. Säve-Söderbergh and Professor Jean Vercoutter for their most generous help in making available unpublished material, reading the manuscript and offering suggestions that enhanced considerably the historical perspectives of this volume. Others who gave unfailing friendship and advice during my visits to Nubia were the late Professor W. B. Emery and Mrs Emery, Tony and Lesley Mills of the UNESCO Group in Sudanese Nubia; Thabit Hassan Thabit, formerly Commissioner for Archaeology in the Sudan, and his successor, Nigmed Din Mohammed Sherif; Dr Louis Christophe of the UNESCO Nubian Unit, for whom no request is too much trouble; Dr H. J. Plenderleith, who initiated me into the mysteries of temple conservation, and Dr F. Hinkel who demonstrated the art of moving them; the late Professor Jaroslav Cerný, whose profound scholarship was always at my disposal; H. A. Nordström and J. Knudstad, both of the UNESCO team working in Sudanese Nubia; Signora Michela Schiff-Giorgini and C. Robichon, whose findings at Solb so fired my imagination; Mme Christiane Desroches-Noblecourt, Professor P. L. Shiner, Dr Labib Habachi and Dr Dows-Dunham; and all those others, prehistorians and classical scholars alike, who submitted to my questioning and gave freely of their knowledge.

I am indebted, too, to colleagues and friends in the UNESCO Secretariat for their help and encouragement, and the authorities of the Sudan and Egyptian Governments.

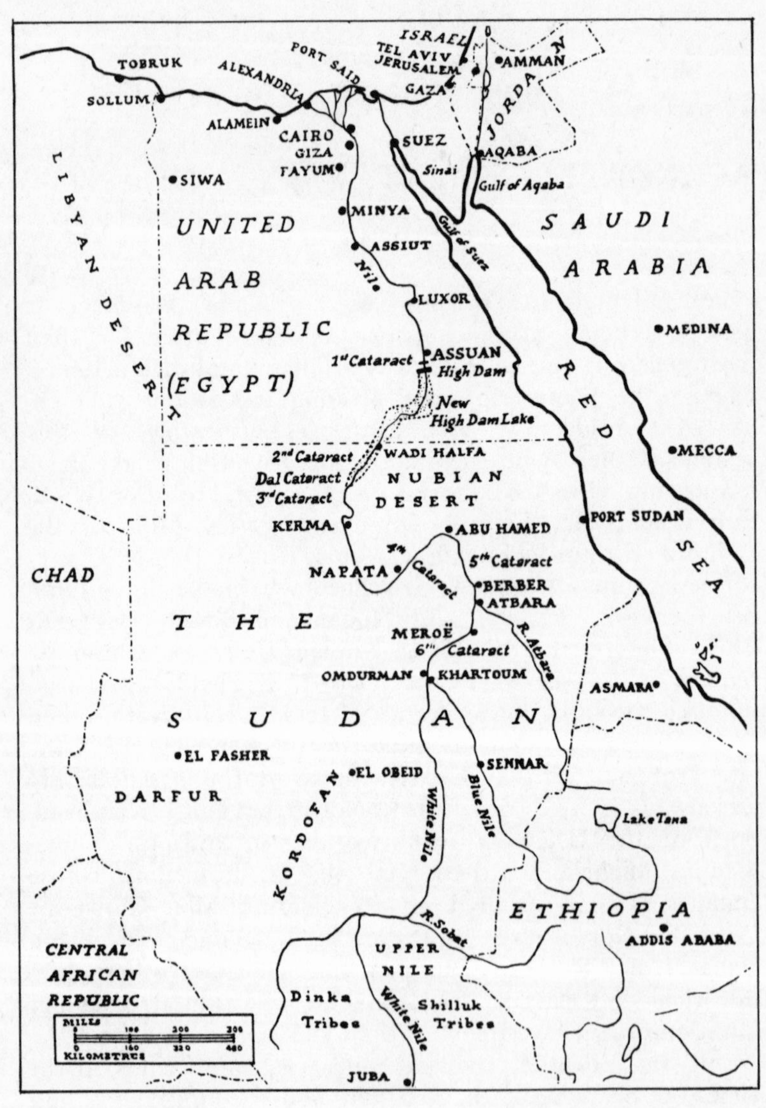
ISRAEL
TEL AVIV
JERUSALEM
AMMAN
JORDAN
PORT SAID
TOBRUK
ALEXANDRIA
SOLLUM
GAZA
ALAMEIN
CAIRO
GIZA
FAYUM
SUEZ
AQABA
Sinai
Gulf of Aqaba
LIBYAN DESERT
SIWA
MINYA
UNITED
ARAB
REPUBLIC
(EGYPT)
SAUDI
ARABIA
ASSIUT
Gulf of Suez
Nile
LUXOR
MEDINA
1st Cataract
ASSUAN
High Dam
RED SEA
New
High Dam Lake
MECCA
2nd Cataract
WADI HALFA
Dal Cataract
NUBIAN
3rd Cataract
DESERT
KERMA
PORT SUDAN
ABU HAMED
4th Cataract
5th Cataract
CHAD
NAPATA
BERBER
ATBARA
THE
MEROË
R. Atbara
6th Cataract
OMDURMAN
KHARTOUM
ASMARA
SUDAN
EL FASHER
SENNAR
EL OBEID
DARFUR
White Nile
Blue Nile
Lake Tana
KORDOFAN
ETHIOPIA
R. Sobat
ADDIS ABABA
CENTRAL
AFRICAN
REPUBLIC
UPPER
NILE
Dinka
Tribes
White Nile
Shilluk
Tribes
MILES
0
100
200
300
0
160
320
480
KILOMETRES
JUBA

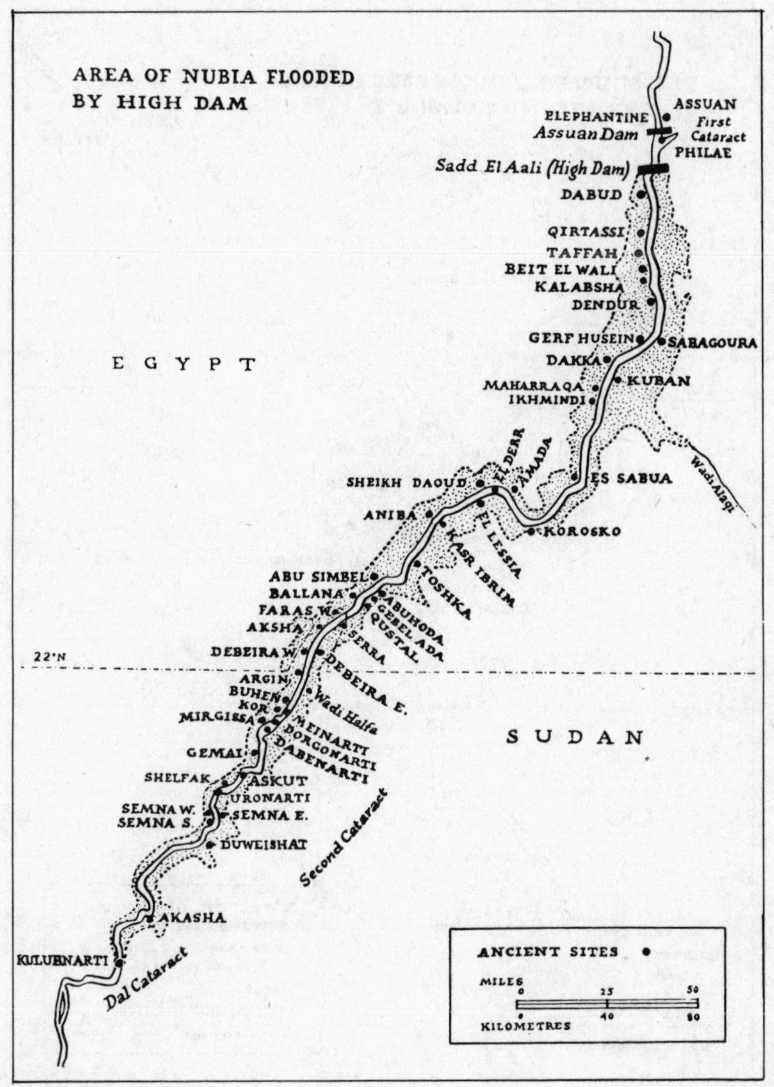
AREA OF NUBIA FLOODED
BY HIGH DAM
ASSUAN
ELEPHANTINE
First
Cataract
Assuan Dam
PHILAE
Sadd El Aali (High Dam)
DABUD
QIRTASSI
TAFFAH
BEIT EL WALI
KALABSHA
DENDUR
GERF HUSEIN
SABAGOURA
DAKKA
KUBAN
MAHARRAQA
IKHMINDI
EGYPT
EL DERR
AMADA
ES SABUA
Wadi Alaqi
SHEIKH DAOUD
ANIBA
EL LESSIA
KOROSKO
KASR IBRIM
TOSHKA
ABU SIMBEL
BALLANA
FARAS W.
ABUHODA
GEBEL ADA
QUSTAL
AKSHA
SERRA
22°N
DEBEIRA W.
DEBEIRA E.
ARGIN
BUHEN
KOR
Wadi Halfa
MIRGISSA
MEINARTI
DORGONARTI
DABENARTI
SUDAN
GEMAI
SHELFAK
ASKUT
URONARTI
SEMNA W.
SEMNA S.
SEMNA E.
DUWEISHAT
Second Cataract
AKASHA
KULUBNARTI
Dal Cataract
ANCIENT SITES
MILES
0
25
50
0
40
80
KILOMETRES

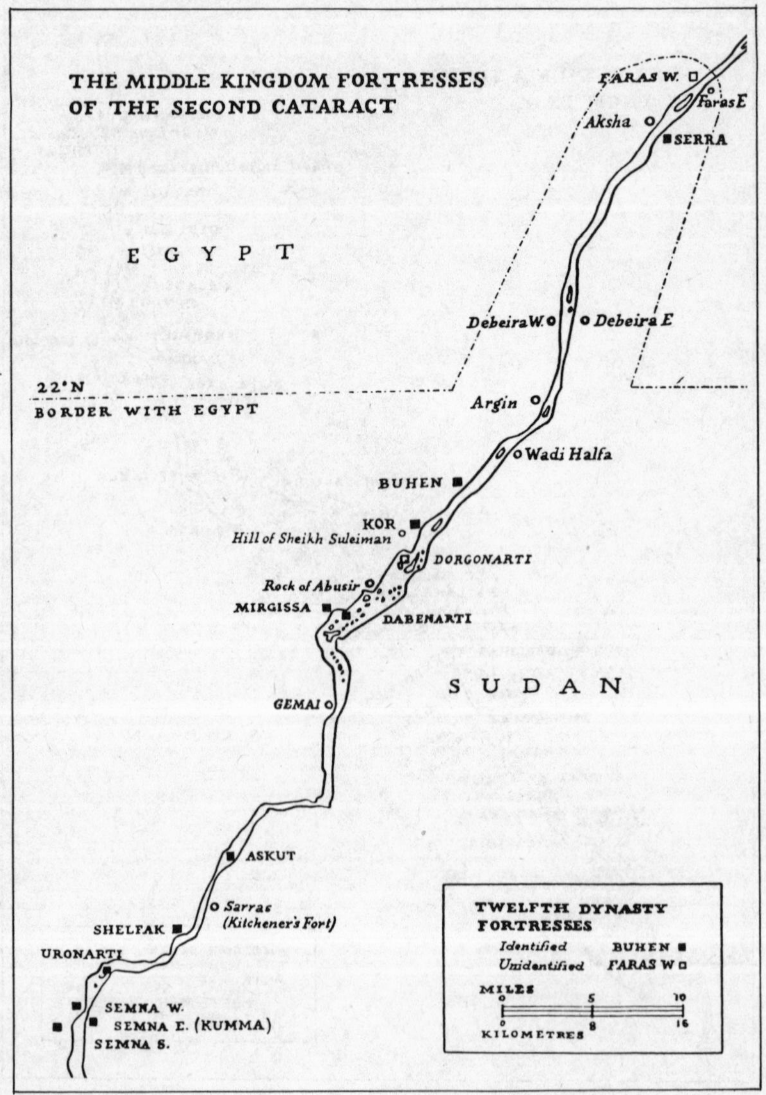
THE MIDDLE KINGDOM FORTRESSES
OF THE SECOND CATARACT
EGYPT
SUDAN
22°N
BORDER WITH EGYPT
FARAS W.
Faras E
Aksha
SERRA
Debeira W.
Debeira E
Argin
Wadi Halfa
BUHEN
KOR
Hill of Sheikh Suleiman
DORGONARTI
Rock of Abusir
MIRGISSA
DABENARTI
GEMAI
ASKUT
Sarras
(Kitchener's Fort)
SHELFAK
URONARTI
SEMNA W.
SEMNA E. (KUMMA)
SEMNA S.
TWELFTH DYNASTY
FORTRESSES
Identified
BUHEN
Unidentified
FARAS W
MILES
0
5
10
0
8
16
KILOMETRES

CHAPTER 1

Rescue without Precedent

A river threads its way across three hundred miles of waterless desert bordered by a strip of cultivation never more than a few hundred yards wide. Along its banks 100,000 people coax some sort of a living from soil on which rain never falls. Such is, or was, Nubia, and it is a description undeniably accurate but about as near the truth as to describe a beautiful woman as a bony framework clothed in tissue. That three hundred miles of river was a reach of the legendary Nile and wherever a cataract broke the placidity of its majestic course the resulting beauty would have moved Coleridge to ecstasies. Moreover the cultivation along its banks concealed relics of man's past in such profusion as to constitute a seemingly endless ribbon of museum. As for the Nubians who lived in this watery, antique landscape, they could claim, although it would never occur to them to do so, descent from the hunters who roamed across the valley long before civilisation drew men into settled communities. Nubia, astride a great cultural artery of the world–the Nile–was unique, something to be treasured. Why then did it have to be destroyed and its people dispersed? Fecundity was the cause of its destruction, human fecundity, but not, ironically, of the Nubians themselves. They and their land were victim to the upsurge of population in Egypt, the northern neighbour.

As the century advances we are likely to witness the extinction of many more Nubias, as population pressures build up across the world. For so much of his short history was homo sapiens the victim of natural forces beyond his control but now, when the "subjugation" of his natural environment is within reach, he seems hell-bent on its destruction. Pollution of land, water and air has become a melancholy area of debate with which we are increasingly familiar but there is less awareness, because it is more subtle, of a form of pollution which is not so easily seen for what it is and which is affecting the human psyche as profoundly as the physiological damage done to us by the pollutants of industry. Cultural pollution is inevitable among societies devoted to the pursuit of material gain and scant heed is paid by those who claim to act in the name of progress to the handiwork of our forebears that has somehow survived the attentions of man and nature. Consequently old buildings and other remains are terribly vulnerable for, apart from the rarity value of some which is marketable, their appeal is to the intellect and to the senses. Instinctively our forebears, certainly men of the ancient world, built for eternity or at the very least for posterity since they had little reason to doubt the permanence of their institutions. Hence the splendid temples and the public buildings that have come down to us. The built-in obsolescence imposed on us by contemporary purveyors of buildings and merchandise is a concept unimaginable to the architects and craftsmen of not so long ago.

The lengths to which a country is prepared to go to protect and conserve the remains of its past is a measure of the extent to which its people are able to rise above the prevailing climate of materialism. Meanwhile with every year that passes, the ways in which ancient sites and monuments are menaced by public and private works proliferate. Several years ago UNESCO (United Nations Educational, Scientific and Cultural Organisation) convened in Paris a meeting of interested states to discuss the drawing up of international regulations for the protection of cultural property, and on that occasion a list was prepared which placed on record the principal offenders. First among them, and the most spectacular, is dam construction for irrigation or flood control and the generating of hydroelectric power. A dam can be particularly destructive because of the huge areas of land it may ultimately engulf with its reservoir. A dramatic example is the new Assuan Dam which has created a reservoir that covers 5000 square kilometres of Egypt and the Sudan. Scarcely smaller are the Kariba and Volta Dams in Africa and the Gandhi Dam in India, and shortly the Syrians will be damming the upper reaches of the Euphrates River and in so doing will obliterate whole pages of man's history in the form of monuments, town-sites, settlements and cemeteries. In America, the Missouri River drainage plan has submerged all the known sites of five major prehistoric cultures. The list is endless. Hundreds of dams have been built across the world over the last half century. Occasionally the mass media will report on unfortunate side-effects of a new dam but when they do, attention usually focuses on the harm done by the reservoir and seldom do we hear of the subsidiary works which can be equally destructive to ancient sites and free standing monuments. The network of access roads, for example, and the camps to house construction workers, which in the case of a major dam can reach the proportions of a township. And if the dam is one that uses earth and rock fill, then hundreds of thousands of tons of these materials must be excavated from the nearest source, and should this happen to contain an ancient town site or prehistoric settlement, the bulldozers will take care of it.

Fortunately, there are signs that people are becoming increasingly exasperated by the mindlessness of industries and institutions which regard reminders of our forefathers' presence on earth as obstacles to 'progress' and as such to be eradicated. Produce more, consume more, and to the devil with cultural consequences! Moreover, having learned nothing from the rape of its own environment, the developed world cajoles the Third World to do likewise. "Industralise" says the siren voice, "for there is no other road to prosperity and the good things of life". And the under-developed world—two-thirds of mankind—is falling for it. For most of them the "good things of life" mean little more than one guaranteed square meal a day for a man and his family and an old age that stops short of actual misery. Yet these are the very countries which gave birth to so many of the great monuments of the past. Scattered and remote, often smothered in sand or jungle, they are poignant reminders of a time when beauty, often splendour, were naturally the handmaidens of utility, when artists and craftsmen worked in harmony with nature, drawing on natural forms for inspiration, so that still today their handiwork can beguile our senses and the destruction of any one of their creations can arouse feelings of personal reproach. Yet destroyed they are as more and more of the earth's surface is 'subdued'.

However, it must be admitted that financial gain is not always the motive. What, for example, should the government of an underprivileged nation do if faced by the choice, say, of building a technical institute or health centre or of preserving a crumbling temple? Egypt and the Sudan were confronted by just a dilemma when in 1955 the decision was taken to build a High Dam at Assuan. To rescue the many temples and other ancient structures standing along the three hundred-mile length of the river Nile which would be transformed into a lake, not to mention the scores of sites below ground, was a task far beyond the resources of the two countries concerned. They turned to the world for help and their appeal was destined to establish the new and wholly admirable principle that great monuments of the past should not be the exclusive property of any one country but were the heritage of all mankind. From this followed acceptance that the comity of nations should shoulder at least part of the financial burden of their preservation.

What forced Egypt to build a new dam knowing that an unavoidable result would be the destruction of Nubia? The decision was Egypt's; the Sudan's only concern in the affair was to protect its rights in the use of the Nile waters and to obtain adequate compensation for the loss of a hundred miles of territory which the new Egyptian reservoir would inundate. The Nile, generous in its bounty, nevertheless is a temperamental river and always it has been the dream of every Egyptian to tame the Nile by somehow conserving the abundant water of the good years against the inevitable lean years when the inundation would fail to rise. To the earliest Egyptians the Nile rose somewhere in the Land of Ghosts, the dreaded abode of the dead. Why its waters should rise in the hottest month of summer, continue in flood for a hundred days and then subside, they had no means of knowing.

Quite simply, they were grateful for its bounty and their gratitude was reflected in religious observances and customs, even to our day. Until very recently the arrival of the inundation at Cairo was the occasion for a public holiday and the launching of a procession of decorated boats filled with singing people who would cast garlands of flowers into the brown flood as a thanks-offering to the river. However reverence for the Nile did not deter the ancient Egyptians in their attempts to tame it. Within the limits of their technology they accomplished wonders in irrigation works. An example is the canal they dug from Middle Egypt to the Fayum Oasis west of modern Cairo, where it emptied into a lake, Moeris, which thus became a flood regulator. This canal, the Bahr el Yussuf dug around 2000 BC, is in use to this day. However, Egypt had to endure the vagaries of the Nile until the Industrial Revolution brought engineers and their machines from Europe to build flood barrages and plan a modernised system of irrigation canals that was to bring new prosperity to the ancient land. The first such barrage, the Mohammed Ali Barrage north of Cairo, was built in 1842. It was one of a series that culminated in the construction of a dam at Assuan by British engineers, completed in 1902. There, at the ancient frontier between Egypt and Nubia a granite barrage 130 feet high brought into being a reservoir which flooded a large part of Lower Nubia for about half the year. The flooded area was extended with the subsequent raising of the dam in 1912 and again in 1934 when the dam reached its maximum possible height. The builders of the dam had the foresight to include in the estimates a sum of money sufficient to protect, at least partially, the many stone temples which would be affected by the rise and fall of the water level in the reservoir. That those ancient buildings successfully resisted so many years of submersion is a tribute to the excellence of the protective measures taken in the early 1900s, measures which made it possible for the architects and civil engineers of half a century later to rescue these relics of the past by removing them bodily beyond reach of the waters.

To conserve the Nile flood and thus increase the country's prosperity by making available more irrigated land for cultivation had been the motive behind a century of increasingly ambitious hydrological works, but already in the 1930s a new threat to Egypt's well-being was discernible. At the turn of the century when work began on the Assuan Dam Egypt's population stood at around ten millions, a figure roughly comparable with that of pharaonic Egypt. At the final heightening of the dam in 1934, the population had risen to 16 millions, a figure within the limits, although only just, of the country's food resources. Then came the Second World War and with it the introduction of the new life-saving drugs—penicillin and the sulphonamides. The result was a dramatic fall in infant mortality which in 1945 had been as high as 168 per 1000 births, and it was coupled with an increased expectation of life. This was, of course, a pattern repeated elsewhere in the underprivileged world, but for Egypt with few mineral resources and dependent for her very existence on the climatic vagaries of the distant highlands of Central Africa and Ethiopia, the outlook was bleak indeed. By 1961 the population had jumped to close on 28 millions and estimates showed that within twenty years Egypt would be struggling to support 40 million persons. By 1960, the "land of plenty", long an exporter of corn, fat and vegetables had become an importer of all those commodities. Attempts to control Egypt's burgeoning population had met with scant success and now there was the spectre of 20 million additional mouths to feed in the next twenty years. Only the creation of a new storage reservoir of far greater capacity would make possible the reclamation of more land desperately needed for food and the introduction of a new source of power for industry. Against those sombre statistics, the political manoeuvrings of the 1950s involving the USSR, the USA and Egypt which resulted in the USSR agreeing to build a new, high dam to supplant the old Assuan Dam, are seen in perspective. The decision to build the High Dam was basically humanitarian, not political as has been so often represented.

The High Assuan Dam is keyed into a granite outcrop of the Nile Valley known as the First Cataract. To build it, some 30,000 men laboured round the clock for five years in one of the fiercest summer climates on earth. It stands 360 feet high and the road on its crest is 2¼ miles long. Incidentally, someone with a taste for irrelevancies has calculated that the volume of the dam is 17 times that of the Great Pyramid. The generating capacity of its 12 turbines is in excess of Egypt's foreseeable needs for years to come. The reservoir behind the dam (known as Lake Nasser) is long and narrow, covering an area of three thousand square miles and extending across two hundred miles of Egyptian territory and a hundred miles over the border into the Sudan, and it will bring two million more acres of land under cultivation. Unquestionably the benefits are great, but it must be said that the building of the High Dam is the first example of large-scale interference with a major river system and the adverse effects on the environment will become the subject of study by ecologists the world over. However, that is a subject outside the scope of this book.

In the face of the overwhelming advantages to Egypt in purely human terms, what chance did 100,000 Nubians and a collection of weathered monuments have? Nubia had to be sacrificed and its people moved elsewhere. The question was how best to save the maximum possible number of its ancient remains? The 'open air museum' of Nubia was known to contain some twenty stone temples and shrines, at least a dozen fortresses of mud brick, several town sites, around thirty churches dating from the early years of Christianity and dozens of tombs; but archaeologists who knew the area were convinced that the alluvium deposits lining the Nile's banks must conceal hundreds of sites hitherto unsuspected—and time proved them to be right.

Here was an archaeological rescue operation on an unprecedented scale and the two Governments involved, while concerned to do the right thing, had to admit that the magnitude of the task and the probable cost were beyond them. So it was that in 1955 UNESCO was asked to find a solution. Within a few months the Egyptians with UNESCO's help had organised the Documentation and Study Centre for the History of the Art and Civilisation of Ancient Egypt, and both Centre and the Egyptian Antiquities Service were instructed to concentrate their efforts on surveying, copying and photographing all threatened monuments and sites which lay within the Egyptian stretch of Nubia, UNESCO arranging for the French Institut Géographique National to carry out a photogrammetric survey of this area for the preparation of essential maps. These were admirable activities but far short of the effort needed. In 1959 UNESCO took the first major step by calling together a group of leading authorities in various fields of archaeology and architecture to make recommendations. This committee of thirteen was drawn from eight countries and it had to consider how the excavations should be handled, how the monuments could be removed to safety or possibly, preserved *in situ*, what the work would cost and any other measures that might be found necessary. First, the group visited Nubia to go over the ground and then met in Cairo where the United Arab Republic's Minister of Culture announced that his government would cede to foreign excavators the half of all finds made during excavation, excepting only those considered unique or essential to Egypt's national collections. Moreover any country sending an archaeological expedition to Nubia would be authorised to dig in Egypt itself—this was an important concession since foreign excavation in Egypt had been virtually at a standstill for years. Finally Egypt would be prepared to allow the transfer abroad of certain Nubian temples, and various antiquities from the State reserves. The Government of the Sudan offered similar concessions.

The report submitted by the committee revealed for the first time the true dimensions of the undertaking, making plain that only assistance and cooperation on a world scale could carry it through. On 8th March 1960 UNESCO's Director General, Dr Vittorino Veronese, launched the appeal which set in motion over the succeeding years a chain of events that in many countries was to modify official attitudes towards what had come to be vaguely categorised as "man's cultural heritage". Without doubt it was the object lesson of the Nubian Campaign that caused many nations to join in the formation of the International Committee for the Preservation of Cultural Property Endangered by Public and Private Works, a somewhat daunting title for a body that may be expected to exert increasing influence as cultural pollution gathers momentum.

The text of Vittorino Veronese's appeal is given here in full:

Work has begun on the great Assuan dam. Within five years the Middle Valley of the Nile will be turned into a vast lake. Wondrous structures, ranking among the most magnificent on earth, are in danger of disappearing beneath the waters. The dam will bring fertility to huge stretches of desert, but the opening up of new fields to the tractors and the provision of new sources of power to future factories, threatens to exact a terrible price.

True, when the welfare of suffering human beings is at stake, then if need be, images of granite and porphyry must be sacrificed unhesitatingly. But no one forced to make such a choice could contemplate without anguish the necessity for making it.

It is not easy to choose between a heritage of the past and the present well-being of a people, living in need in the shadow of one of history's most splendid legacies; it is not easy to choose between temples and crops. I would be sorry for any man called on to make that choice who could do so without a feeling of despair. I would be sorry for any man who, whatever decision he might reach, could bear the responsibility for that decision without a feeling of remorse.

It is not surprising, therefore, that the governments of the United Arab Republic and Sudan have called on an international body, on UNESCO, to try to save the threatened monuments. These monuments, whose loss may be tragically near, do not belong solely to the countries who hold them in trust. The whole world has the right to see them endure. They are part of a common heritage which comprises Socrates' message and the Ajanta frescoes, the walls of Uxmal and Beethoven's symphonies. Treasures of universal value are entitled to universal protection. When a thing of beauty, whose loveliness increases rather than diminishes by being shared, is lost, then all men alike are the losers.

Moreover, it is not merely a question of preserving something which may otherwise be lost. It is a question of bringing to light an as yet undiscovered wealth for the benefit of all. In return for the help the world gives them, the governments of Cairo and Khartoum will open the whole of their countries to archaeological excavation and will allow half of whatever works of art may be unearthed by science or by hazard to go to foreign museums. They will even agree to the transport, stone by stone, of certain monuments of Nubia.

A new era of magnificent enrichment is thus opened in the field of Egyptology. Instead of a world deprived of a part of its wonders, mankind may hope for the revelation of hitherto unknown marvels.

So noble a cause deserves a no less generous response. It is, therefore, with every confidence that I invite governments, institutions, public or private foundations and men of goodwill everywhere to contribute to the success of a task without parallel in history. Services, equipment and money are all needed. There are innumerable ways in which all can help. It is fitting that from a land which throughout the centuries has been the scene of—or the stake in—so many covetous disputes should spring a convincing proof of international solidarity.

> "Egypt is the gift of the Nile." For countless students this was the first Greek phrase which they learnt to translate. May the peoples of the world unite to ensure that the Nile, in becoming a greater source of fertility and power, does not bury beneath its waters marvels which we of today have inherited from generations long since vanished.

Dr Veronese's successor, René Maheu, supported the Nubian Campaign with equal enthusiasm and carried it through to its successful conclusion.

UNESCO's first concern was the formation of a permanent committee which would meet regularly to examine difficulties as they arose and recommend solutions. Committees are notoriously ineffective and often exasperating but the quality and standing of those serving on the Nubian Executive Committee, and on the two consultative committees of the United Arab Republic and the Sudan, respectively, scholars such as the late Professor W. B. Emery of London University, Professor T. Säve-Söderbergh of Uppsala, Mme Desroches-Noblecourt of the Louvre Museum, Professor John Otis Brew of the Peabody Museum, Harvard and Professor Jean Vercoutter of Lille, to name only a few, ensured the formulation of policies that over the years were to bring the Nubian Campaign to a triumphant conclusion. The Executive Committee is still in being but its efforts nowadays are directed towards the saving of the monuments of Philae, also threatened by the rise and fall of the Nile but downstream of the High Dam.

UNESCO had now embarked on the most spectacular and, as events proved, the most successful of the many projects undertaken since its foundation in 1946. For the members of the Secretariat who were involved it was an odd experience. They were starting from a platform of total inexperience in a field that was the province of scholars, a body of men reputedly impatient of official procedures; even more alarming, they had no precedents on which to draw and that is a situation which civil servants and especially international ones will go to any lengths to avoid. Yet somehow the Nubian Campaign was different; it became a challenge which aroused quite remarkable enthusiasm inside the Secretariat. Quickly a Nubian Unit was formed in Paris headed at first by a Dutchman, Van der Hagen and subsequently by a very able Italian, Ali Vrioni. A professional archaeologist, Louis Christophe, was stationed in Cairo to handle day to day problems there, while in the Sudan, W. Y. Adams, an American archaeologist, had since 1959, been attached to the Antiquities Department of that country to assist in organising an archaeological survey in preparation for the excavations to follow.

With little difficulty intellectual and artistic circles were persuaded to support the campaign and the role played by leading figures from many walks of life in serving on committees organised in many countries became vital, especially in the collection of funds.

Soon it became evident that the campaign would naturally follow two divergent paths: excavation and conservation, with scholarship and historical investigation on the one hand and civil engineering on the other. So far as UNESCO was concerned the excavation element had few financial implications, although I hasten to add that the Nubian Trust Fund maintained in Sudanese Nubia at least one and at times as many as three archaeologists to assist the Sudan Department of Antiquities for no less than eleven years. However the cost was chicken feed compared with the sums disbursed in safeguarding the temples. In the year following the Director General's appeal the universities and archaeological institutes which were expected to send teams to excavate in the threatened area showed some reluctance to venture into Nubia. To all but a handful of archaeologists it was *terra incognita* and was reputed to be poor in sites and unlikely to yield artefacts suitable for museum display. It was a misconception soon righted by the first expeditions to work there and eventually some thirty expeditions from twenty-four countries discovered how ill-founded was Nubia's reputation; the prehistorians, in particular, found Nubia an astonishingly rich depositary of artefacts of early man. The build-up of excavation was rapid so that by 1963 both Egyptian and Sudanese Nubia offered scenes of unparalleled activity. Camps were everywhere along the river, some in houseboats, others in tents or village houses, their "digs" betrayed by clouds of dust. Land Rovers laboured through the sand carrying prehistorians and epigraphists in search of "benches", rock drawings and inscriptions. Long neglected temples buzzed with animation as engineers, architects and draughtsmen dodged masses of carved stone swung by cranes or carried on 'deccaville' rail hoppers. Nubia was experiencing the biggest archaeological rescue operation the world had yet seen.

The evidence subsequently yielded by the many excavations showed that the Nile Valley had been used by men as a corridor between inner Africa and the Mediterranean over an immense span of time and that it was in Nubia that the record of their movements had been miraculously preserved.

The Organisation's main pre-occupation in the campaign was in the salvaging of Nubia's many temples. To dismantle and remove buildings rendered fragile by many centuries of sun and abrasive wind calls for great expertise and much money, and it was here that the conservation element came into play. In Egyptian Nubia, the Graeco-Roman temple of Kalabsha was successfully dismantled by German engineers—20,000 tons of stone in all—and re-erected at a point several miles from its original site; the transfer was completed in the record time of 18 months and was paid for by the Federal German Republic. France assumed responsibility for moving the much smaller temple of Amada but, true to the French tradition of being different, they lifted the building bodily onto rails and dragged it uphill out of harm's way. Other smaller temples were dismantled by Egypt's Antiquities Service, while in Sudanese Nubia the removal of Buhen temple to Khartoum became the financial responsibility of Britain's Egypt Exploration Society. The two temples at Semna, also in the Sudan, were taken to Khartoum by the Antiquities Service of that country using funds provided by the Governments of Holland and Belgium. All this was accomplished only by dint of much prodding and pleading.

Everybody concerned had recognised as early as 1960 that the focus of the campaign would inevitably be the two temples of Abu Simbel located just inside Egypt's frontier with the Sudan. While the other temples of Nubia were interesting and archaeologically significant, the Abu Simbel monuments were unique: in all her history Egypt produced nothing comparable in size and splendour. Long neglected by tourists because of its remoteness and difficulty of access, Abu Simbel made a spectacular entry into the modern world via television, film and press. To the purveyors of the mass media Rameses II's rock-cut temples offered everything—grandeur, romance and above all a challenge to technology. Various plans for salvaging them were considered including the favourite which would detach the temples from the mountain in which they were hewn, encase each in a concrete box (the larger of the two was estimated to weigh a quarter of a million tons) and lift them by jacks to a height of two hundred feet, beyond reach of the lake. This plan foundered on the estimated cost: $70,000,000. The scheme finally adopted and successfully carried out was less dramatic but much less expensive. The overlaying cliff was first removed and the temples then sawn into pieces for reassembly on the plateau above. The Abu Simbel operation was one of the outstanding feats of civil engineering of our time. The cost was $41,774,458 and long before the whole sum was subscribed many financial crises arose so that fund-raising became paramount. However, after several years of experience we in UNESCO were getting the hang of it; governments were cajoled while radio and film, television and the press were tempted into playing their part in the world pattern of mass persuasion to save Abu Simbel. And it worked, to the relief and secret surprise of all of us who were directly concerned.

All 23 temples and shrines were saved and re-erected elsewhere. Four of them, from Egypt, went overseas; the temple of Dendur now stands in New York's Metropolitan Museum of Fine Art, Taffeh has come to rest in Holland where it may be seen at Leyden, Ellesyn is in Turin and Debod at Madrid. In 1969 the archaeological survey team working in the Sudan reached the Dal Cataract, the extreme southern limit affected by Lake Nasser. Their work had ended and a year later the last two expeditions in Sudanese Nubia were forced by the rising waters to leave. By 1971 Nubia had passed into history.

CHAPTER II

The Nubian Corridor

The stretch of the river Nile that used to be known as Nubia began just south of Assuan where a mass of granite forces its way up through the overlying sandstone to form a natural barrier. This is the First Cataract. At the southern extremity of this granite outcrop the immense bulk of the High Dam is dwarfed by the wilderness of splintered hills that seem to enwrap it as they press in from east and west. For the next two hundred miles the Nile flowed placidly enough across a landscape of sandstone and desert relatively flat, past a crag with the ruins of the Kasr Ibrim fortress clinging to its summit, until 180 miles above Assuan a bend in the river revealed a cliff with a group of colossal figures hewn into its face—the rock-cut temples of Abu Simbel. Twenty miles on and the frontier was crossed into the Sudan. Another thirty miles upstream and a sandstone promontory, known as the Rock of Abusir, heaves its bulk from the river and once more the underlying granite broke through the Nubian sandstone to turn the Nile into a chaos of broken water cascading among islands and rapids. This was the Second Cataract, and of all the many reaches of the Nile in its four thousand mile journey from source to sea, it was by far the most beautiful. Rapids and islands followed in bewildering variety until at Semna, forty miles upstream from the Rock of Abusir, the granite closes in on the river, driving it into a channel less than fifty yards wide. From then on the landscape was convulsed into a series of ridges known in Arabic as Batn el Hagar—the Belly of Stone—and never was anything more aptly named. From Semna to the Dal Cataract, a distance of

55 miles, the Nile ran swiftly between steep walls of rock which now and again drew away, as at Akasha, to give place to an alluvial plain studded with boulders. At Dal the granite subsides and once more the river runs softly across a wide expanse of desert and sandstone. Dal marks the southern limit of the High Dam reservoir. Along this three hundred miles of river countless floodings had deposited alluvium wherever the rocks permitted and it was on these pockets of fertile soil that the Nubians grew their meagre crops and built their picturesque villages.

That description of Nubia still held good in 1960 when I first saw it. Since then the whole stretch of river between Dal and the High Dam has been transformed into a narrow lake. The villages and cultivation have vanished and so, too, have the many islands and the tumultuous corridor of the Second Cataract. Only the Belly of Stone remains, as harsh and forbidding as ever.

Although the term "Nubia" has always been used along the Nile Valley, you will not find the name in any atlas. Geographically it was a corridor of the Nile linking the northern part of the Sudan with Assuan, the southernmost point of ancient Egypt. Lower Nubia was the name given in our day to the two hundred miles of river between the First Cataract at Assuan in Egypt, and the Sudanese frontier. Upper Nubia in the Sudan is the series of reaches of the Nile between the former Second Cataract and the Fourth Cataract. Politically, therefore, Nubia was divided, at least in our time, but in language and traditions it was always one country with a single cultural identity. The ancient Egyptians themselves recognised the Nubians, who were known to them as Kushites, as a people whose origins like their customs and attitudes were different from their own. Nevertheless, the two peoples were linked by geography and no matter how strongly the Nubians felt about it, never could they wholly break free of their powerful neighbour, although the archaeological and written record of four thousand years shows how they never ceased to try. Only during those periods when Egypt herself suffered disruption through internal dissention or military attack from abroad did the Nubians find themselves free to manage their own affairs. And not always then, for Nubia was a cockpit of the ancient world, a battleground seldom free from foreign soldiers. Since the beginning of recorded history Egyptian armies and expeditions used the Nubian corridor in attempts to penetrate the lands to the south, and in their turn the peoples of the south pressed north into Nubia, their eyes on Egypt with her fertile soil and legendary wealth. Inevitably, from time to time one or other of the contending peoples would occupy the corridor, sometimes for generations, indeed Egypt eventually came to colonise Nubia for close on fifteen hundred years.

However, colonisation in the form of annexation came late in the chequered history of Egypt and Nubia. To an early Egyptian the peoples and animals of the upper river were the stuff of legend, dwellers on the edge of the awesome Land of the Ghosts. None but the most courageous of men would dare to brave the perils that awaited any who approached the realm of the dead. Let us now in imagination, try to follow in the footsteps of one man who did make the journey to the south despite its hazards. His name was Herkhuf, Prince of Elephantine, an extraordinary character who steps briefly from the pages of history to project himself vividly across a gulf of 42 centuries. He lived at the peak of that splendid flowering of Egyptian civilisation known to us as the Old Kingdom. Sometimes called the Pyramid Age, it was the most creative period of Egypt's long history. Great engineering enterprises ranging from flood control to the construction of immense stone pyramids were executed with brilliance and confidence. Art flourished, sculpture in particular reaching heights never again to be equalled in Egypt. Towards the latter part of the Old Kingdom period the Kings of the Sixth Dynasty (2340–2180 BC) had turned interested eyes towards the lands of the south. Explorations made during earlier dynasties had revealed that many desirable commodities could be found far up the river, wonders such as ivory, ostrich feathers, leopard skins, incense, rare stones, ebony and other hardwoods. In the time of the Old Kingdom Egypt's southern frontier was Elephantine Island at Assuan and the flourishing little town sprawled across the southern tip of the island was responsible for the security of the great country at its back. Not for nothing did the Princes of

Elephantine bear the title, among many others, of "Keeper of the Door of the South". We can imagine, then, Herkhuf summoned to the Court in Memphis, then the capital city of Upper and Lower Egypt (the Two Lands), where Merenré, who has only recently become king, receives him with kindness and tells of his wishes. Herkhuf will fit out an expedition at Elephantine, lead it into the Land of Kush and bring back all the produce he can lay hands on for the king's pleasure. If he does this successfully he will be richly rewarded. We can see Herkhuf, filled with pride, leaving the presence of the god-king and setting off on the return voyage of five hundred miles that separated Memphis, near where Cairo stands today, and his native Elephantine. The procession of vessels borne against the current by the prevailing north wind presents a gay spectacle, garlanded and decorated with banners. Each day as the sun slips below the western hills the little fleet puts in to one of the many towns along the river's banks for provisions and shelter, and there the local governor and officials welcome Herkhuf with the respect due to one of his rank, a man second only to the king himself and moreover high in the royal favour. Does he not bear the titles of "Overseer of Upper Egypt", "Ritual Priest", "Overseer of all the Desert in the Head of Upper Egypt who set the Terror of Horus in the Foreign Lands", "Caravan Conductor", "Overseer of Dragomans" and above all "Keeper of the Door of the South"?

The day comes when preparations are complete and Herkhuf is ready to leave. For the little metropolis of Elephantine it is an occasion for feasting, a day of joy though tempered with apprehension that their Prince may never return to his native city. Herkhuf, his bodyguard, servants and pack donkeys–the camel and horse are as yet unknown in Egypt–are ferried across to the west bank. A steep climb up a rocky slope brings them to a massive rock, shaped like a crouching toad, overlooking the river. It is the Rock of Offerings, sacred to Khnum the ram-headed. Here Herkhuf pauses to pay homage to Khnum as god of the cataract and to pray for a safe return from his perilous journey. There on the rock he must have seen similar prayers engraved by earlier travellers. His followers pile up little cairns of stones, each covering an earthenware offering pot.

Some 42 centuries later I, too, made my little cairn of stones before setting out on the same journey—but by Land Rover. The road which Herkhuf took is still to be seen, about three hundred yards of flattened desert curving past the Rock of Offerings before losing itself among the sandhills. Over the millennia, travellers in Herkhuf's footsteps have covered every inch of the Rock's surface with prayers to Khnum, and the little cairns of the more humble wayfarers cover acres of surrounding desert. Such is the world's oldest highway, deserted now as sand and wind conspire to smother the footprints of five thousand years.

The thoughts of Herkhuf at that moment must surely have centred on the glittering metropolis below, its streets thronged with figures, gay pennants fluttering above its temples in the sunshine. And so with the north wind at his back he sets his feet on the Nubian Highway. What could he expect to encounter on the journey? The people of Wawat (Lower Nubia) must have been well known to him; only recently the King himself, Merenré, had come to Elephantine to inspect the frontier and to order the cutting of five canals through the granite barrier of the cataract, and the chiefs of the Mazoi, of Irthet and of Wawat had come to Elephantine to pay him homage. Herkhuf need expect few obstacles there; it was the Kushites beyond the Second Cataract whom he had reason to fear. They were the unknown quantity. Following the course of the river along the west bank and skirting the granite tangle of the First Cataract the caravan moves south across what is now a rainless desert where the sole source of water is the Nile. There is reason to believe that in Herkhuf's day the climate was more clement with a rainfall sufficient to support vegetation suitable for grazing animals. Some five days' march from the Rock of Offerings the expedition would have come abreast of a line of sandstone cliffs falling sheer to the river two hundred feet below. There on the cliff edge one seems suspended between river and sky; the Nile below is broad and placid and its majestic path can be followed to north and south for fully thirty miles, so transparent is the atmosphere. Assuredly a point of vantage such as this would have attracted Herkhuf if only to spy out the land, for he was drawing close now to the Second Cataract and the territory of the Kushites. Also there is reason to believe that the "high place" of Abu Simbel was sacred to the gods long before Herkhuf's day and he could be expected therefore to have made a suitable offering there on the very cliff which one day would be shaped on the orders of a pharaoh as yet unborn into two of the most magnificent structures ever to be created in a valley of magnificent buildings. Here, a thousand years later, the sandstone below Herkhuf's feet would be hewn into four colossal figures in the semblance of a great king, Usi-ma-re, Rameses II.

Two days' march beyond Abu Simbel the caravan comes abreast of the ruins of a town. Did Herkhuf walk through the streets littered with fragments of reddish pottery, come across the remains of kilns, note the broken moulds and heaps of copper ore scattered on all sides? Assuredly he would have recognised this as a town built and lived in by Egyptians. Was he aware that for some two hundred years Egyptians had smelted copper at this place, called Buhen, and that its furnaces were alight when the Pyramids of the Fourth Dynasty and the Sphinx itself were rising above the plateau of Giza, nearly three centuries before his day? Did he know all this or had this outpost of Egypt been so long abandoned that all record of it was lost? If he did not know, then this eloquent ruin must have surprised Herkhuf as much as it did the late Professor W. B. Emery when he unearthed it in 1962. Until then Egyptologists had accepted that no Egyptian settlements were founded in Nubia (Kush) before the Middle Kingdom, that is to say, before *c.*2000 BC. Emery's discovery was, therefore, startling. Certainly Herkhuf made no mention of the town in his account of his journey so it is reasonable to assume that he had no prior knowledge of its existence.

Within sight of Buhen is a conical hill, known to the modern Nubians as Gebel Sheikh Suleiman. This too seems to have been a holy place so it is likely that Herkhuf climbed it. He would have received another surprise for there on its summit was a large rock bearing an inscription engraved some seven centuries before his time. Assuming he could decipher the archaic hieroglyphs Herkhuf would have learned that there before him was the record of a military expedition sent to Kush by Djer, the second king of Egypt's First Dynasty. There is some doubt about the reading of the name "Djer" although there is no doubt of its being inscribed by a king of Egypt's Archaic Period. For Herkhuf it would have been an emotional experience to see what was, in effect, the signature of one of the god-kings who founded sacred Egypt. On the other hand one can imagine Herkhuf the explorer being taken aback to discover that dreaded Kush had apparently been peopled by Egyptians for centuries; but he could at least have consoled himself with knowing that his was no punitive expedition sent to capture Kushite towns but a purely trading venture. More than likely the little caravan passed by the Djer inscription in ignorance of its existence.

However, Herkhuf could hardly have escaped seeing the great cliff a few miles further on. It commanded glorious views of the Second Cataract and its summit much later would bear scores of inscriptions cut by travellers from pharaonic times to our own day. Herkhuf was now in Kushite territory. As he passed among the rocks he must have noticed the shapes of many unfamiliar animals engraved on their surfaces and wondered about the people who carved them and when they lived. We can assume that it would have taken Herkhuf and his cavalcade at least two days to cover the next forty miles of splintered rock and sand-drifts to Semna where the river thundered through the gap in the granite barrier. Semna was a natural strongpoint and three centuries after Herkhuf's death it was destined to become Egypt's southern frontier; on either side of the gorge powerful fortresses would be built by the Pharaohs of the twelfth Dynasty and behind them a line of strongholds stretching far downstream into Wawat. The historical record shows how the Kushites were to develop into formidable enemies but in 2300 BC Herkhuf seems not to have found them so, at least on this his first expedition. Beyond Semna we are unable to follow him and he vanishes among the rocks of the Belly of Stone. Seven months later he reappears laden with gifts for his king. It is tantalizing to speculate on how far he penetrated inner Africa, but so far it has proved impossible to identify the various tribes he names as having encountered.

Herkhuf made three more expeditions to the Land of Ghosts before being laid to rest in the modest tomb prepared for him in the cliffs behind Elephantine. On his fourth and last journey he brought back a prize which sent the new king into ecstasies—nothing less than a dancing dwarf. Pepi II had only recently succeeded Merenré and the letter of appreciation he wrote Herkhuf from Memphis is the expression of an excited boy—he was in fact eight years old—and it is one of the most delightful documents to come down to us from ancient Egypt. The intrepid Herkhuf proudly recorded the King's message on the walls of his tomb, together with accounts of his adventures in the Land of Kush. His example was followed by successive Keepers of the Door of the South, and this extraordinary period of African exploration came to an end only with the collapse of the Old Kingdom, which followed the death of Pepi II. Last of the Sixth Dynasty kings, he had ruled Egypt for close on a century—by far the longest reign in history. Thereafter Egypt lapsed into a long period of anarchy and Nubia recedes into the shadows.

Until recently it had been assumed that among the tribes encountered by Herkhuf were the people known to archaeologists as the A-Group, the first of Nubia's settled cultures. However this supposition is now considered doubtful in that there is, as Professor Säve-Söderbergh says, ". . . no proof whatsoever of the existence of the A-Group after the end of the First Dynasty or at most the Second Dynasty". The A-Group were a neolithic culture and their earliest graves date from before 3000 BC. The variety and quality of their funerary objects show that they were well advanced on the path of civilisation. The pottery in particular is of good design and workmanship and appears in a variety of forms. Their dead, usually interred in a contracted position, are often adorned with bracelets and necklaces of shell and cornelian. Boomerangs, grinding stones, copper and flint implements all go to show that these, the first settled inhabitants of Nubia, were far removed from the primitive hunters who preceded them.

Before the advent of the Nubian Campaign little was known of early man's occupation of Nubia. Since 1960 prehistorians and palaeontologists searching far back from the river along the tops of the many rocky outcrops have discovered that Nubia was outstandingly rich in artifacts left by palaeolithic men, so much so that living conditions must have been good for the hunters of that remote age. Thus it follows that the territory over which they hunted a wide variety of animals, including giraffe, elephant and oryx, was very different in appearance from the arid and desiccated landscapes of our time. Indeed there is evidence that 60,000 or 70,000 years ago, when the Nile valley did not yet exist, the plateau was supporting abundant flora and fauna. Returning to the historical record, the A-Group people seem to have remained in Nubia through much of Egypt's Archaic Period, from time to time suffering attacks from their northern neighbour, the expedition of King Djer being one such. Another invasion of Nubia, much more devastating, was launched by Sneferu, first king of the Fourth Dynasty, who recorded how he brought back to Egypt 7000 prisoners and 200,000 head of cattle. For a region so poor in arable land and only sparsely populated, this campaign must have been a crushing blow and it probably put an end to any warlike intentions on the part of the Kushites for generations.

The long centuries of the Pyramid Age under the wise guidance of its god-kings had harnessed the youthful vigour of a great people to the creation of a civilisation notable for its splendid achievements in all fields of endeavour. Indeed in the centuries to come Egyptians would look back to the Old Kingdom with nostalgia, seeing in it a golden age of government, religion and security of tenure. To an Egyptian living in the closing years of the Old Kingdom his was a way of life that must have seemed destined to flow on forever. On earth a bountiful nature offered a plethora of good things and, provided the proper magical formulae were invoked, those good things of life would continue after death in the underworld. At that time you could, most emphatically, take it with you. Therefore when the end came it was to the Egyptians a shock of terrible proportions. The fabric of the society they had believed eternal collapsed about their ears and the resulting lawlessness and violence, so foreign to the Egyptian character, plunged the country into despair. The bewilderment and misery of a gentle and civilised people come echoing down the millennia that divide us from the Pyramid Builders in an account written by a scribe of that unhappy time:

> The Nile is in flood, yet none plough the land... Corn hath perished everywhere. People are stripped of clothing, perfume, oil.... Women are barren and there is no conception. Khnum fashions men no more because of the condition of the land... The heart is violent. Plague stalks through the land and blood is everywhere... The crocodiles are glutted with what they have carried off. Men go to them of their own accord... Laughter has perished and is no longer made. Grief walks through the land... The laws of the judgment hall are placed in the vestibule. Men walk upon them in the street and the poor tear them up in the alley... Great and small say: "I wish I were dead." Little children say: "He ought never to have caused me to live."

For close on two centuries Egypt was torn by destructive forces until around 2000 BC the energetic Pharaohs of what was to become the Middle Kingdom (Eleventh to Thirteenth Dynasties) took control. The administrative structure of the Two-Lands (Egypt) was reorganised and the long-neglected irrigation system that was the source of the country's very existence was restored and extended. An essential step was to restore Pharaoh's influence over the southern lands and thus resume the interrupted flow of commodities and slaves considered indispensable to Egypt's prosperity. However, with the passage of the centuries the face of Nubia had changed. A new culture, a. pastoral people known to archaeologists as the C-Group, had arrived on the scene bringing with them great herds of cattle. The pottery and objects found in the many C-Group cemeteries excavated during the Nubian Campaign have revealed a standard of culture more advanced than that of their predecessors, the A-Group. I should perhaps mention here that the hypothesis of a linking culture between the A and C-Groups put forward first by Dr George A. Reisner of Harvard when he dug in Nubia at the beginning of this century and which he termed B-Group, is no longer accepted by most scholars. This is further discussed–Chapter IV.

The C-Group people, then, were occupying Nubia when the Middle Kingdom Pharaohs moved in to establish Egypt's presence and the indications are that they were unwarlike in character. Who then was the formidable enemy who forced the Egyptians to fight campaign after campaign so that nearly a century was to pass before they were able to establish their southern frontier at Semna where river and rock form the natural strongpoint already described? Even then the occupation of Nubia was so insecure that the Egyptians were able to hold their own only by building a line of 12 fortresses along the sixty-mile length of the Second Cataract. They were probably the most powerful strongholds built in antiquity and are a measure of the military prowess of the Kushite adversary. A culture known as the "Kerma" people has been cast for the rôle by some scholars. They are so called because the focal point of their culture seems to have been at Kerma south of the Third Cataract where between 1913 and 1915 Reisner made some spectacular discoveries. The very distinctive Kerma burials and pottery are found as far north as the Second Cataract and the graves, like Kerma itself, are mostly contemporary with the Middle Kingdom occupation of the forts.

Generation after generation of Egyptian soldiers garrisoned the forts until, abandoned by the homeland, retreat was forced upon them. The Middle Kingdom in its turn had run its course. Lower Egypt had been infiltrated by intruders from the east and the day came when they made themselves masters of the whole country. For the first time in their history Egyptians were subjected to alien rule. This conquest by the Hyksos, as they were called, was regarded by later generations of Egyptians as the greatest disaster ever to befall their land. Egyptologists describe this era, from about 1785–1570 BC, as the Second Intermediate Period.

Again, for about two centuries, the Kushites were left to pursue their destiny undisturbed and there is even evidence that at one time an alliance was established between the Hyksos kings in Egypt and the chieftains of Kush. With the expulsion of the Hyksos the new native rulers of Egypt, founders of the brilliant Eighteenth Dynasty, turned their attention to Nubia and this time they were determined to bring Kush into complete subjection. Nothing less than the outright appropriation of this corridor so vital to Egypt's interests would suffice. It was Thutmose I who conquered

Upper Nubia and he pushed south into the Sudan beyond the old frontier at Semna, for four hundred miles where he "penetrated valleys unknown to my ancestors". There he established his new boundary, a boundary that was to remain unchallenged for nearly eight hundred years. Nubia had been subdued in less than a year. Following the Nubian victory Thutmose I and his successors went on to conquer most of the ancient world, but that is another story. Soon the fortresses of the Second Cataract, fallen into ruin, were rebuilt and enlarged, but now they served as fortified trading posts rather than military strongholds. The enemy so feared by the Pharaohs of the Middle Kingdom had gone, or was no longer considered dangerous. The C-Group people were in Nubia still and the archaeological record of their burials shows that over the years their culture became progressively absorbed by that of the Egyptians so that by 1500 BC C-Group burials are indistinguishable from those of native Egyptians. The Pharaohs had always respected the fighting ability of the Kushites and henceforward men of Kush—called "Medjay" by the Egyptians—became the backbone of the Empire's armies. So many Kushites were engaged on law enforcement in Egypt itself that *medjay* became the term used to describe policemen.

Nubia was now a province of Egypt and to govern it a Viceroy was appointed. The post was of such importance that the holder stood next to Pharaoh himself in the hierarchy. The territory was divided between the two administrations of Wawat and Kush, each being under the control of a deputy and the Viceroy's chief responsibility was to ensure that the annual tribute of Nubia was regularly delivered to Pharaoh's treasury. For close on five hundred years the government of Nubia remained in the hands of the Viceroys. Many were outstanding figures in an age that produced some of the greatest men in Egypt's history. Most of the temples standing in Nubia until in our day the campaign brought about their removal elsewhere were built during the long reign of the Viceroys, including the two rock-cut temples of Rameses II at Abu Simbel.

Rameses II, the last great figure of the Nineteenth Dynasty, was destined also to be last in the gallery of outstanding native Egyptian rulers. His successors, all named Rameses, proved incapable of maintaining authority over a country weakened by the intrigue and dissention which during the reign of Rameses IX culminated in civil war. The last Pharaoh of the Nineteenth Dynasty appointed a high priest of the Theban god Amun to the post of Viceroy of Nubia. His name was Herihor and the wealth and military prowess of the South gave him the power he needed to usurp the throne, which he succeeded in doing in 1085 BC. During the period of confusion that followed Herihor's death Kush became increasingly independent although it is probable that Egyptianised Lower Nubia (Wawat) remained loyal to Egypt. Meanwhile the priesthood of Amun had established their influence deep inside Nubia where at the foot of Gebel Barkal, a sacred mountain near the Fourth Cataract, a magnificent temple was built to the glory of Amun. By the year 950 BC the nearby town of Napata had become the focal point of a kingdom, African in origin but Egyptian in tradition and religious belief. The king even bore pharaonic titles, calling himself Lord of the Two Lands, as if he governed Egypt itself.

It was from Napata more than a century later that Piankhy, first of the Kushite kings to emerge from the shadowy Upper Nile, marched north to subdue the forces of barbarism at large in the venerated homeland. For Egypt was again torn by internal dissention and we know that Piankhy saw himself as an enlightened ruler destined to restore the lost virtues of the great civilisation which he claimed to represent. His subsequent adventures are known in detail from a granite stela set up in the temple at Gebel Barkal. Suffice it to say that he succeeded, in spite of the handicap of his being a chivalrous "liberator" as the Gebel Barkal stela makes plain. Following his coronation as King of Upper and Lower Egypt Piankhy hastened to return to his Kushite capital of Napata. Thus the despised people of Nubia, invariably referred to in Egyptian texts as "Kush the Wretched" or "Kush the Vile" became masters of their former conquerors.

Piankhy's descendents governed Egypt as the Twenty-fifth Dynasty for the next seventy years with varying fortunes. They were able men who might have restored Egypt to greatness had they been given time, but their misfortune was to enter history at the moment of Assyria's rise to power. The Kushites were no match for Assyrian military prowess and with the withdrawal of Tanutamun, last of the line, to Napata the Kushite dynasty in Egypt came to an end.

It may have been the invasion of Napata by the Egyptian Pharaoh, Psamtik II, at the beginning of the sixth century BC that persuaded the Kushites to move their capital upstream from Napata to Meroë near the Sixth Cataract. Egypt had by 525 BC become a Persian province and the conqueror Cambyses was so imprudent as to send an army against the Meroites with such inadequate preparation that most of his troops died of starvation in the Nubian desert.

From now on, for many centuries, the Kushites were destined to be free of invasion. Secure in their fertile bend of the Nile at Meroë they developed a curious bastard culture in which both African and Egyptian, and later Hellenistic, elements were combined. Cut off from the northern neighbour the Egyptian hieroglyphic script became corrupted and its meaning forgotten, although it remained a vehicle for the native tongue; while it can be deciphered the meaning is obscure and will remain hidden from us until a Meroitic equivalent of the Rosetta Stone is unearthed. Meanwhile the Meroitic Empire prospered and grew, spurred on no doubt by the skill its people developed in the smelting and forging of iron implements. As far as Nubia was concerned the Meroitic kings seem to have retained at least a toe-hold in the Belly of Stone, always a corridor of supreme importance in the ceaseless struggle for power between Egypt and Africa. Indeed it seems that during the reign of Ptolemy IV of Egypt the Nubian (Meroitic) king Argamani controlled the Nile as far as Philae, within sight of Elephantine itself. When with the death of Cleopatra in 30 BC Egypt was annexed by Rome, the Romans signed a treaty with the Meroitic king whereby Lower Nubia would become a Roman protectorate while remaining a part of the Meroitic Empire. But the Meroites made uncomfortable neighbours. They were in constant conflict with the Romans and went so far as to inflict a defeat on the soldiers of Caesar and occupy the frontier town of Syene (Elephantine). This was an indignity too great to swallow and a Roman army drove back the Meroites, who were led by a redoubtable queen, as far as Napata which had remained the religious centre of the Meroitic Empire. With the departure of the Meroitic army the Nubians were able to enjoy long years of prosperity under Roman administration. As for the Meroitic Empire, that strange African civilisation after more than a thousand years was nearing its end and with the fall of Meroë around the middle of the fourth century AD Kush, as a kingdom, ceased to exist.

The origin of the next culture to be identified in Nubia is doubtful, hence the name given to it: X-Group. The X-Group may be identified with a troublesome people known to the Romans as Blemmyes or, equally, with another tribe living in Nubia which the Byzantine historian Procopius names Nobatae. For scholars they remain a bone of contention. Any expedition which found in its concession the large circular tumuli characteristic of an X-Group cemetery always dug hopefully in the recollection of W. B. Emery's discovery of the mid thirties when he located near Abu Simbel the tombs of the X-Group kings, the richest "find" ever made in Nubia. Alas, the tombs excavated in the 1960s were nearly always found plundered—with one exception. It was a tomb near Kasr Ibrahim in Lower Nubia and by the luck of the game the discoverer was again Emery.

Worship of the ancient gods lingered on in Nubia until the sixth century of the Christian era, long after the conversion of Egypt to Christianity. It was then that the Byzantine Emperor Justinian ordered the closing of the temples on Philae Island, sacred to the goddess Isis, and with the removal of the cult statues a faith that had seen the passage of nearly five thousand years flickered and died.

The spread of the new religion was rapid and soon three Christian kingdoms were stretched along the length of the Nile, the northernmost, Nabatia, establishing its capital at Faras on the present border between Egyptian and Sudanese Nubia. There in 1962 the Polish Expedition to Nubia discovered the graves of several of the Bishops of Pachoras, the name of the ancient capital, and excavated a cathedral. From its crumbling walls of mud-brick they removed with infinite patience close on a hundred frescoes, among them superb examples of Byzantine art. Christianity in Nubia spanned eight centuries so it is hardly surprising that the largest proportion of Nubia's ancient sites were Christian. Each settlement or townlet would have as its focal point a church and there were dozens of these. Irrigation works and cemeteries were everywhere to be seen and the many fortified villages and islands bore witness to the increasing pressures of Islam as the centuries advanced. With Islam in Nubia the salvage campaign had no concern so that with the fifteenth century AD the archaeological story comes to an end.

The record of field archaeology in the Nubian stretch of the Nile valley is both long and honourable; it provided a solid foundation for the activities of the 1960s and consequently should be given due recognition. It has often been written that the UNESCO Campaign was the first large-scale example of salvage archaeology, but in fact the first operation of the kind was at the beginning of this century, also in Nubia. When the decision was taken at the end of the nineteenth century to build the original Assuan Dam there was considerable agitation in artistic and archaeological circles. Letters were written to *The Times* and lecture platforms echoed to the protestations of the conservationists—and this long before the days of radio and television. The flooding of the Philae Island temples in particular aroused a storm of protest. Perhaps because of public agitation a sum of money was included in the estimates for the dam sufficient to protect at least partially all the temples likely to be affected by the annual rise and fall of the new reservoir. The possibility of dismantling and removing them did not arise at that time; instead the foundations and structures above ground were underpinned and generally strengthened by engineers of Egypt's Ministry of Public Works. That these ancient buildings successfully resisted so many years of submersion is a tribute to the excellence of the protective measures taken in the early 1900s, measures which made it possible for the architects and civil engineers of half a century later to rescue these friable relics of the past by moving them beyond reach of the destructive waters forever.

The work of excavation was confined mainly to the recording of ground plans and no real record was made of pottery or other artifacts found; neither was much published. In this respect Philae suffered grievously, being literally covered in buildings and churches all of mud-brick and all of which were swept away by the floodwaters, although of course the stone temples consolidated with Public Works thoroughness, remain to our day. Philae had come to play a vital role in the last years of pagan worship in the Nile Valley so the loss of the unrecorded town-site was a catastrophe for Egyptology.

The decision to raise the height of the Assuan Dam taken some years later sparked off the first systematic archaeological salvage operation ever undertaken. Called the "First Archaeological Survey of Nubia", the name was misleading because in fact it involved full-scale excavation of every site found. Again the Ministry of Public Works was the organiser but on this occasion an archaeologist, Dr Reisner, was appointed to head the mission. Around him he gathered a brilliant team of scholars, including two men of international renown to take care of the anthropological elements: Dr G. Elliot Smith and Dr Douglas Derry. Reisner has been described as the greatest archaeologist and excavator the United States has ever produced. His name will always be associated with Nubia and comes up again and again in this book. He it was who on the evidence yielded by a single large necropolis at the beginning of the survey, was able to formulate the sequential pattern of Nubian cultural history, a pattern that was still being followed by scholars sixty years later. Since then, inevitably, some modifications to Reisner's conclusions and dating have had to be made in the light of recent discovery. Here is Reisner's sequence as it applied to Nubia:

	BC
Early Pre-dynastic	*c.*4000–3600
Middle Pre-dynastic	*c.*3600–3400
Late Pre-dynastic	*c.*3400–3200
A-Group	3200–2680
B-Group	2680–2258
C-Group	2258–1600
D-Group (New Kingdom)	1600–1085

(*above*) Assuan: the original dam, completed in 1934 and situated a few miles downstream of the new High Dam. (*below*) Abu Simbel: dismantling the heads of the Rameses II colossi which formed the façade of the rock-cut temple. Behind can be seen the scar in the cliff where the 250,000-ton temple was cut from its interior for re-assembly 200 feet higher.

(*above*) Elephantine Island: the ruins of the ancient metropolis of Upper Egypt are to the right of the picture. They represent some forty centuries of building. (*below*) Rock of Abusir: overlooking the entrance to the Second Cataract – now vanished – the Rock bore hundreds of graffiti ranging from the nineteenth century BC to the nineteenth century AD.

The Gap (Napata)	1085–332
Meroitic-Ptolemaic	332–AD 30
Meroitic–X-Group, Roman	AD 30–324
X-Group, Byzantine	324–565

I had the good fortune to know Reisner in the last years of his life, and to visit his house among the Old Kingdom tombs near the Great Pyramid that he had spent years excavating and recording was always a delight. Afflicted by blindness, nevertheless he continued to work on his notes and records assisted by his daughter Mary. Reisner's method of recording excavations under pressure of time, in particular cemeteries, was so well founded that it was followed by Emery in the Second Survey and later by others during the UNESCO Campaign. When Reisner left the Survey Cecil Firth, his former assistant, took over and it was Firth who brought it to its successful conclusion.

In all, the Survey lasted from 1907 to 1911. Probably its most striking excavation was the clearance of the large Middle Kingdom (*c.*1900 BC) fortress of Ikkur, but it was dwarfed by the solid record of achievement revealed when the final report was officially published in no less than seven folio volumes. The Survey stopped short at the limit of the area to be flooded, which was at Wadi es Sabua about halfway between Assuan and the Sudanese frontier. Despite all pleas, no funds could be found to carry the Survey up to the frontier and the result was calamitous. Professor W. B. Emery has commented that no sooner had Firth closed the excavations and departed than into Nubia came teams of illegal diggers sent by the Luxor dealers in antiquities so that when 18 years later Emery was conducting the Second Survey south of Wadi es Sabua, he found cemetery after cemetery stripped and plundered. It was the old and bitter lesson that every field archaeologist must learn: once you open up a site it must be cleared completely and recorded fully.

The Second Archaeological Survey came about because of the second heightening of the Assuan Dam, the effects of which would be felt two hundred miles upstream from Assuan as far as the Sudan frontier. Accompanying Emery as sub-director of the Survey was L. P. Kirwan who is now Director of the Royal Geographical Society. The Survey picked up from where the First Survey left off at Wadi es Sabua in October 1929, and from there worked south to the Sudan frontier, a distance of about a hundred miles. As with the First Survey one of the highlights was the excavation of a Middle Kingdom fortress. Kuban fort stood at the mouth of Wadi Alaqi and was intended to protect the gold mines worked there. Emery has described how beneath the great mounds of rubble inside the fort they found many of the buildings with the original brick-vaulted roofing intact; some even had the upper stories in place and in one of them was a fireplace still containing charcoal. They had planned on three seasons of work, but fate ruled otherwise. On the last season they stumbled on one of those discoveries that all archaeologists dream about in their less lucid moments but seldom realize. For Emery and Kirwan it was the finding of the tombs of the X-Group kings at Ballana and Qustol and it was far and away the most sensational find ever made in Nubia. Two more years were to pass in excavating and recording the innumerable objects yielded by the tombs before they could write *finis* to the Second Archaeological Survey of Nubia. Details of the Ballana and Qustal excavations are given in a later chapter. In 1935 and 1938 the official reports of the Second Survey and the Ballana/Qustal excavations were published in four quarto volumes by the Egyptian Antiquities Service.

Meanwhile 12 temples of Egyptian (Lower) Nubia had been recorded, and published in 15 folio volumes, while other scholars contributed 19 volumes devoted to temples, churches and archaeological sites in the same area. In all, more than forty volumes and innumerable published papers were available to leaders of those expeditions electing to work in Lower Nubia at the start of UNESCO's Nubian Campaign and subsequently many a blessing was called down on the Egyptian Administration of the first part of the century for its archaeological foresight.

Obviously then Egyptian Nubia had been well explored and documented. With Sudanese (Upper) Nubia the situation was very different; in archaeological terms it was *terra incognita*. In 1959 Dr Jean Vercoutter, then Commissioner for Archaeology in the Sudan, pointed out somewhat ruefully that along the hundred mile-length of the threatened area in the Sudan only ten sites had been excavated, and those only partially, and that no full archaeological survey had ever been made. He himself had carried out a preliminary survey of part of the threatened area in 1955 and 1956 and this had resulted in the discovery of 25 new sites. By 1969 when the Sudan Archaeological Survey of Nubia was completed the number of sites had risen to the staggering figure of a thousand and more, surely a situation unique in the annals of field archaeology. The teams of excavators who decided to work in Sudanese Nubia were thus projected into the field of salvage archaeology with a vengeance and it is a measure of their adaptability and ingenuity that they were able to respond so well.

The Sudan then, unlike Egypt, had to start from scratch. An essential and as it turned out invaluable preliminary was an aerial survey of the Valley between the Egyptian frontier and the Dal Cataract, a hundred miles upstream. This was carried out by the Sudan Survey Department in 1956 and 1957. To interpret the photographs and organise the aerial maps Dr W. Y. Adams was sent out by UNESCO at the end of 1959 and under his direction a second aerial survey was made at a lower altitude thus providing a larger-scale coverage than the first. A special type of camera, mounted so that it shoots vertically down through the belly of the aircraft, fires off automatically every 5, 10, 15 or 20 seconds according to the height of the aircraft and its flying speed. The aircraft flies along a succession of parallel lines so as to produce photo strips which have to overlap by at least 30 per cent. It demands most accurate piloting, as I observed when I accompanied Adams on one of his survey flights. When developed and printed the individual photographs can be mounted as part of a mosaic which becomes in effect a single photograph of the entire region surveyed. The mosaic as shown to me was about forty feet long. An ingenious stereoscopic device uses overlapping photographs to exaggerate human binocular vision, so that the smallest configuration stands out prominently from the surface. The series of aerial photographs relevant to each concession was made available to each expedition as it arrived to start work.

Scores of new sites were revealed by the aerial survey and mapped accordingly. However, no survey from the air can reveal sites hidden beneath heavy layers of silt or sand, neither can it spot tell-tale sherds lying on the surface which could indicate a hidden site nearby. There is in fact no substitute for walking over the ground, so the next step was a detailed ground survey and this was undertaken by Adams who later was joined by two other archaeologists both sent out by UNESCO. Eventually as more and more expeditions arrived and pressure of work built up, Adams became "our man in Nubia" for UNESCO. From his headquarters at Wadi Halfa he conducted the Survey on behalf of the Sudan Antiquities Service, supervised excavation of those sites which fell outside the concessions granted to foreign missions, acted as liaison between them and the Sudan Government and kept an eye on the photographic laboratory which had been set up with equipment supplied by UNESCO for the use of everyone working in the rescue operation. This dark room with its air-conditioner–the first and only one ever to be seen in Nubia–proved of inestimable value. Photography is an essential tool of field archaeology and the abrasive dust, lack of clean water and great heat at certain times of the year, would have raised severe problems for individual expeditions continually on the move had it not been for the Wadi Halfa dark-room. Before long the laboratory came to resemble a club where archaeologists from any of a dozen nations would drop in from time to time to collect mail and exchange news and information about their work. Many were the rumours sent flying up and down the river from this source. One such, firmly believed I remember, was that someone had discovered an unrobbed New Kingdom tomb complete with an excellent mummy, gold mask and all. I took the trouble to follow it up and found it no different from a score of similar burials and as for the mask, it consisted of a fragment of gold foil overlooked by the ancient robbers of the tomb.

The Scandinavian Joint Expedition was not only the biggest expedition to work in Sudanese Nubia but it had the largest concession, and the Scandinavians undertook to carry out their own ground survey between the frontier on the east bank and Gemai and Abka, about forty miles to the south. From 1960, as the Survey proceeded—and here I would emphasise that from first to last it was conducted by archaeologists made available by UNESCO, although all other costs such as equipment and materials, labour and transport, were supplied by the Sudan Antiquities Service—the locations of all sites found were mapped and passed on to the various expeditions who would then deal with the excavation of them. In 1966 Adams who, as chief of the Survey operation since the beginning of the campaign, had been a tower of strength in Nubia, returned to the United States to take up a Chair in the University of Kentucky. A. J. Mills, a Canadian, who had been working on the survey since 1964 now assumed full charge and, assisted from time to time by other archaeologists appointed by UNESCO, carried it through to its conclusion in 1969, when the Dal Cataract was reached.

During those five seasons of work Mills and his colleagues located about 650 additional sites of all periods; they included campsites and middens, villages and churches, cemeteries, forts and rock carvings. The method used in the Survey was for each archaeologist accompanied by a labour force of up to fifty men to inspect a selected area of ground. When surface indications were found, test diggings were made at once, sufficient to give the date, type and degree of preservation of the site. Those sites which revealed something out of the ordinary—an unplundered cemetery for instance—were given full excavation. All records made and objects found became the property of the Sudan Antiquities Service. Ideally every site should have been fully excavated but lack of time and manpower made this impossible. Nevertheless all the sites revealed by the aerial and ground surveys, more than a thousand in all, were adequately cleared, with two major exceptions which will be discussed in other chapters.

Nubia had straddled one of the great cultural corridors of the world. I liken it to a railway with one terminus on the Mediterranean and the other in inner Africa. A section of the line vanished under water but not before we were able to observe a number of signals and all of them pointed in one direction: south. In this book, therefore, it is my intention to confine myself to the work done in Sudanese Nubia, between the years 1960 and 1969. However, from time to time, unavoidably, the reader will find himself crossing the border into Egyptian Nubia, so intertwined were the destinies of the two countries over a span of years that embraces the whole of man's recorded history.

CHAPTER III

The Nubians

In the winter of 1966 after thirty uncomfortable hours, I shook the dust of the Khartoum train from my hair and stepped out into the Nubian sunshine. The air was cool and clear and the sunlight seemed to dance and sparkle. Clearly the old magic was at work and suddenly Europe with all its frustrations and preoccupations seemed very far away. Even the gritty throat which had bothered me for weeks felt easier. Admittedly, ever since leaving Khartoum two days before I had been fearful of what I might see and now here was the realization. In the two years since I had last set foot in this enchanting land it had changed almost out of recognition. The vitality of Nubia, the unhurried, unpressurised vitality that sprang from a close accord between man and environment, had ebbed. Even the Nile had changed, swollen now to the dimensions of a lake. It was the Nile that had given shape and substance to the Nubian way of life, its bounty sometimes abundant, sometimes withheld. To the dwellers on its banks the river was a stern reminder that to adapt to nature meant survival, to resist was to invite disaster. It bred a people who took life as it came, were friendly to all and envious of none. To the end, Nubia remained untouched by the twentieth century which effectively by-passed it when Kitchener's railway to Khartoum struck off into the desert instead of following the Nubian bend of the Nile. It left unsullied a museum as rich in memories of the past as in monuments.

An attachment to one's native land is natural. Among Nubians it is particularly strong and this is hard to explain because Nubia offered them nothing of wealth and little comfort; so poor was it in natural resources, in particular arable land, that most Nubians were compelled to pass a large part of their working life abroad in order to support their families at home in Nubia. Yet, always with advancing years they would abandon the attractions of the big cities of Cairo, Alexandria and Khartoum where most of them worked, to seek the simplicity of their homeland.

And now they were gone, this ancient people so dignified and calm, so independent of mind, so hospitable and tolerant towards strangers. Their grasp on the land had never been strong and what little of themselves they had imposed on the harsh landscape was fast vanishing. From the banks of the Nile the houses of abandoned villages, stripped of doors and windows, stared out at the swollen river like empty eye-sockets. That characteristic sound of Nubia, the part-screech part-groan of the ox-driven saqia wheel lifting water to the thirsty soil, was no longer heard and the irrigation channels were becoming choked with sand. Desert and flood had drawn close and at the points of their meeting all signs of man's husbandry ceased. The strips of cultivation on islands and river bank were yellowing and withered and above them the palm trees drooped, fruit ungathered—the tree valued by the Nubians almost to veneration, for it gave them forty different products from dates to ropes. Yet in another guise life was returning. Grasses and undergrowth with no voracious goats to eat out the roots grew higher than I had ever seen them; wild flowers and bushes sprouted from plantations once given over to barley and sorgum, and the air was alive with birds and insects. Yet this burgeoning of nature could be no more than a final flamboyant gesture. I knew that in five years when the new lake would reach its maximum level the waters would have closed over every scrap of vegetation, every remaining building and every patch of alluvial soil.

At a certain spot on the river I stood staring across at the opposite bank and memory carried me back to the spring of 1962 when I had first made close contact with Nubians. For a month I had lived among them in one of their villages and it was then that I formed an attachment to Nubia and its people which was to grow with each subsequent visit and which will remain with me as long as I live. So strong were my impressions during those weeks of tranquillity that I recorded them in detail as the days slipped away.

Only four days have passed since I arrived in Abd-el-Qadir yet already I seem to have slipped into the pattern of life here. The mantle of history which envelops this corner of Nubia is almost palpable. Within sight, to north and south, are two of the strongholds built 40 centuries ago by Egypt's Pharaohs to dominate the Cataract; a thousand years earlier an Egyptian military expedition had come this way and left an account of its passing on the summit of a rocky hill overlooking the village; five miles to the south a pinnacle of limestone shoulders itself out of the river, the Rock of Abusir, and its inscribed flanks bear witness to the procession of travellers, soldiers and traders who over the millennia have moved along this reach of the Nile between Egypt and inner Africa.

Yet with the past the villagers of Abd-el-Qadir are unconcerned. Our village—I call it 'our' because the others of the small UNESCO team living here have formed, like myself, a strong attachment to the place—is no more than a hamlet, as are most Nubian villages. A dozen houses lie scattered along a shelf of sand and rock on the river's west bank. From the water's edge the ground rises to a mound surmounted by the tomb of a holy man, the tomb of Abd-el-Qadir, which gives the village its name. Our house is within a stone's throw of the river and from the porch we can look beyond a row of palms lining the bank to a scene of rare beauty. Fully a dozen islands are in view, some a few square yards in area, others like Meinarti directly facing us as much as a quarter of a mile from tip to tip. Every island is clothed in many shades of green, the green of grasses and reeds, the green of miniature plantations sprouting corn, beans and clover, tobacco and castor plants. Here and there dom palms and acacias stand high above the islets—a dozen shades of green and all framed in beaches of sand so white as to dazzle the eyes.

Two feluccas sail back and forth across the river bearing passengers and animals. Needless to say no timetable is followed and passengers wait patiently in the dust. One of the boats is owned by our landlord. His patriarchal figure, tall and hawk-featured, can often be seen moving between the houses with dignity, as befits the owner of the only radio in the village. An incongruous note is struck by the pipe stuffed with evil-smelling local tobacco which he smokes incessantly. Alongside his door stands a shelter constructed of reeds and in it a goat and her brood gambol and whinny all day long. Cocks and hens as skinny and undernourished as the Nubians themselves, scrabble on the water's edge, noisily dodging the feet of the women who go down to the river and sway back up the bank under the weight of laden water jars balanced effortlessly on their heads. The older among them are swathed in black garments and they are inclined to avert their faces as they pass but the younger women have adopted bright colours; their bold stares usually dissolve into giggles. The many children, when not rolling one another in the dirt, display a shy curiosity towards us; the girls shake their fuzzy mops of hair and laugh without restraint while the little boys stare with great liquid eyes. Tethered outside each house is a camel and every morning at the first flush of sunrise the ungainly beasts are led protesting noisily down through the acacias to drink at the Nile. As they go they disturb the wild geese nesting on the island off-shore, and up river they fly towards the Rock of Abusir, honking clamorously in competition with the piping call of the hoopoe bird which always heralds the dawn. The dawn chorus grows into pandemonium, a chain reaction started by the camels and picked up by goats, cocks and donkeys above all, which throw back their heads to bray with unrestrained enthusiasm. The rising cacophony is the signal for the water boy to empty the tins of drinking water he has dragged up from the Nile into the huge pottery jars immediately under my bedroom window. After dawn sleep in our village is impossible.

As the sun lifts from across the river, the men of the village gather to squat by the wall of our house which offers them shelter from the probing wind of the winter months. There they sit like a row of images, robes and turbans freshly washed and startlingly white against the sombre mud wall. Inside the house the courtyard is full of activity with Hassan noisily preparing breakfast while the potsherd boy prepares refills of water for the tin bowl which he will use for the rest of the morning to wash the dirt of centuries from the bits of pottery collected on yesterday's 'dig'. They lie in baskets along the walls, thousands of dun-coloured fragments. This is a typical Nubian house with an open courtyard as large as all the rooms opening off it. Two pillars of solid mudbrick support horizontal beams that in turn support a thatch of palm fronds. Surprisingly, among the beams are two iron girders made in Birmingham some seventy years ago and which are, in fact, rails taken from the railway line built by Kitchener along the Nile from Wadi Halfa during the River War against the Dervishes. That event was at the turn of the century and all the rails have long since been incorporated into scores of Nubian dwellings. In this dry climate not a speck of rust shows on the iron. However, most of the beams are palm trunks split lengthwise. Palm-frond thatch is effective in filtering the sun's rays but does nothing to keep out the endless rain of mud-dust and fine sand stirred up by the perpetual north wind and it deposits itself on objects and persons alike, day and night, especially night. The walls of mud-brick are plastered over with liquid mud and add their quota of dust so that the interior of a Nubian house is never free of it. Yet the houses are attractive in design and comfortable enough, their spaciousness and thick walls going far to offset the blistering heat of summer. The massive doors rest on flat stones and are secured at the top by a length of rope passed over a projecting beam; they incorporate an ingenious wooden latch which in design dates from Roman times. Two years later when I wanted to bring one of these extraordinary latches back to Europe, I was unable to find any wieghing less than sixteen pounds. The windows are tiny and have been knocked through the walls for our benefit. Most Nubian houses do not have windows but should you need one you simply knock out a few mud bricks, insert a wooden frame using mud plaster and it is ready. Indeed, to enlarge your house you gather mud from the Nile, pour it into wooden brick moulds to dry in the sun and in a few hours the job is done. Where mud and desert are inexhaustible as in Nubia, building problems are non-existent. Fortunately it is a rainless land, which is as well, otherwise the villages would melt back into soil. Our beds, called *angarib*, are wooden frames on four legs with palm fibres stretched lengthwise and they are of the same design as those found in Tutankhamun's tomb. They are totally lacking in comfort.

The days pass and the sandbanks in the river enlarge. One by one the small islands merge to become bigger islands as the falling water level causes the channels dividing them to disappear. In our village nobody hurries except perhaps the children and, of course, the baby goats that frolic around from dawn to dusk. It is in the evening when we get back from a long and tiring day at the 'dig' that the peace and tranquillity of the place takes hold of us. The smaller animals are back in their straw pens, the camels are tethered, and one by one the men on their donkeys pad silently up through the sand to squat in the last rays of the sun and talk in monosyllables of the day's doings. The figure of our landlord comes into view moving towards the river; beneath a palm he pauses and drops to his knees, face turned towards Mecca. The two feluccas, their sails furled, move gently to the drift of the current. Nearby three women are washing clothes, their movements leisurely and deliberate.

The honking of the wild geese dropping onto the island for the night raises mournful echoes. The sun sinks ever lower behind the ragged silhouette of a church raised on the hillside a thousand years ago, and the colours on the river intensify and change until the moment comes when the sun finally dips over the earth's rim and the sky is suffused momentarily with unearthly light. This was the moment dreaded by the old Egyptians, the 'in between time' when malign spirits were given power to take possession of the living. In Nubia night falls swiftly and within minutes the stars are rushing out. The river stirs with the rising wind and a chill creeps into the air. By now the village has surrendered to the night. The silence of the desert closes in on Abd-el-Qadir until the first rays of tomorrow's sun will reactivate a cycle of living unchanged since man first settled on the banks of the Nile.

The memories faded as I stared across the mile or so of water to Abd-el-Qadir. Only the Hill of Suleiman which had held the inscription of Djer for 5000 years showed where the village had once stood. Houses and trees alike had vanished below the waters. Even the islands with their honking geese were gone and the lake stretched, its surface unbroken, from my feet to the flanks of Gebel Sheikh Suleiman. At last the twentieth century had caught up with Nubia and had destroyed the land I cherished above all others.

In the crisp sunshine my spirits rose as I bumped back along the track to New Wadi Halfa, to a township which officially had no existence since old Wadi Halfa vanished under the lake. Out in the desert beyond reach of the creeping waters lived three thousand or so Nubians who had refused to leave when their great exodus ended six months before. The ramshackle shanties they had fabricated out of plaited reeds, old railway sleepers, even flattened petrol cans, were pitiful travesties of the beautiful and commodious dwellings traditional to Nubia. There was even an hotel knocked together from odd wooden planks; it was the one hotel in my experience where not only could I hear my next door neighbour but actually see him. For all that it was a brave effort. Unable to abandon these hardy individualists, the Government had compromised by constructing a spur of track to connect this non-existent township with the Khartoum railway. The line ended in a welter of shanties and the sand round about was strewn with a variety of objects dumped there by the weekly train. These people were eking out a living in trade between Egypt and Dongola some three hundred miles to the south. The goods brought from Egypt on a shabby little steamer were on-carried by a fleet of even more dilapidated trucks, so battered that only miracles of improvisation enabled them to endure the shattering surface of the desert track they were obliged to follow.

Next morning I took a boat to old Wadi Halfa. It was a hazardous voyage, for the boat like much of new Wadi Halfa, was made largely of flattened petrol tins which leaked at the joints; moreover a sandstorm was whipping up the surface of the lake into sizeable waves. We puttered on, heading north until the boatman pointed downwards: "Nile Hotel" he announced. I looked down through the water and could just distinguish a flat expanse of stonework, the roof of the comfortable little hotel where countless travellers had passed the night while awaiting the departure of Sudan Railways' 'Express' steamer to Assuan in Egypt or the arrival of the extremely slow train to Khartoum. Over a span of sixty years the two modes of travel were never able to coincide. It was from this same hotel several years before that I had embarked on the 'Express' steamer for Egypt. We were approaching Abu Simbel which is some thirty miles downstream from Wadi Halfa, when I heard my name called by the steward. With three separate groups of tourists aboard the boat was packed. I identified myself. "Sir", said the steward, a gigantic Sudanese, "I have here a telegram from our office in Khartoum instructing us to call at Abu Simbel to pick you up." 'Express' boats, I should explain, did not call at Abu Simbel on the regular run. "I changed my plans" I explained, "and did not go to Abu Simbel. So you won't have to call there," I added brightly. "But we must" was the reply, "the instructions are clear." So an hour or so later the ponderous floating structure consisting of four Mississippi-type passenger boats lashed together, drew in towards the sandy shore. The temples looked magnificient; the night was moonless and the floodlights were switched on. Bemused, I watched a gangplank lowered. There came an excited rush and a hundred and fifty or so delighted tourists disappeared into the darkness, hardly able to believe their luck. It took a distracted crew all of two hours to round them up. Consequently we missed the Egyptian Customs at Assuan and had to spend an extra night aboard the 'Express'. Food and drink ran out, air and train connections were missed and the worst national characteristics of several groups of Europeans were given full rein, to the distress of the Egyptian officials who were, of course, entirely innocent in the affair.

From the submerged hotel we splashed along an avenue of tall palms that had been the pride of Wadi Halfa. I reached out and picked several withered dates as we passed over the Commissioner's house where nearly seventy years before Kitchener had planned the strategy of the River War. And so to the docks and railway yards, invisible now beneath twenty feet of water. The minaret of a mosque and the dome of the Coptic Church, apparently floating on the surface, were the only clues to the whereabouts of an administrative capital that had housed 15,000 people.

In Upper Nubia the deposits of alluvial soil dropped by the Nile in its annual floodings were seldom more than a hundred yards wide and even less at those places where the river is confined by rocky banks, as in the Cataract. Only in the region of Wadi Halfa where the hills fall back had the river created a sizeable plain. It enabled Wadi Halfa and the 13 surrounding villages to support no less than 42,000 people. The remaining 8,000 or so Sudanese Nubians lived south of Wadi Halfa in hamlets scattered along the ninety miles of river between the beginning of the Second Cataract and Dal which marked the extreme southern limit of the flooded area. Here was a pattern of settlement that had changed little over the millennia so that the villages of today were often built on top of, or very close to, the settlements of long ago. The expeditions soon learned that the most likely sites for excavation were to be found in the vicinity of present-day villages. I remember an incident in the Nubian house which was the headquarters of the Scandinavian Expedition. We were enjoying the evening meal when abruptly my chair leg went through the top of an ancient tomb that lay unsuspected under the mud floor beneath the dining table. Many a time an expedition's Land Rover bogged down in a concealed grave; it was one of the hazards of driving near villages.

In Egypt and the Sudan the pace of life is very different from that of Europe or the United States and decisions tend to be made slowly, but no delays were acceptable with the fate of a hundred thousand people in the balance. From the moment the first loads of equipment arrived at the High Dam site, the days of the whole of Lower Nubia and a hundred miles of Upper Nubia were numbered and it is to the credit of both governments that the action taken was swift and decisive. In each country there were about fifty thousand persons to resettle. On one point Nubians on both sides of the border were adamant, they would move only if each village, each community, was preserved as a single group;

piecemeal resettlement they rejected outright. In Egypt the move was relatively simple. Komombo, the site selected, is only about fifty miles downstream from the High Dam with an environment little different from that of Lower Nubia—the Nile, the crops, the date palms, the desert and the climate being much the same, so that most of the familiar elements of life would continue unbroken. The houses, though, were very different, with each village laid out in rows of concrete structures, neat and hygienic. Admittedly the Nubians of Egypt would be forever separated from their fellow Nubians of the Sudan but their communities were kept intact and compensation in the form of land and money had been generous. In short, the phychological difficulties of social re-adjustment were minimal.

For the Nubians of the Sudan no similar solution could be found. The Northern Sudan is far less fertile than Egypt and nowhere along the Nile was there enough land to support an additional 50,000 people. The site chosen after much deliberation was at Khashm-el-Girba which is in the eastern part of the Sudan, near the Ethiopian frontier. It is known as the Bhutana and is the Sudan's largest grazing area. However, there was an inescapable snag: Khashm-el-Ghirba is nine hundred miles from Wadi Halfa and its soil and crops, climate and landscape are utterly different. People accustomed to the confined, intimate scale of Nubia would have to adjust to endless prairies and wide horizons. Unaccustomed crops would have to be cultivated in a heavy clay soil very different from the light easily worked alluvium of Nubia. For the first time in their lives they would experience thunder and the heavy rains of the monsoon; many of them had never seen water fall from the sky. Would their health deteriorate in an atmosphere so different from the bone-dry air of Nubia, and how well would they resist the malaria prevalent in Khashm-el-Ghirba? How would they feel about the Atbara, their new river, a smallish tributary of the venerated Nile? Evidently, unlike the Egyptian Nubians, the Sudanese would face a psychological adjustment that could be devastating in its effects.

It says much for the Nubians that they showed little resentment that the loss of their ancestral land sprang not from any economic problems of their own country, the Sudan, but from the pressures of a neighbouring state. Never were a proud and independent people more victimised by circumstance or less prepared psychologically and socially to adapt to fundamental change. Fortunately the dilemma of the Nubians was appreciated by those in authority so that everyone concerned was determined to make the transition as easy for them as possible.

On the Bhutana plain villages and a new town sprang up, the town of New Halfa, with some 2,000 houses and buildings. The surrounding villages, each of 250 houses, were named after settlements back in Nubia and as each became ready for habitation so the population of the corresponding village in Nubia was evacuated and transported to the new homes. The enforced movement of minorities is always a sad and harrassing affair and the Nubian exodus was no exception. Trainloads of as many as 600 persons, preceded by freight trains carrying their movable property and livestock (in all, 25,000 animals were transported) set out each week on the 40-hour journey. Only camels and household pets were left behind. Each train incorporated a mobile hospital and carriages were reserved for pregnant women and the aged. Food and pocket money were provided for every traveller, each of whom had been medically examined and inoculated. Nobody was coerced into leaving but every incentive had been used to persuade; in Wadi Halfa an exhibition showed models of the villages and houses in the new settlement, and deputations of villagers were taken to Khashm-el-Ghirba to demonstrate that the place really existed and was not a device of Government to trick them. The organisation behind the move was first-rate and in the event the Nubians "joined hands" with the authorities and left without fuss when their turn came. Most of them, that is. Some 3,000 stayed behind to build New Wadi Halfa as I have already described, and as late as 1969 I came upon little pockets of Nubians still living along the Batn-el-Haggar in ramshackle hutments, convinced that in Allah's good time Nubia would live again.

The Government of the United Arab Republic had contributed ten million Egyptian pounds to the cost of resettling the Nubians of the Sudan but it proved to be far (*above*) Assuan: the Elephantine Road to the south, probably the world's oldest highway. On the left is the Rock of Offerings, sacred to Khnum, surrounded by scores of stone cairns erected by ancient travellers setting out for Kush. (*right*) Sahaba: A-Group burial, *c.* 3000 BC. Observe ostrich-feather fan and palette (centre) and leather cap on skull.

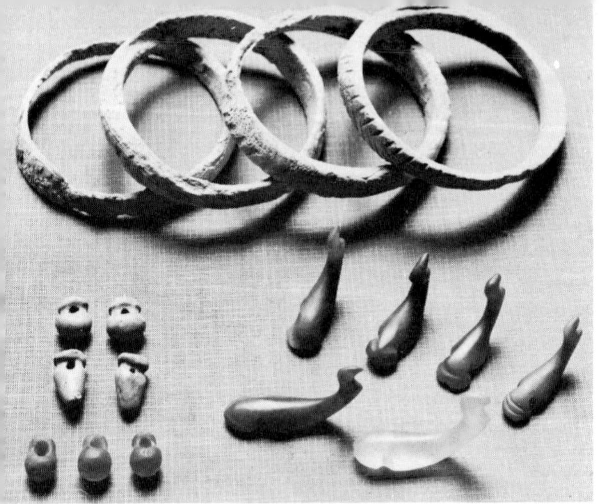

(*top left*) Second Cataract: jewellery from A-Group burials. (*below left*) Hill of Sheikh Suleiman: archaic inscription by Djer, third king of Egypt's First Dynasty. About 5000 years old, it is the earliest found in Nubia and records a military expedition and the capture of two towns. (Djer's name is at extreme left of boulder.) (*bottom*) Nubian Village, its inhabitants evacuated. The village is now far below Lake Nasser.

too little and the balance had to be made good by the Sudanese Government. Some Halfawi with houses worth a few hundred dollars in Halfa were given new dwellings at Khashm-el-Girba that cost $6,000 to $7,000 apiece to build. For each acre of land owned in Nubia they were given two acres, and in addition every able-bodied man was encouraged to become a tenant-cultivator of 15 acres of government-owned land on which to grow cotton, wheat and groundnuts in a three-year rotation. Obviously people cannot move into a new environment and immediately be self-supporting, so to tide them over, one million dollars was made available to them under the World Food Programme of the United Nations in the form of a balanced diet of food distributed free to every family.

In material terms the Nubians "never had it so good": 125,000 acres of potentially rich soil in exchange for 10,000 miserable acres that had given them no more than a marginal existence, plus brand new houses, schools, roads and social amenities. Indeed, Sudanese elsewhere in that vast country have cast envious eyes on the Nubians for their good fortune in being "victims" of the most radical and ambitious resettlement scheme ever attempted in Africa. Yet, with all this, let the Nubians of Khasm-el-Girba be offered the opportunity to return to a magically resurrected Nubia and I am pretty sure what the joyful response would be. The price they must pay will be the erosion of a culture with roots far back in the history of the Nile Valley. Nubian is not a written language, and although most of the men know and even write Arabic, the women speak only Nubian. So theirs is an aural tradition unlikely to survive the abrupt transplantation from the motherland which was the source of its continuing renewal.

It is fortunate that two experts were at hand to study the customs and traditions of Upper Nubia before the villagers were moved elsewhere. The field work, which occupied three seasons, was undertaken under the aegis of the Sudan Antiquities Service by the Viennese anthropologists, Dr and Mrs A. Kronenberg, and it is to them that I am indebted for much of what is included in the rest of this chapter.

Who are the Nubians and where did they originate? At first

Dr Kronenberg found it not at all easy to pinpoint a 'genuine' Nubian. Through marriage to Nubian women an extraordinary variety of ethnic groups seems to have been incorporated into Nubian society, including lineages of Turkish, Arab (several different tribes) and curiously, Magyar, origin. These latter may well have been Hungarians serving with the so-called Bosnians who garrisoned the fortress of Ibrim in Lower Nubia until 1811 when they were driven out by the Mamelukes, themselves in flight from Egypt's Mohammed Ali. However there seems to be wide agreement that the majority of present day Nubians are descended from the X-Group people who were converted to Christianity in the sixth century. By the fifteenth century Islam had taken over and Christianity as a living faith was dead. Still, 800 years is a long time and many traces of the old faith linger on in Nubian observances. To this day the sign of the cross is painted on the forehead of a child for the first seven days after birth. In Serra a quarrel over ownership of a date palm would be settled if one of the disputants cut a leaf from the tree in question and declared "Oh wood of Mary, what I say is true", an invocation nobody would dare to dispute. The Virgin Mary is also invoked by women in childbirth.

Other customs have origins much further back in history. An example is the presentation of a child, if born on the expected day, to the sun in a complicated ceremony and is probably carried down from pharaonic times when worship of the sun was, of course, an important feature of Egyptian religious belief. As with birth so with death. In Nubian cemetaries a bowl or pot is placed at the head of each grave and it is supposed that birds will drink the water it contains. Here, probably, is another link with ancient Egypt where the soul of the deceased was believed to take the shape of a bird which could seek sustenance in the form of life-giving water. Again, anyone who has seen an inscription in hieroglyphs will have noticed that certain groups of signs are enclosed in an oval box known as a cartouche. It usually denotes the name of a king and its purpose was to protect the name, and therefore the king's spirit, from malign influences for eternity. In Gemai, the villagers pursued the same idea when they drew a line around a newly-closed grave to keep evil spirits at bay. In other parts of Nubia they placed little collections of plants around graves at festival times, presumably as offerings to the dead—another link with ancient Egypt. Dr Keith Seele, leader of the expedition organised by the Oriental Institute of the University of Chicago, had often noticed the modern Nubian custom of covering graves with little white pebbles, round and smooth. One day just over the border in Egypt he came upon a C-Group cemetery and on excavating it was astonished to find similar collections of white pebbles placed between the big stones of the grave superstructures. That cemetery he dated to around 1600 BC. Subsequently he found deposits of white pebbles in A-Group graves of 3000 BC.

Customs and traditions were remarkably localised even in so small and restricted an area as Upper Nubia. Until the evacuation, the villagers of Mattokiya were still building into their houses architectural elements that were common in Old Nubian settlements of many centuries earlier, elements such as vaulted roofs, niches and windows, ovens and doors, and stone shelves built into the mud walls; indeed in the whole of the Sudan, Mattokiya was the only village to construct that particular type of Old Nubian vaulted roof. The islands of the Second Cataract, notably Nobennarti, Gummarti and Askombe were inhabited by people of Koki lineage who traditionally never marry outsiders—a Nubian living only 50 yards away on the mainland would be classed as an "outsider"—and on their islets they followed customs and traditions long since meaningless or forgotten elsewhere in Nubia.

Tony Mills, the young Canadian archaeologist who was responsible for conducting the archaeological survey from south Gemai to Dal, had worked for a time with Emery at Buhen and while there he came across an astonishing survival of an ancient belief. Two hippopotamus skulls unearthed while digging out the pharaonic fortress were taking up valuable space in the storeroom, so Mills on impulse stood them on the gateposts outside. In a day or so he noticed that women from nearby villages were coming to the expedition's headquarters to touch the skulls and the daily procession continued until the skulls were removed. Generations must have gone by since a hippopotamus was seen even as far north as Khartoum, 800 miles up-river from the Second Cataract, so not from personal experience could the women have known what it was they were touching. The point of the story lies in the mythology of ancient Egypt. The patroness of childbirth was the goddess Teuert who often took the form of a hippopotamus.

Nubia produced many surprises during the campaign and one of the most remarkable was Dr Kronenberg's idea that there may have been early cultural connections between Nubia and Europe. He based this view on the close affinity in themes of European folk stories with those of Nubia and he cites as examples "Gold Mary and Pitch Mary", "Cinderella", "Hansel and Gretel". It is the women who relate the tales, never men. Indeed women are the force behind the preservation of the traditional ways in village life. It is they who remain behind in Nubia to care for the plot of land, the children and the aged, while their men work abroad. They speak only Nubian and this too must be a powerful factor in their resistance to change and foreign influences.

Unlike the Copts (Christians) in Egypt who lost their language but preserved their religion, the Nubians lost their Christian faith but retained their language. Its origins and connections with other African tongues are obscure; Nubian deserves close linguistic examination and analysis because at one time it was a written language. Extant documents in Old Nubian show that it was widely used for biblical texts during the time of the Christian kingdoms of the Upper Nile Valley. Some date from the seventh century and this means that Nubian was the oldest written alphabetic language in inner Africa. Excavating for the Egypt Exploration Society in Lower Nubia at Kasr Ibrim, Professor Plumley recently found a veritable treasure trove of documents, several among them written in old Nubian.

The foregoing is no more than a random selection made from the many links with the past brought to light during the Campaign. Now for a look at how the conservative Nubians, while not accepting the twentieth century, managed to come to terms with it. An entire book would hardly suffice to describe the complicated ramifications of relationships between kin and fellow inhabitants of a hamlet, all with a clearly defined set of personal and communal obligations based on mutual help and cooperation, obligations that nobody dared neglect without incurring shame and disgrace. Briefly, then, the backbone of Nubian Society is the system of social security it has evolved, a system to which "self-help" Samuel Smiles would have given unqualified approval. Responsibility is shared by all so that, for example, the death of one member of a community becomes the concern of the rest, and all contribute to the cost of the burial and, where the deceased was the wage-earner, the support of his family. Should a farmer die during the time of cultivation his fellow-villagers are bound to grow and harvest the crop for the benefit of his surviving relatives. Marriage celebrations in Nubia are long and expensive affairs so all members of the community must assist with gifts and money. The pattern is repeated with birth and religious ceremonies.

All the events described would call forth financial contributions from the corresponding Nubian association or 'club' abroad. The communal pattern in village life had its exact counterpart in Cairo, Alexandria and Khartoum where the majority of able-bodied Nubian men worked to supplement the inadequate income from the minute plots of land farmed by their families back home. Each club represented a village or group of hamlets and any changes in interrelationships between individuals and between communities were faithfully reflected in Cairo, Alexandria or Khartoum. In short, social ties as they operated in the home village were transferred to the place of wage-earning.

Membership of the association or club was more or less obligatory for a newcomer from the village but at the same time he would be helped to find a job and, if necessary, be supported until work came his way. The clubs provided effective economic security for their members in time of sickness or unemployment. Taking financial responsibility for damage or misfortune in the home village was another of the club's responsibilities; should a house burn down or a ferry boat sink the club was bound to step in and help. Some of the wealthier clubs of Cairo and Alexandria have gone further. The Serra West Association which owed allegiance to ten hamlets–incidentally the 1960 census showed 655 residents in Serra West and 644 absentees–established a school and a dispensary, a cooperative irrigation pump scheme and a cooperative mill back in Nubia. Could voluntary social service go further? Of course, in the strictest sense, none of this is voluntary; it is enforced by the unwritten code which makes non-conformism unthinkable, just as it is unthinkable for a Nubian to offend against the accepted code of social behaviour. To do so would cover not only himself but his entire family with shame. So everybody behaves with courtesy, voices are seldom raised, violence is almost unknown. And so is dishonesty. In Nubia the houses had no locks, only latches, while in the big cities outside not notable for their rectitude in money matters, the honesty of Nubians is proverbial.

While the remarkable stability of the Nubian character undoubtedly owes much to social cohesion, there is another factor in Nubian life which may be even more significant; the mystic notion of *awi*, which expresses and assures solidarity. *Awi* is common to all relatives and residents in the same village and by uniting them in a mystical sense tends to lift disputes, ideas of vengeance and hatred out of the arena of everyday life into a transcendental sphere. *Awi* unquestionably adds to the high degree of social equilibrium that is so striking a feature of Nubian village life. Moreover it bridges distance for it is the strongest of the bonds linking the clubs with the homeland.

Abroad, Nubians keep very much to themselves, the clubs providing recreation and amusements in the form of football and other sports, boy-scout troops, folk music groups and dancing. Most Nubians work as cooks and *safragis* (butlers) or janitors of the many apartment buildings. Generations of Europeans in Egypt would have been lost without Nubians to run their houses, and I was no exception. In Cairo I employed the same Nubian cook for ten years and during that time five young relatives passed through his hands for training in the arts of cooking and housekeeping. He was a great demonstrator of the communal give and take among Nubians, sometimes with embarrassing results. On one occasion I had invited a rather important man and his wife to dinner for the first time. During the meal I noticed the wife eyeing the crockery which even to my bachelor eye seemed vaguely unfamiliar. At our next meeting she revealed that the crockery had been hers. My cook had borrowed it from a fellow villager who by coincidence happened to be my guest's cook.

Nubians are also famous as sailors and generations of crews on the river steamers of the Nile have come from the land of the Cataracts. Like the domestic workers, they are well organised and insist on conforming to time-honoured rules and customs. The tradition of leaving the village to work abroad is by no means recent among Nubians. As early as the middle of the thirteenth century, Cairo had its Nubian Quarter, *Haret el Noubi,* but it was the construction of the first Assuan Dam in 1902 that precipitated a large migration of Nubians to the Egyptian capital. Mostly they were from Lower Nubia where a considerable area of cultivable land was inundated. More land vanished with the first heightening of the dam in 1912 and more yet in 1934 when the reservoir was extended for the second time. With each shrinkage of arable land more Nubians were forced to leave until now the High Dam has driven out not only the remaining able-bodied men but their families as well. Possibly the new opportunities for prosperous farming offered at Khasm-el-Girba will persuade the men to abandon the cities and remain with their families to work the land themselves. A result would certainly be a weakening of the conservative influence of the women and this could bring about profound changes in the long-established structure of Nubian society as I have attempted to describe it.

As for those left behind in Nubia, their tenacity may be rewarded. The intention is to re-open the important commercial link between Egypt and the Sudan which after 60 years or so of continuous operation was severed in 1964 with the closing of the High Dam across the Nile. The plan, which is part of an ambitious scheme for the economic development of Lake Nasser using funds and expertise provided by the United Nations Development Programme (UNDP) and the Food and Agricultural agency of the United

Nations (FAO), envisages the construction of harbours and docks at Assuan and in the district of Wadi Halfa, where the town will be rebuilt. If all goes according to plan the traffic of freight and passenger steamers will be resumed and once more it will be possible for a traveller to step off the train which has carried him 700 miles from Cairo to Shellal just south of the High Dam, embark on a steamer for the next stage of the journey–the 200 miles of Lower Nubia–to Wadi Halfa, and there pick up the Sudan Railways train for the 600-mile run to Khartoum. Wadi Halfa itself, re-instated as the terminal point of river and rail, will re-appear on the maps and prosperity will surely follow. Undoubtedly many Nubians will return to rebuild the little businesses that used to thrive on the regular traffic between their country and Egypt. Also at a later stage when the Nile silt begins to form new areas of fertility around the shores of the reservoir, others will follow, not a large number probably but enough to re-establish a Nubian presence on the Nile.

CHAPTER IV

Prehistoric Nubia

A century ago a sailing dahabieh was beating its way up the river Nile, the north wind billowing the triangular sail against a cloudless sky. Aboard it was a group of people who could be said to typify the travellers of the day. In that other world of the early 1870s, the wealthy and the influential of Europe would turn their well-clad backs on wintry rain and snow and seek the warmth and sunshine of Upper Egypt and Nubia. They ate well and travelled comfortably in paddle steamers and the delightful dahabiehs that once belonged to Mr Thos. Cook and nowadays lie rotting in the Nile mud around Cairo. They travelled to Luxor, Assuan and Philae and even further up-river to Abu Simbel and Wadi Halfa at which point the rocks of the Second Cataract effectively barred their venturing any further south.

Armed with Baedeker, sketch pad and watercolours and, of course, notebook and pencil, they overlooked no temple, shrine or tomb then visible no matter how insignificant. Their interests were both catholic and practical. Anthropology and geology, the flora and the fauna, all engaged their earnest attention. Above everything they revelled in the romance tinged with melancholy that the stony remnants of long-dead civilisations so often inspire. And on return to Europe at the end of the Season their notes and diaries would sometimes blossom into romantic novels or what nowadays we would call travel books–illustrated as often as not, charmingly if not always accurately.

Typical then was the little group of people reclining on the deck of the dahabieh labouring against the current towards the Sudan frontier. Among them was a Miss Amelia Edwards. Miss Edwards, author and traveller, was an unusually handsome woman with a passion for Egyptology; the day was to come when she would endow London's University College with the Edwards Chair of Egyptology but now as the Abu Simbel temples slipped astern Miss Edwards' eye was drawn to the curious rocky hills that spring up from the desert in those parts with dramatic effect.

> Of all the strange peaks we have yet seen, the mountains hereabout are the strangest. Alone or in groups, they start up here and there from the deserts on both sides, like the pieces on a chess-board. . . As regards form, they are weird enough for the wildest geological theories. . . One is four-sided, like a pyramid; another, in shape a truncated cone, looks as if crowned with a pagoda summerhouse; a third seems to be surmounted by a mosque and cupola; a fourth is scooped out in tiers of arches; a fifth is crowned, apparently, with a cairn of piled stone; and so on with variations as endless as they are fantastic. . . They are for the most part conical; but they are not extinct craters, such as are the volcanic cones of Korosko and Dakkeh. Seeing how they all rose to about the same height, . . the Writer could not help fancying that, . . . they might be but fragments of a rocky crust, rent and swept away at some infinitely remote period of the world's history, and that the level of their present summits might represent perhaps the ancient level of the plain.

Amelia Edwards had the makings of a geologist. She was very nearly right in her speculations. Those strange formations have since revealed how and when the Nile itself was born. If Miss Edwards had been taken to the summit of any of those curious peaks by a group of geologists and palaeontologists, as I was, the mystery would have been explained. Those conical hills are all that remain of a great plateau, hard rocky cores left behind after the softer sandstone and gravels had been eroded away by wind and water. Across this plateau flowed great rivers. Then, around 30,000 years ago, one of them started to cut through the sandstone until it reached the level of today. That river is the Nile.

But long before our Nile was born men were living and hunting on the plateau and making stone artifacts. Miss Edwards, I feel sure, would have been deeply stirred by the sight on that summit of an Old Stone Age "workshop" lying on the surface undisturbed, with the finished or half-completed tools and waste flakings lying just as they were abandoned, perhaps 100,000 years ago. The river levels exposed on the flanks of the hills are known as terraces and they have enabled the pre-historians to trace the movements of palaeolithic man as the Nile dug ever deeper into the plateau. In classical archaeology the deeper you dig the older your finds are likely to be but for pre-historic Nubia the very opposite seems to be true. As the Nile sank ever lower in its bed so early man, in his need for water, followed it down to its present level. Consequently the "industries", as they are termed, exposed on the highest level turn out to be the oldest and they grow progressively younger as today's level is approached.

On my first visits to Nubia, classical archaeologists were predominant but by 1964 I found it impossible to move through the Second Cataract region without constantly coming upon little knots of men marking out grids on the desert surface or chipping away at the flanks of wadies. And back from the river the gravel plains were criss-crossed with the tyre tracks of their Land Rovers, for they seemed to be always on the move. In all, about fifty specialists concerned with pre-history, mostly American, were at work on both banks of the river and to seek them out you had to be prepared to venture into the most inaccessible corners of that inhospitable landscape. Even then you would have difficulty in understanding their vocabulary for they spoke in terms of denticulates, burins, cores, microliths, lunates, horizons, benches and so on (see Figure 1). Moreover their expeditions seemed to embrace an astonishing variety of disciplines. One, for example, had on its strength two prehistorians, two geologists, two biologists, one invertebrate zoologist and one vertebrate zoologist.

The institutions from five of the countries participating in the pre-history rescue operation in Nubia decided from the outset that the only effective approach to an emergency such as that imposed by the rapidly rising water was a joint operation. So the Combined Prehistoric Expedition came into being. In Egyptian Nubia their concession took in the entire west bank of the Nile, and in the Sudan not only the

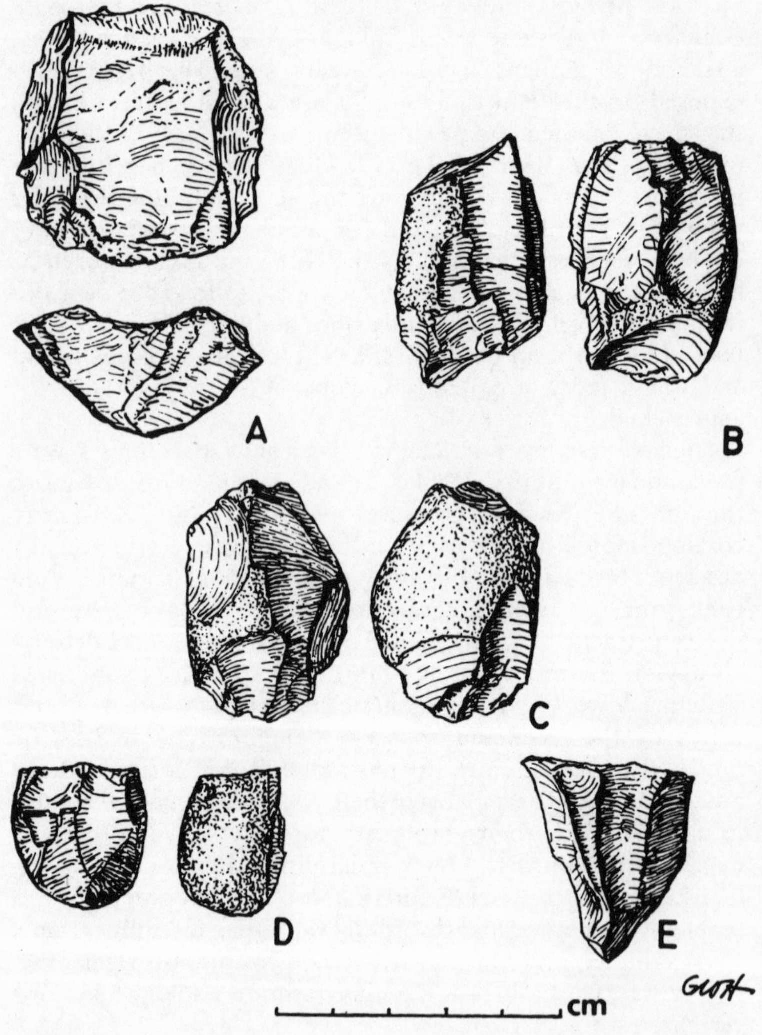

Fig. 1. SITE 11-I-16. MISCELLANEOUS CORES
(A) Levallois core with overshot removal, yellow chert; (B) double-ended core, brown chert, (C) brown chert, from gravel layer; (D) struck in one direction, brown chert; (D) pyramidal core, greenish-brown chert-jasper breccia, from gravel layer.

west bank but most of the east bank as well–some four hundred miles of territory in all. The Scandinavian Joint Expedition, which in the Sudan was responsible for the remaining section of east bank between the Second Cataract and Egyptian border, in practice made over their prehistoric findings to the Combined Prehistoric Expedition. In Egyptian Nubia the east bank was the responsibility of a joint expedition sponsored by the Peabody Museum of Yale University and the National Museum of Canada.

First the concessions had to be surveyed and where necessary excavated, and all from ground level; the aerial surveys which proved so useful to the classical archaeologists offered nothing to the pre-historians. The team approach was carried to its logical conclusion with the collective publication of all the final reports. Edited by Dr Fred Wendorf of Southern Methodist University, Dallas, the three large volumes appeared in 1969. Thus, almost simultaneously with the ending of the archaeological phase of the Nubian Campaign a comprehensive corpus of Nubian prehistory had been drawn up and made available to scholars everywhere. It was a *tour de force*. They provided an object lesson in how large-scale salvage archaeology can be organised and conducted to extract the maximum of data when time is strictly limited, and, moreover, to make maximum use of it by speedy publication.

That having been said, I trust my pre-historian friends will forgive me for the compression and oversimplification which a book of this nature imposes on the writer. In less than one chapter it is impossible to do justice to the awesome range of expertise involving so many disciplines that was drawn into the structuring of Nubian pre-history. The resources of science have become a powerful aid in the interpretation of evidence drawn exclusively from the stone fragments fashioned by man into "tools" and from the conformation of the rocks themselves. Computer technology and statistical analysis together with intricate systems of dating, of which carbon-14 is only one, are some of the means used by pre-historians of today in their efforts to follow the long march of homo sapiens and his predecessors to the threshold of recorded history. It is a far cry from the scientifically-orientated pre-historians of today to the amateur antiquarians of a century ago with their notebooks and pencils.

Nubian pre-history divides into four epochs

DATE	EPOCH	INDUSTRY
Pre 50,000 BC	Early Stone Age	Acheulian
c. 45,000–33,000 BC	Middle Stone Age	Nubian Mousterian, Denticulate Mousterian, Nubian Middle Palaeolithic
c. 25,000–16,000 BC	Upper Stone Age	Khormusan, Gemaian and Sebilian
c. 18,000– 3,500 BC	Final Stone Age	Halfan, Ballanan, Quadan, Arkinian, Shamarkian (microlithic components dominate all industries)

The Nubian Ceramic Age, when pottery first appears, has been dated 4500–4000 BC.

The terms Acheulian and Mousterian have been borrowed from European pre-history for convenience, and the industries they represent in Europe differ in many ways from the Nubian counterparts. All the other industries mentioned, and their offshoots, are local and distinct and this discovery bears out a remark made by Professor Joel L. Shiner, leader of the University of New Mexico group. He was puzzled by the absence in Nubia of a single line of development. Rather there seemed from earliest times to be groups of people living independently with little or no interchange of information or ideas. Thus in the making of tools each group carries its own tradition, evolving gradually but nevertheless discernible over thousands of years.

The population appears to have stabilised into a Nubian Nilotic culture once the Nile river had become established. This momentous event seems to have taken place about 25,000 years ago—only yesterday in terms of geological time. The complexities of the pre-Nile river system have yet to be reconstructed but it seems that geological changes in the landscape stabilised around 50,000 years ago resulting in a main depression which ultimately became the Nile bed; Middle Acheulian artifacts found buried at that level provided the dating. Some 25,000 years later, during the Upper Stone Age, a sudden discharge of water from the south forced its way around the edge of the Batn-el-Hagar bringing gravels and minerals and forming ponds below what became the Second Cataract. The subsequent phases are too complex to follow here beyond saying that the modern alluvial floodplain of the Nile was formed around 3000 BC.

Most of the prehistorians I met admitted that before coming to Nubia they expected to find little of interest. Nubia it seems had the reputation of being a backwater in the development of early man. How wrong they were excavation quickly revealed. Their method of work was to seek out industries and wherever possible associate them with geological formations or deposits. Very occasionally sites would contain organic material such as bone or even wood and this would provide a date by laboratory analysis. "Industries" are so called because they are concerned with the shaping of stone "tools" by hammering, chipping and flaking, and it is the study of shape and size and, above all, the method of manufacture, that enables the prehistorian to label each artefact and slot it into a time scale.

The artefacts range from the earliest of tools–pebbles with one end flaked to a rough point–to the ultimate in Stone Age technology: the elegant, pear-shaped hand axe, known in its most advanced form as the Acheulian axe. In between these there emerged a wide variety of specialised tools for cutting, scraping, drilling and, of course, killing. Early man was exclusively a hunter and animals were his primary source of food; their skins kept him warm and their bones had many practical uses. Bare hands alone were able to achieve little, but a rapidly evolving intelligence developed artificial extensions to the hands which enormously increased their efficiency in the endless search for food. Nature provided the raw material in the shape of flints and stones and man's inventiveness provided the technology, the same inventiveness that has brought the world in our day to the brink of catastrophe. It is salutary to note Jacquetta Hawkes's comment on man as he was about 700,000 years ago during the Pleistocene Age. It was then that he first began to chip away at pebbles and she points out that in any one year probably not more than ten thousand brains on the entire planet were well enough equipped to design and execute even so simple a tool as that.

In the early part of the Pleistocene Age man was a rare

being. In Nubia however he lived and hunted in comparatively large numbers especially in the latter part of the Old Stone Age. Professor Shiner was astonished by the number of sites and the quantity and variety of tools found in them. He explained that in America one might dig for a month and find a dozen tools, or in an extremely rich site perhaps fifty, whereas in Nubia they were finding hundreds of artefacts in one day. He showed me an excavation not more than a metre square that had yielded close on 300 pieces of worked stone of which 50 were finished tools. Dr Fred Wendorf describes a habitation site 30 metres by 20 which produced no less than 21,391 artefacts. These were mostly flakings, chips and cores, but included 1149 blades and 1001 tools. These figures suggest that the site was occupied by a group of people for a fair span of time, long enough for considerable camp debris to accumulate. The habitations of these early men were roughly of three types. One used natural rock formations to provide wind shelters which usually faced north-east or south-west; a second category also took advantage of natural features such as large boulders lying in partial circles, circles which could be completed and enclosed by man; the third type was what pre-historians call "workshops" because they contain a high concentration of stone tools and flake debris. Whether any of these "habitations" were roofed, or protected from the weather by walls of brush or twigs is impossible to say since no trace has survived.

One site consisted of more than a hundred hearth areas each indicated by fire-cracked rocks. Surrounding dunes which had once contained ponds must have provided shelter and water and, therefore, a comfortable camp site for the people who came here to fish in the adjacent river. Fish remains yielded by the hearths suggested that the bulk of a catch was smoked on the spot and eaten elsewhere. The place seems to have been a semi-permanent camp to which people returned again and again.

The many habitation sites show that life on the plateau was congenial for early man and this view is supported by evidence of game animals in plenty. Remains of wild ox and wild ass, giraffe, hartebeest and gazelle have been found in areas of total desert, as much as twenty miles back from the

(*top left*) Abka: one of the individualists who refused to leave their ancestral *Batn-el-Haggar* as the waters rose to engulf dwellings and patches of cultivation. (*top right*) Abka: typical Nubian house in the Second Cataract area, abandoned and soon to be swallowed by the rising Nile. Wood is so scarce that the owners invariably took away with them all doors, windows and frames. (*below*) Wadi Halfa: the river front of the former capital of Sudanese Nubia, now completely engulfed by the reservoir.

(*top left*) Wadi Halfa: collection of objects from A-Group cemeteries: pottery palette, golden handle, figurine, copper axes. (*top right*) Wadi Halfa: two masterpieces of early art in unburnt clay (*c.* 3000 BC), found in a woman's tomb of the A-Group period. They represent a mature female and a young girl: note the curious pattern around the loins. (*below*) Wadi Halfa: Professor Torgny Säve Söderbergh, leader of the Scandinavian Joint Expedition, measuring an A-Group grave before recording and clearing the contents.

Nile. Only savanna or steppe can support such animals so the climate of those times must have been much less rigorous than today's, although over so long a period of time quite wide variations must have been experienced. Pollen and invertebrate studies point to a belt of Mediterranean flora right across the central Sahara as late as the Nubian Final Stone Age around 10,000 years ago, and this implies a steppe environment with a comparatively moist and mild climate. Such an environment, while unfavourable for permanent settlement, would have provided easy movement for nomadic hunters.

By 18,000 BC the Nile was probably a well established river supporting hippopotami and crocodiles and well stocked with fish. Along its banks a fringe of dense vegetation harboured a variety of small animals while in the savanna to east and west roamed numerous large herbivores. This was the environment enjoyed by the Khormusan people. These Upper Stone Age Nubians seem to have been organised into small bands and tended to return to the same areas again and again for their campsites. Khormusan sites were never found beyond the belt of Nile alluvium which indicates that although hunters, these people preferred to stay close to the river. They were selective in their use of lithic materials and knew where in the Second Cataract to find what they wanted. They knew, for example, the region's only source of haematite which they could have used for decorating their bodies, because this red oxide was present in every Khormusan site excavated. They used wood extensively and probably reeds but there is no evidence of either of these materials being employed for constructing shelters. Nevertheless the number of burins found does imply the development of a wood and reed-work industry on a substantial scale. The foregoing is a tentative picture of one of the Nubian Stone Age cultures drawn from the findings of the pre-historians and geologists. The Khormusans came into the Second Cataract region around 25,000 BC and remained there for about ten thousand years before passing into oblivion. It has been suggested that they were driven out of the Second Cataract by an influx of hunters from the north. If this is so then a group of newcomers may have been the victims of a grisly drama that was played out near the northern end of the Second Cataract some time between 12,000 and 10,000 BC. At the head of a small wadi Dr R. Paepe and Dr Jean Guichard found fragments of three human skeletons in a shallow pit covered by thin sandstone slabs. Subsequent excavation disclosed more graves, some containing as many as four burials. In all 58 skeletons were recovered, both male and female, adult and infant. Most were buried in a contracted position with hands before the face. Here follows an extract from Dr Wendorf's report.

> One of the unusual features of the burials was the direct association of 110 artifacts, almost all in positions which indicate they had penetrated the body either as points or barbs on projectiles or spears. They were not grave offerings. Many of the artefacts were found along the vertebral column, but other favoured target areas were the chest cavity, lower abdomen arms and the skull. Several pieces were found inside the skull, and two of these were still embedded in the sphenoid bones in positions which indicate that the pieces entered from under the lower jaw. Other artifacts were found during the screening of the fill; many of these may have been weapon points, too, but their original positions in the graves are not known.

This is a scientist's way of saying that more than half of a group of men, women and children had died violently. Some had been repeatedly cut about on the limbs and no distinction had been made by the killers between males, females and children. Dr Wendorf has the final word:

> There is no direct evidence available on the factors which were responsible for the violence seen in Nubia at this time. The ferocity evident in the deaths of many of the individuals indicates that the situation was more serious than that which leads to the occasional friction between neighbouring groups. One possibility, if the graveyard is correctly dated, is that the population pressures may have become too great with the deterioration of the Late Pleistocene climate and the effects which this had on the herds of large savanna-type animals which were the primary source of food at this time. With this situation, the few localities which were particularly favourable for fishing would have been repeatedly fought over as other sources of food became increasingly scarce.

Subsequent examination of the skeletons by the Southern Methodist University's Anthropological Research Centre has revealed that the skulls of these Late Palaeolithic Nubians bear a resemblance in general morphology to those of the Cro-Magnons of Europe; in particular they resemble strongly the skulls of men who were widely distributed through North Africa, known as the Mechta type. Here then is an indication of movements across the Sahara shortly before the end of the Pleistocene Age. More to be expected were influences penetrating Nubia along the Valley from south and north, and such penetrations have been confirmed by the findings of the pre-historians.

One other group of pre-historic burials came to light; they numbered 39 but with one exception all appeared to have died naturally.

Another problem for pre-historians to ponder has been raised by the discovery of grindstones in Nubia. For food production grindstones had to be fabricated to mill the wild grains into flour for baking into bread, all related inventions but nonetheless notable for that. South-West Asia has long been accepted as the favoured environment where, with the domestication of wild grains and animals village life began. It seems now that the technique of using grindstones was known in Nubia around 13,000 to 12,000 BC, some two to three thousand years earlier than in South-West Asia. Why then did the Nile Valley inhabitants of that time fail to exploit this source of food growing along the river by domesticating it and settling into permanent communities? A clue may lie in shifts in the pattern of Pleistocene vegetation between 10,000 and 8,000 BC; the lessening rainfall at that time could have brought about a corresponding change in the wild grasses on which the grain gatherers depended. If this hypothesis is correct it provides an interesting demonstration of the interaction of man with his environment in the days before he learned how to manipulate it. A slight change in climate and the immense potential of his new technology was neutralised and the appearance of permanent villages in Nubia delayed, probably for several millennia.

In 1948 and 1957 O. H. Myers excavating at Abka in the Second Cataract found sites which seem to provide a bridge between Upper Palaeolithic man and his Neolithic successors. He identified both Mesolithic and Neolithic occupations and his findings have since been confirmed by pre-historians of the Combined Expedition who agree with Myers' contention that Sudanese "Neolithic" was developed locally and was not imported from Egypt, as most scholars have maintained. Among the many rock drawings on the site, Myers identified several which are especially interesting in that they give a further indication of the kind of climate and vegetation that Nubia enjoyed at that epoch: elephant and rhinoceros, oryx, warthog, ostrich and lion. Another significant drawing was that of a baobab tree and the most interesting a fish-trap built of stones, of the kind still used in the area up to the evacuation of the population in the 1960s. The date assigned to the earliest of the drawings is around 7500 BC and this probably makes them the earliest dated drawings in Africa.

The Scandinavians took me to see the drawings, in particular the oldest group which I can best describe as abstract whirls and curls. They also showed me a desolate valley nearby where they had discovered a veritable picture gallery of early man. Across the granite boulders marched animals by the thousand. The recorders had stuck a little white label above each pictograph for enumeration and since there were so many of them the spotted effect in that valley of brown rocks was bizarre in the extreme. The archaeologist who showed me the carvings pointed out that they were on both walls of a series of narrow canyons through which the animals would have to pass from their feeding grounds to find water, and here the hunters could wait, effectively concealed by the many boulders.

From the Abka sites Myers recovered organic material that was subsequently dated by the carbon-14 process: *c.*7350 BC and 6300 BC for the Mesolithic, *c.*4000 BC and 2550 BC for the Neolithic sites. The latter date brings us well into the historical period of Nubia which according to Reisner's classification begins with the A-Group culture. Before the Nubian Campaign so little was known about these people that Dr A. J. Arkell, now of the University of London, was able to write in 1955 that only two of their cemeteries had been scientifically excavated in the Sudan, one at Faras and the other at Gemai although sherds of A-Group type pottery had been picked up south of the Dal Cataract and even further south, on Sai Island.

The years of excavation during the Campaign has broadened our knowledge of the A-Group culture although we still do not know where it originated and have not much more idea of how it ended. Neolithic pottery of the types known as early Khartoum and Shaheinab was found mixed with A-Group pottery in many Nubian A-Group settlements during the 1960s. Khartoum and Shaheinab are some seven hundred miles south of the Second Cataract and the view now held is that the A-Group is a cultural facet of the Khartoum Neolithic and that the A-Group were direct descendents of the Neolithic peoples of the Sudan. They appeared in Nubia as a distinctive culture around 3200 BC. Their settlements were in the nature of campsites since no evidence of buildings of mud-brick or stone has survived. However, traces showed that they did live in huts made of perishable materials, probably of woven reeds of brushwood; several well-preserved fireplaces were found.

A-Group cemeteries appeared along the whole length of Lower Nubia in Egypt and over the Sudan border right through the Second Cataract region. There was a falling off between the inhospitable crags of the Belly of Stone and the Dal Cataract where the Survey ended, and there has been much speculation as to whether the A-Group might have penetrated further south. At the time of writing there is news of the discovery of a cemetery indisputably A-Group at Solb about 60 miles up-stream from Dal. But in between Dal and Solb and beyond, how many more sites might there be? Here is yet another reason for a survey team to walk along the whole seven hundred-mile length of the Nile between Dal and Khartoum.

Reisner's classification of a separate B-Group culture contemporary with the A-Group is no longer accepted. The general view now is that these people were poor relations of the A-Group, at a lower level of development.

The level of civilisation reached by the A-Group is reflected in the funerary objects recovered. Apart from a wide variety of pottery, some of which is extremely attractive in design, there are leather garments, ostrich feather fans, copper weapons and palettes of quartz, and grindstones, to mention only a few.

A-Group cemeteries were often difficult to find. Unlike the cemeteries of later periods few of the graves showed surface indications. Many indeed were buried under layers of hard-packed gravel dropped by successive Nile floodings over the millennia and only prodding with iron rods could locate individual burials. Unquestionably this is what saved them from the attentions of robbers and is the reason why a remarkably high number of A-Group graves were found intact. A typical A-Group burial was No. 62 of a cemetery near Wadi Halfa excavated by the Scandinavian Joint Expedition and the following is a description of the grave as I saw it. Incidentally not one of the 66 graves excavated had been plundered, because of the hard silt overlay. The skeleton lay on its side in a contracted position. Near his head–it was a male–lay a largish red-polished jar with a narrow neck probably intended for water. Behind his neck a small palette of stone bore traces of green material which was ground on it and then used as a paste to adorn the eyes. Remains of what was once a kind of leather kilt lay under the legs near the pelvis and beneath that again were slight traces of the straw mat in which the body was laid. His left foot was touching one of the beautiful black-topped jars with incised bands that are characteristic of the A-Group. Next to it, two medium size dishes and two smaller ones represented the food he would need beyond the grave, and at the other end of the body near the skull lay two largish jars with a smaller beaker which could have been meant for beer. I watched the archaeologists first measure the grave, then photograph it and finally, mark up a diagram showing exactly where the objects lay in relation to one another and to the skeleton. Each was then lifted, numbered according to the number on the diagram and placed in a plastic bag. When the objects had been cleared the ostiologist got to work, measuring and noting the position of the bones and then lifting them for removal in the ubiquitous plastic bags.

From an A-Group grave in the Scandinavian concession came two figurines, unique in burials of this period. Moulded from unburnt clay they represent a mature female and a young girl just emerging from childhood. Round the loins is a pattern which may represent either tattooing or a loin cloth.

They are masterpieces of early art. Again it was the Scandinavians who found a puzzling A-Group interment. Buried with the man was a mineralogical collection of the many varieties of stones found in the neighbourhood–ochres, chert, amethyst, carnelian, quartz, granite and so on. This was at Abka near where Myers had excavated his Mesolithic and Neolithic sites.

Across the border in Egyptian Nubia, Dr Keith B. Seele hit upon an unplundered A-Group cemetery which yielded some exceptionally fine pottery. One pot in particular was a masterpiece, as delicate as porcelain. There were several attractive bowls decorated in a pattern of white spots and a burnt clay hippopotamus head about nine inches across; unfortunately the body of the animal or the vessel of which it may have been a handle was missing. The outstanding treasure of this small cemetery however was a set of wonderfully preserved copper implements which included chisels and something that resembled a razor. A parallel with the Abka man and his mineralogical collection was provided by one of Seele's A-Group burials which contained thousands of beads, some of shell, others of bone. Many beads were unfinished or unpierced and Seele suggested that here was the burial of a bead-maker and that on his death his relatives buried with him his entire stock-in-trade.

Evidence in plenty came to light to show that the A-Group were in contact with intruders from Egypt from the earliest times. Apart from imported Egyptian pottery and other artifacts, several early Egyptian sealings have been found in A-Group burials by Nordström in the course of the Survey and Mills too, towards the end of the campaign showed me an Archaic Period cylinder seal from an A-Group grave near Sarras.

The foregoing examples are but a few of the multitude of objects recovered by most of the expeditions from the many A-Group cemeteries excavated in the 1960s. It has been pointed out, and the observation is significant, that in all the thousands of graves excavated along the banks of the Nile in Nubia few can be convincingly dated to the period between the end of Egypt's First Dynasty and the beginning of the Sixth Dynasty and that this must surely mean that for a period of about five hundred years there were few settled communities in Nubia. What then became of the promising A-Group culture? The answer may be engraved on that elongated rock which lay on the top of Gebel Sheikh Suleiman at the entrance to the Second Cataract (see Figure 2). It is the oldest inscription ever found in Nubia and it records in archaic hieroglyphs the capture of towns in the area. The man who carved that rock was a member of the military expedition sent to Nubia by a king of Egypt's First Dynasty, possibly Djer. Below the boat, typical of the First Dynasty in design, several corpses are shown, and a figure tethered by the neck to the boat has been taken to represent the people captured and deported to Egypt. King Djer's name occurs again on a rock not far removed from Gebel Sheikh Suleiman. The vast collection of objects found in Djer's northern tomb at Saqqara near Cairo and the jewellery recovered from his southern tomb at Abydos seem to indicate that Egypt enjoyed increased prosperity during his reign. It is also of interest that human sacrifice was still in vogue, for the Abydos tomb was surrounded by rows of subsidiary graves numbering 338; most were of women and all were put to death at the time of the royal burial.

Fig. 2 The Inscription of King Djer at Sheikh Suliman.

Whether Djer's was an actual conquest or a punitive raid like those of his predecessor Hor-Aha it is impossible to say. About two centuries after Djer a Second Dynasty king,

Khasekhemui, sent a military expedition to Nubia following which the country seems to have been left in peace for another two centuries. Then Sneferu, founder of the mighty Fourth Dynasty of pyramid builders, descended on Nubia, and as already described, deported 7000 prisoners and 200,000 animals. It is difficult for us in our overcrowded world to envisage how few people there were in 2500 BC and how utterly they depended on animals and basic agriculture for their continued existence. How many people were settled in Nubia at that early period cannot even be guessed but assuredly their numbers were considerably less than those of the C-Group people of Middle Kingdom times. The forcible removal of so many of the inhabitants, quite apart from those killed, together with close on a quarter of a million beasts from so circumscribed and poor an area must have been a catastrophe for settled life in Nubia. An interesting footnote to this episode is the reputation Sneferu left behind of an ideally good-natured and beneficent monarch; that he commanded considerable resources is obvious from the huge stone pyramids he built—no less then three—at Darshur and Meydum.

In Nubia itself Sneferu left no record of his campaign or if he did the exhaustive surveys of the 1960s failed to discover it. The sole evidence for the raid comes from the Royal Annals, otherwise known as the Palermo Stone, after the Sicilian capital where it is now preserved. It is a fragment of diorite no more than 18 inches long—other smaller pieces are in the Cairo Museum, in London and elsewhere—and it is of outstanding importance in the chronology of the early Egyptian kings. The Palermo stone was compiled in the Fifth Dynasty and was not, therefore, far removed in time from Sneferu's day. Still one should bear in mind that in ancient times as much as in modern, there was an urge to exaggerate gains and play down losses; rather like the number of aircraft claimed by both sides as shot down in the Second World War. Nevertheless, many scholars take the view that the figures as stated on the Palermo Stone should be accepted. If the people were pastoralists as seems likely from the large number of animals carried off by Sneferu, then the survivors with their remaining animals might have moved out of their permanent settlements in the Valley into the savanna on either side where today there is desert. Credence to this hypothesis is given by a mace from Nubia which dates from the Archaic Period. The head is of stone but the gold handle is inscribed with pictures of animals, among them an elephant, a giraffe, a lion, a zebra and an antelope. The inference to be drawn is that such animals with their supporting habitat could still be found in the Nubia of 3000 BC.

A picture that begins to take shape is that of a people emerging from the Stone Age and the semi-nomadic life of hunters to settle in communities, with domesticated animals and grain crops to sustain them. Inventiveness among them is high so that soon they develop pottery of distinctive designs and a whole range of decorated objects of considerable artistic merit! Unfortunately for them their entry into civilisation coincides with the unification in the north of highly gifted groups of people into a single kingdom, a kingdom which from its innovation demonstrated great powers of social organisation and possessed of a technology that gave its people mastery in the fashioning of stone and metals. Between them and the Nubians stretched an invitingly broad highway, the Nile, and from the very beginning the A-Group must have been familiar with the movement of Egyptians through their territory either as traders, prospectors in search of minerals or simply as pillagers, as we have seen. One can picture this unfortunate people on the threshold of civilisation exploited and finally decimated by their powerful northern neighbour. Many of the survivors take their flocks out of the Valley, probably not to return. Meanwhile a steady influx of cattle-breeding people from the south has begun, people racially akin to the A-Group and classified by Reisner as the C-Group. The weakened A-Group is unable to resist and although the burials show that for a time the two cultures existed side by side, and indeed had much in common, the time soon comes when the A-Group as a distinctive culture drops out of the archaeological record. Here I must point out that most of the foregoing is pure hypothesis and many historians would dispute it for lack of archaeological evidence but it does fit much of the known data.

We have no monuments, no remains of permanent settlements and no contemporary documentary evidence to provide clues to the social and political organisation of the A-Group. All that we know of them comes from graves and the pitiful debris of campsites. Little enough, but sufficient to show that had the A-Group civilisation been left in peace to come to its full flowering it might have made a notable impact on the later history of the Nile Valley.

No hypothetical reconstruction, however, is needed to interpret the discovery made by Professor Emery on the west bank of the Nile at Buhen. Sound archaeological evidence revealed a new and totally unexpected episode in the history of Egypt in Nubia. It all began in 1960 with an archaeologist's wife walking her dogs along the river bank and noticing pieces of greenish stone lying on the surface. Mrs Emery realised that what she had found was copper-ore. The place was about a half mile north of where Emery and his assistants were excavating the Middle Kingdom fortress of Buhen for the Egypt Exploration Society. Emery started trenching and almost immediately came across brick walls and large quantities of red-ware of the type known as Meydum bowl, so-called after the ancient site in Egypt where it was found in great quantities. (Meydum, as mentioned, is where one of the three stone pyramids of Sneferu is located.) This pottery is the hallmark of Egypt's Fourth and Fifth Dynasties and eventually a fragment of this red-ware turned up with the name of a Fifth Dynasty king named Kakai on it in black ink. Then there emerged clay sealings of the types used to seal jars or to close the bindings around rolls of papyrus and on them, one after another, Emery found the names of the kings of the Fourth Dynasty who raised those immense monuments on the desert plateau at Giza, and others of the Fifth Dynasty. Thus the site was firmly dated and it was unequivocally a purely Egyptian settlement—very little local pottery was found among the vast quantity of Egyptian ware. Moreover the time span covered by the sealings, which amounted to several hundreds, showed that the place had been continuously occupied for at least two centuries. The town was of considerable size but its limits, unfortunately, were never determined because the northern and southern extremities had been obliterated by floodings and erosion. The reason for its foundation was the smelting of copper as the great quantities of copper-ore and slag, even charcoal, scattered around the site, made plain. Here then deep inside Nubia Egyptian vessels were being loaded with copper ingots at the quays of an Egyptian town at least two centuries before the first of the great caravan captains of the Sixth Dynasty was born.

Emery's assistant, David O'Connor, took me on a fascinating tour of this industrial town that was literally going full blast when Khufu's (Cheops) architects were laying out the foundations of the Great Pyramid. I examined several of the furnaces and extraordinarily well preserved they were. At the bottom of each circular structure was a brick plinth which supported a brick construction reminiscent of a wheel and on this, presumably, the crucibles of ore were placed for smelting (see Figure 3). Close to the furnaces was a series of cubicles with pounding stones set in the floor; stone hammers lying nearby showed that this was where the ore was pounded into manageable fragments for filling the crucibles.

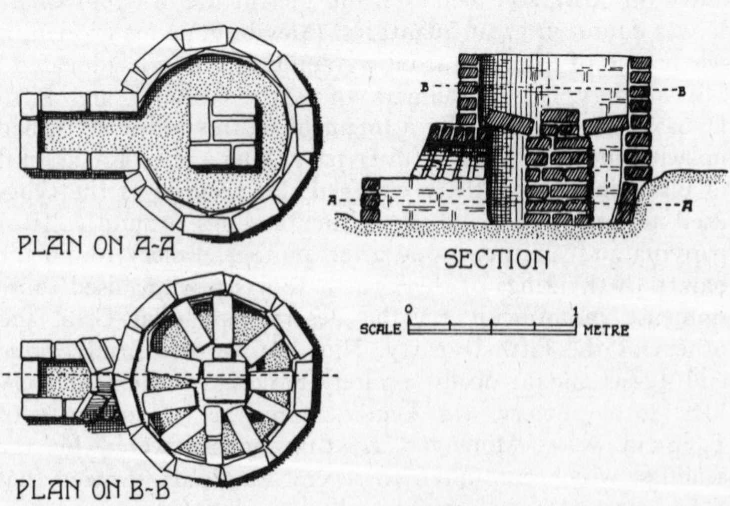

Fig. 3. Smelting furnace Buhen.

Fragments of these lay around in hundreds; many contained slag and one I picked up had pure copper splashed around the edge. Also there were hundreds of little flint blades obviously associated with the industry although O'Connor was unable to suggest how they were used.

Copper was for Egypt a basic factor in the astonishingly rapid development of her arts and crafts, in particular stone-masonry. From the earliest times copper was fashioned into a wide variety of tools and of course weapons. Undoubtedly therefore, one objective of Egypt's many expeditions up-river was to locate deposits of the metal. The curious thing is that prior to Emery's discovery the Sudan had given no indication of copper deposits. Back in the United Kingdom the Buhen ore was assayed and pronounced to be of high quality. This, coupled with evidence that the furnaces had been fed without interruption for about two hundred years, made it certain that a rich vein of copper was located in the vicinity of Buhen since the Egyptians always processed their copper as near as possible to its source. Present-day Sudan is poor in mineral resources and a copper deposit would have been a splendid spin-off from an archaeological dig. Emery and his colleagues searched for the mine but without success. There is a postscript to this story. During the evacuation of the Nubians from Wadi Halfa a passing archaeologist was told by a local man that he knew the whereabouts of a copper deposit back from the river between Buhen and Mirgissa–just the right location! Unfortunately the archaeologist failed to act at once by insisting on being guided to the spot but instead reported it later in Khartoum. By then it was too late, the informant had left Nubia and was untraceable.

While exploring the east side of the site, Emery and his assistants, one of whom at that time was Anthony Mills, came across a construction built of large bricks similar to those commonly used during Egypt's Second Dynasty. Also of Second Dynasty type were jar sealings and pottery. These finds together with fragments of stone bowls of the Archaic Period found in the nearby fortress led Emery to suggest that the town went back to a much earlier period, perhaps to the First or Second Dynasty. Until the Buhen discovery the colonisation of Nubia was assumed to have started at the end of the Eleventh Dynasty around 2000 BC, when the Second Cataract fortresses were built. Now we have proof that the Egyptians were colonising Nubia at least five hundred years before that and possibly much earlier. The only protection provided for the Buhen smelting settlement was a roughly built stone wall and this lack of defence precautions indicates that the Egyptians working in Nubia had nothing to fear from the local inhabitants. That may have been because there were few of them left in the Valley–the paucity of locally-made sherds in the Buhen excavations upholds this supposition–and it supports the hypothesis put forward earlier in this chapter that the Nubians had already 'taken to the hills' to escape the attentions of the intruders from the north.

The abandonment of the copper town more or less coincides with an increase in the numbers of C-Group people arriving in the Second Cataract region and one could speculate whether it was they who caused the Egyptians to withdraw to their homeland. Another, possibly more cogent, reason could of course be the exhaustion of the mine that fed the furnaces.

CHAPTER V

Mirgissa

Whenever I think of Nubia, it is Mirgissa Fortress that comes to mind. That improbable mass of brickwork perched above the wildest and most dangerous stretch of the Second Cataract fires the imagination. The audacity of its builders in even attempting so prodigious a construction deep in hostile territory is hard to credit, until one recalls that those who toiled to raise the battlements and towers of this the largest of the Kush strongholds, were descendants of the Pyramid builders. Which leads one to the question: why did the military commanders of 1900 BC choose that particular site and why did they build such strength into it? These were long-standing puzzles and the French Archaeological Mission seemed well on the way to solving them as they laboured season after season to clear the site of the mountains of sand that smothered it. Some of the discoveries they have made could turn out to be of outstanding importance in the study of relationships between Middle Kingdom Egypt and inner Africa, but at the same time have raised other awkward questions for Egyptologists to mull over.

However, before describing the findings of Professor Jean Vercoutter and his colleagues, it would be helpful to examine the work done at Mirgissa by others before him.

The first to investigate Mirgissa was Major Lyons in 1892. It is interesting to note that Howard Carter searched the Valley of Kings for ten years before he found Tutankhamun's tomb; Lyons, with acres of untouched site at his disposal, dug into it almost at random and immediately uncovered two stelae bearing the name of Senusret III, the only Middle

Kingdom stelae ever to be found there. Such is the luck of a field archaeologist! In 1894 Somers Clarke examined most of the forts of the Second Cataract, Mirgissa among them, but the excavations he made were limited in extent. Not until 1931 was there any intensive clearance when Dr Reisner of the Harvard-Boston Expedition to Nubia delegated Noel Wheeler to work at Mirgissa during the 1931-2 season. Wheeler had a keen eye for detail and was a methodical worker but in the short time at his disposal he was able to clear little more than the north-east corner of the fortress and draw up an outline of its overall construction. Even more unfortunate was his disappearance from the archaeological scene without having published his findings and conclusions.

So serious a lacuna did this leave that when the Nubian Campaign got under way Dr Dows-Dunham of the Boston Museum of Fine Arts took the unprecedented step of authorising the publication of the field notes made by Wheeler during his 54 working days of excavation–the only record extant–and it appeared in the 1961 edition of *Kush*, the annual publication of the Sudan Antiquities Service. The diary is such an admirable example of day by day field recording that I have followed the precedent set by Dr Dows-Dunham and here reproduce those pages of it which cover the first and last days of the excavation.

MONDAY, 23 NOVEMBER 1931

N.F.W. and Handrick to Mirgissa, 8 a.m. About 9.15 we proceeded by motor-boat, with Hussein, Saman, and Mursi, to Dabenarti. The route is quite clear, but at Dabenarti there is a cataract some 100 m. north of the landing place.

Dabenarti Fort is very much denuded, and the whole area within appeared to be down to rock. We found no more than *4 potsherds* in the whole area of the Fort. It certainly looks as though the area never contained interior buildings, and was only an emergency defence area into which troops from Mirgissa could be put temporarily when the need arose.

On returning towards the motor-boat, we saw it well from the landing-place, and drifting rapidly down stream with Hussein in it. He appears to have been moving the boat along the bank of Dabenarti without having the engine running, with Saman on shore, and got adrift somehow just before we appeared. He tried to get the

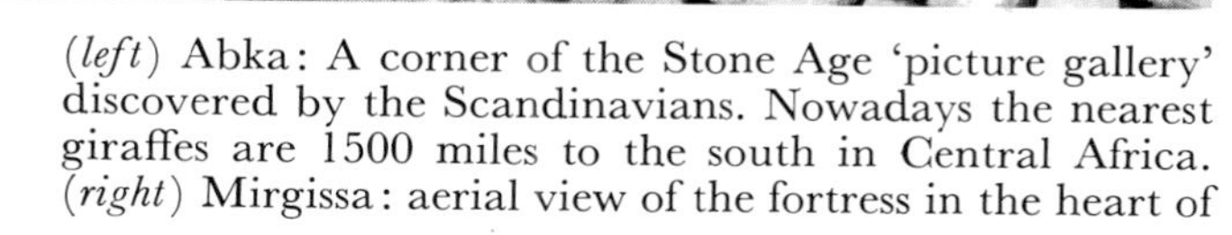

(*left*) Abka: A corner of the Stone Age 'picture gallery' discovered by the Scandinavians. Nowadays the nearest giraffes are 1500 miles to the south in Central Africa. (*right*) Mirgissa: aerial view of the fortress in the heart of the Second Cataract before the Nubian Campaign began. Excavation revealed a whole complex of fortifications and a military town along the river to the left (north) of the fortress.

(*above*) The most important Mirgissa discovery: the wooden tablet found in the Hathor shrine (*left*) of the upper fortress bearing the text "Hathor Lady of *Ikn*". Ikn is the long-sought Egyptian entrepot in Kush during the Middle Kingdom occupation. (*below*) Two of the many fertility cult figurines from the Hathor shrine in the upper fortress.

engine going, but we could not hear whether he succeeded; he managed to get the boat round, meaning to go through the cataract head-on–but before the boat was much more than broadside-on to the stream he was in the cataract. The boat went down at once, and Hussein jumped or was thrown clear–as we saw him once swimming–below the cataract. After that he was not seen, and the local men say that he must inevitably have gone into a second cataract, which is only about 150 m. below the first. When last seen in the boat, Hussein had got his coat off, and was at the tiller trying to hit the rapids bows-on.

After some difficulty, we got into communication with Mirgissa by calling, and within half an hour about 20 of the local men (*Nas Koki*) had come to us on Dabenarti–having swum the rapids from the north on goat-skins. They had searched the shores of the islands for some couple of miles north of Dabenarti but had found nothing. Some small fragments of the woodwork from the boat were seen in the stream and, later, a part of the wooden gunwhale was retrieved and brought to us at Mirgissa. The boat, being iron, is not likely to be seen again, unless low-water uncovers it.

We eventually got a boat from Abka, by sending a messenger about 4 or 5 miles south on the west bank, and returned to Mirgissa. Leaving the locals to search, we got all our men but two or three to continuing building. All the necessary reports were made in Halfa when we returned.

TUESDAY, 24 NOVEMBER 1931

N.F.W. and Handrick at Mirgissa on Building operations. Examined site of Buhen Fort and South Buhen Town, both of which cover a large area. Buhen Fort is only partly excavated, and there would appear from McIver's *Buhen* that there remains much to be done. South Buhen is untouched and covers a very considerable area–the length being somewhere about ½ mile, or more.

WEDNESDAY AND THURSDAY, 25–6 NOVEMBER 1931

Building house.

FRIDAY, 27 NOVEMBER 1931

Building house. At 5 p.m. the Sheikh of the *Nas Koki* reported to me in Halfa the finding of Hussein's body some 4 or 5 miles north of Dabenarti. As the spot was not reachable by other than amphibians–such as these locals appear to be–he was properly buried there. Our men are unanimous in their appreciation of the way these locals have helped in the whole affair.

SATURDAY, 28 NOVEMBER 1931

Two rooms finished in house, and the workroom almost ready for roof.

SUNDAY AND MONDAY, 29–30 NOVEMBER 1931

Putting in the floors of rooms in house, and plastering walls inside.

TUESDAY, 1 DECEMBER 1931

N.F.W. and Handrick moved to Mirgissa. Completed house except extra bedroom, verandah, garage and W.C.

All the workmen occupied building dark-room.

WEDNESDAY, 2 DECEMBER 1931

Unpacking office material, etc., and getting house in order. Men given a day off—their first since starting work. Taking preliminary photographs of Outer South Wall of Fort, preparatory to commencing excavations tomorrow.

THURSDAY, 3 DECEMBER 1931

1st Day of Work

Work on:	1. Outer West Wall.	Locals: 27	Time: 6.0–4.30.
	2. Building	Weather: Fine.	Temp.: 76° at 3 p.m.

1. *Outer West Wall.* Examining the ground about 20 m. south of the southern extremity of this wall, in order to dump on it. The ground consists here of 1 m. of wind-blown sand, deposited in five horizontal layers, some of red sand and some of grey; below which is hard decayed rock dust. Outer West Wall is entirely covered with drift-sand and surface stones, except for the northern end. This wall has taken the full force of wind and sand, and has protected the Inner West Wall to such an extent that the latter is standing to a good height throughout its length.

FIG. A. shows a rough dimensioned plan of the Fort, with the allocated names for the various parts.

Uncovered the south-west corner of Outer West Wall. The debris south of this consists of about 2 m. of mixed drift-sand and fallen mud-bricks; sometimes in clear layers, and at others completely mixed.

The debris here, and the present profile of Outer West Wall, as also that of Outer South Wall, reveal clearly the process of disintegration of the walls. In plan view, Outer West Wall is shown in FIG. B.

In three places a modern 'snake' of drift sand, clean and red, has been deposited to leeward of the wall by the prevailing northerly winds. The widened portions of Outer West Wall are the only remaining *surface* indications of the bastions.

In section the Outer West Wall is shown in FIG. C.

On the surface of the deposited drift-sand is a thin layer of small stones, from 1 cm. to 3 or 4 cm. in size, and potsherds. Under this is a mixture of drift-sand and disintegrated mud from the bricks. The small stones on the surface extend only a few metres to windward of each wall, but considerably more to leeward—as they can be

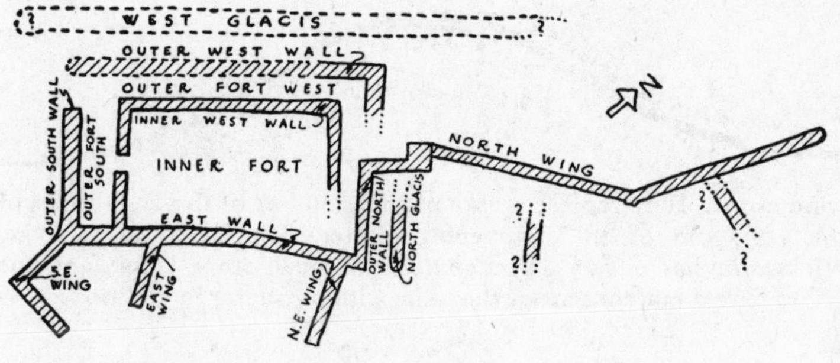
WEST GLACIS
OUTER WEST WALL
OUTER FORT WEST
INNER WEST WALL
OUTER SOUTH WALL
OUTER FORT SOUTH
INNER FORT
NORTH WING
EAST WALL
OUTER NORTH WALL
NORTH GLACIS
S.E. WING
EAST WING
N.E. WING
N

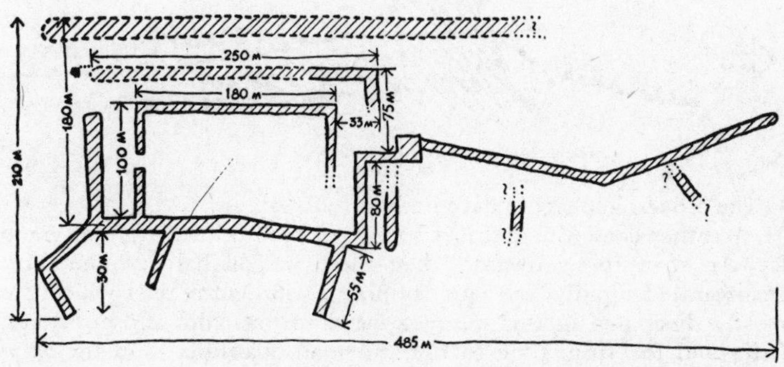
250 M
180 M
180 M
100 M
33 M
75 M
210 M
80 M
30 M
55 M
485 M

Fig. A.

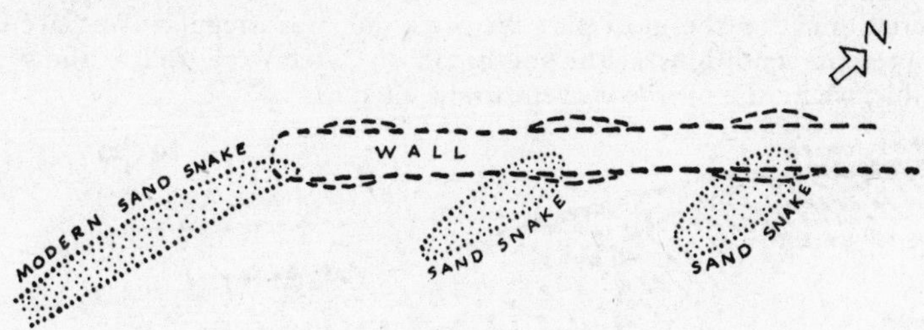
N
WALL
MODERN SAND SNAKE
SAND SNAKE
SAND SNAKE

Fig. B

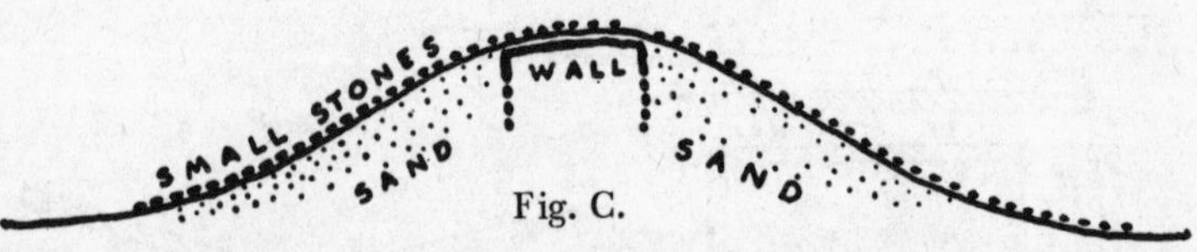

Fig. C.

wind-borne. They represent the original content of the mud-bricks of the wall, and of the intervening plaster. The latter, in surviving brickwork, has a very large content of small stone chips, and the bricks have a fair content of the same with potsherds in addition.

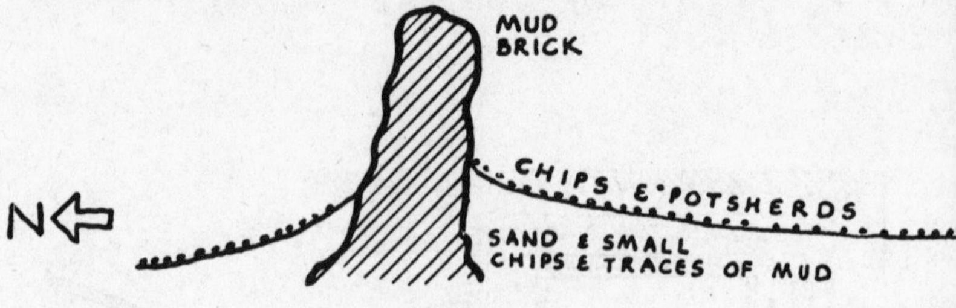

Fig. D.

The process appears to have been as follows:

I. Weather caused mud-bricks to fall, or to 'run' with rain, more to leeward than to windward. When these fell on hard ground, they disintegrated rapidly, the mud forming a wind-borne dust which was mostly dissipated in this way, leaving the stone-chips and potsherds. Drift-sand fell from time to time in small quantities, and the chips 'floated' to the surface. This resulted in the present condition of Outer South Wall, the profile of which is now as shown in FIG. D.

II. When, however, the first falling of bricks was on to ground already sand-silted the process was different. The first bricks fell on sand and were more or less rapidly buried, before they could disintegrate much; so that a mixture of drift-sand and large parts of brick resulted. Occasionally a heavy fall, either of bricks by *habub*, or of mud by rain, made a distinct 'layer' in the drift-sand; but this also was rapidly covered, and for the most part the brick-wall was irregular. We have the present conditions at the south end of Outer West Wall to show for this, where the profile is as shown in FIG. E.

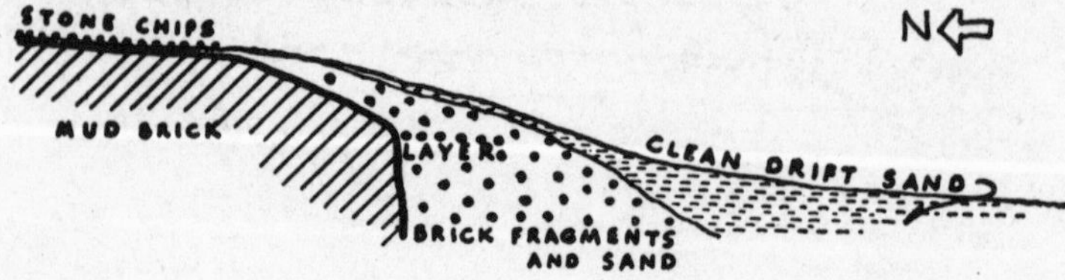

Fig. E.

FRIDAY, 4 DECEMBER 1931 *2nd Day of Work*

Work on: Outer West Wall.

Locals: 28, plus Time 6.30–4.45.

2 camels and 2 donkeys.

Weather: Fine. Temp.: 76° at 3 p.m.

Outer West Wall. Clearing debris at south-west corner of this wall. Uncovered a mud floor, about 3 to 4 m. below the present top of the wall. This floor goes westwards and southwards; possibly this is the floor of the 'ditch' between Outer West Wall and West Glacis. I do not propose going farther west here, now that the south-west corner of the wall is visible. The south end of Outer West Wall is now uncovered, and is being cleared eastwards to reach the Outer South Gate—clearing the floor southwards from the wall for a distance of 2 m. only. The debris here of drift-sand, sand and bricks, sand and mud, is about 2.5 m. deep. The south end of the wall appears to be in line with the south face of Outer South Wall—which was to be expected. *Levels.* A base for levels has been made on one of the stones of the stone-lined room in the north-west corner of the Inner Fort—on Somers Clarke's plan—and this point is 35 m. above present water level and 32 m. above modern H.W.L. of the Nile.

It would appear possible that ancient H.W.L. came over the present river bank, and to within a short distance of the foot of the Fort cliff. There is mud in the sand here which could not have arrived by other means, and the foundations (rubble) of the Dabenarti walls are clearly water-worn to a height of about 5 m. above modern H.W.L.

TUESDAY, 2 FEBRUARY 1932 *53rd Day of Work*

Work on:

1. North-east Wing. Locals: 39. Times: 6.45–5.0.

Weather: Fine. Temp.: 64° at 1.30 p.m.

1. *North-east Wing.* Clearing drift-sand from ditch of wing.

Clearing north of North-east Wing. Debris: potsherds, charcoal, ashes, etc. Uncovered Rooms 56–60.

Room 24 (sic). Two small magazines.

Room 56. North of Room 51. Cleared.

Room 57. Walls broken down. North of Room 54. Doors on east and west. Two magazines.

Room 58. East of Room 55. Found: One pot with handle. Cleared to floor.

Room 59. Walls broken. North of Room 58. Magazine of mudbrick.

Room 60. North of Room 59. Clearing to rock surface.

WEDNESDAY, 3 FEBRUARY 1932 *54th Day of Work*

Work on:

1. North-east Wing. Locals: 40. Times: 6.45–5.0.

Weather: Fine. Temp.: 64° at 1.30 p.m.

1. *North-east Wing.* Continued the clearance of North-east Wing, and the area north thereof—including the outer face of East Wall of Fort.

This area has been very puzzling, owing to the distribution of debris, and its nature; but the sequence is now fairly clear.

The area of small rooms (nos. 51–60) is built largely on debris of potsherds and ashes, but partly on rock. The debris over these rooms was almost entirely small rubble, to a fair depth.

In East Wing itself the ditch contained mostly drift-sand with, in the lower levels, debris of mud-brick from the fallen walls. The north wall, lining the ditch on its north side, is built on debris of potsherds. A series of walls of one-brick thickness against the north side of this wall appear to be retaining walls for rubble and are built on potsherds and debris. Above them was a metre of small rubble debris.

The 'glacis'-slope of mud, built against the lower part of the South Wall of the Wing is built on debris, as is also the similar slope against the outer face of East Wall and its buttresses.

The sequence of construction work would appear to have been:

I The entire Inner Fort with its walls and buttresses, on rock.

II The South Wall of North-east Wing, with its buttresses, on rock.

III The 'glacis'-slope against the lower part of the north face of the South Wall of North-east Wing, and against the lower part of the outer face of Inner North Wall of Fort, built on debris of mud-bricks with an inner core of large rocks between the buttresses.

IV The northward extension of East Wall of Fort, and the entire Outer Fort Walls, with their buttresses.

During one of the above periods the area north of North-east Wing was occupied by workshops of some sort and the ground covered with ashes, charcoal and potsherds. The potsherds are almost entirely of one type of pot, the so-called 'drain-pipe' or 'crucible' which is certainly neither of these things. None show the traces of heat which a crucible would show; and a very large number are unpierced in the base—precluding the possibility of their being pipe sections. Their exact purpose remains problematical.

V The cutting of a 'ditch' in the rock against the north face of North-east Wing. The rock chips from this work were used to fill the small retaining walls north of the ditch.

The northward turn of the east end of North-east Wing wall may have been made at this period or earlier.

The entire Ditch system of the Fort may also have been done at this time and the only stone 'glacis' made.

The small rooms north of North-east Wing may have been built at this time or earlier.

VI The ditch of North-east Wing was cut deeper. The stone chips from this work were dumped over the Rooms 51–60 and over the small retaining walls south of them.

VII The mud-brick 'glacis'-wall was built on the northern edge of the North-east Wing Ditch—the previously dumped stone debris being used as a backing thereto.

The mud-brick 'glacis'-slope against the outer face of the north extension of East Wall of Fort may have been built at this period or earlier. It is on potsherd debris.

The East Wing and South-east Wing were presumably contemporary with North-east Wing (no. II above); but there is, so far, no evidence for or against this.

Between the terse notes made on those first and last days lie 50 days of meticulous clearance, observation and deduction, of the kind familiar to all field archaeologists.

Wheeler uses the inner west wall with its overall length of 184 metres to illustrate how the entire fortress was put together and the ingenious devices that went into its construction. Each course of mud bricks was finished throughout the entire length of the wall before the next course was started. Each twelfth course of bricks was topped by a layer of 'halfa' grass with the stalks laid lengthwise through the thickness of the wall. When the wall was completed therefore, it embodied halfa "sandwiches" at regular heights for its full length and to reinforce it still further logs of wood were laid directly on to each halfa grass layer at intervals of between 2 and 3½ metres. All were tree trunks with the bark in place and they pierced through the wall's thickness, which means that the length of each log varied from 7½ metres at the base of the wall to 3½ metres at the top. The logs were staggered so that one was never immediately above another, making altogether a most effective device to prevent mining up through the wall by an enemy under cover of darkness. The logs when I saw them looked as if cut only yesterday but one touch and they crumbled to powder—the termites had long since eaten their fill. Another puzzle: where in that wilderness of sand and rock did the builders find the thousands of logs they used? However, the most interesting revelation was the modern method of 'ventilating' walls that had been built into the Mirgissa fortifications to good effect. In constructing each wall the builders left open air ducts through its full thickness from outer to inner fort, and each duct intersected other air channels running lengthwise, in the instance of the west wall through its entire 184-metre length. In 1960 at its denuded height the wall had preserved no less than three levels of such intercommunicating systems of ventilation, while at its original height there were probably five. The air ducts were one brick-course in width and two brick-courses in height. Wheeler noted in his Diary that not only did the ducts serve to keep the walls dry—which implies his belief that the climate of 1900 BC was different from that of today—but ensured a supply of cool air for the streets inside the fort. The architects must have foreseen that the towering walls of the fortifications would exclude the prevailing north wind which alone makes life tolerable in a Nubian summer. After 4000 years I could stand at the end of the inner west wall, crumbling and battered though it was, and feel a strong current of air flowing from the ducts. Mirgissa is the only one of the twelve Second Cataract forts to incorporate this feature. The construction of those massive walls demanded a high degree of accuracy for not only did they incorporate the ventilating systems, the halfa 'sandwiches' and the layers of timber, but were built on a surface of uneven rock which varied considerably in height.

Wheeler's sketches show that Mirgissa's strength sprang from its location on a bluff facing the river. The steep cliff below the fort would deter any attacker, and the defences constructed on the east side facing the river are relatively weak; an attacking force could hardly cross the Nile at this point nor for several miles to north and south because the river would carry them into the most dangerous rapid of the Second Cataract—it was here that Wheeler lost his labourer. Moreover on an island immediately facing Mirgissa stood the subsidiary fortress of Dabnarti. Any enemy willing to brave the rapids would find himself trapped between the two forts. In the south-east gateway Wheeler found the original doorway of the fort with the lower 30 centimetres or so of the wooden door and doorposts still in position. The face of the door was composed of six vertical planks of timber each 30 centimetres wide and 7 centimetres thick. It seems a small door for so large a fort! Gullies running up the cliff from the river protected the double line of fortifications to north and south. Almost the only assailable point was the western side of the fortress and as one would expect it was here that the fortifications were strongest with a deep ditch between the outer wall and a substantial glacis. A long spur of denuded brick running from the north gate of the fortress for a considerable distance parallel with the Nile is given no more than a passing reference in Wheeler's Diary and it was Vercoutter who thirty years later discovered its significance.

Since attack might be expected from the west, it is interesting to learn from the Diary that Wheeler drove some ten kilometres due west from the Nile to Gebel Sula, a rocky outcrop which stands high above the surrounding desert and commands views for many miles in every direction. On the summit he discovered a look-out post of well-built stone huts each with a door at the back. From them he removed a quantity of potsherds, all ancient. This could have been an outpost of the Mirgissa garrison and one would like to know what became of the sherds which might have given the huts a firm date.

Wheeler visited the fortress on the island of Dabnarti opposite. He found it much denuded and concluded it had never contained interior buildings and was probably no more than an emergency defense enclosure which could be activated from Mirgissa as the need arose. The area enclosed by the denuded walls is considerable, 230 metres by 60, yet careful search produced no more than four potsherds. In 1963 Dabnarti was investigated by Dr Jay W. Raby of the California Archaeological Expedition to Nubia, with Ernest Chandonet as architect. After a thorough investigation they confirmed Wheeler's conclusion that the fortress was never finished and possibly never occupied.

Now we must leave Noel Wheeler and his Diary but before doing so it is interesting to note that, prudently, he made no attempt to analyse or even conjecture which part of the area excavated dated from the Twelfth Dynasty period and which belonged to the Eighteenth Dynasty.

When Professor Vercoutter and his colleagues arrived at Mirgissa the sand of thirty years had covered most traces of Wheeler's work. In fact the entire site was one vast area of drift sand and for six years, between 1962 and 1968, the French expedition which at times numbered as few as three and never more than eight, laboured to clear it. Less than a tenth of the inner fort had been cleared by earlier digging and in normal circumstances the remaining nine-tenths in itself would have absorbed most of the expedition's time; but events were to reveal that the fort on the cliff was no more than one element in an array of buildings spread over acres of landscape until now effectively concealed by the sand. However, circumstances were not normal. With the rapid rise in the level of the reservoir, time was running out; moreover in Nubia the season is short because of the intense heat and fieldwork becomes impossible after April and seldom begins before November.

First they attacked the sandy plain that lay between the foot of the cliff and the river and almost at once struck buildings below the northern end of the fort. An imposing array of fortifications emerged from the sand, many in an astonishing state of preservation. As the excavators moved north parallel with the river, foundations of yet other defence works appeared which proved eventually to encircle a town; from the layout of its houses and streets it was of a military character. Beyond the fortified 'girdle' wall lay another town of poorer construction but of considerable size; in fact the excavators never did reach its full extent. By now it had become obvious that Mirgissa was something very different from the other fortresses of the Second Cataract, much more in fact than a stronghold. Vercoutter had his own ideas on the subject and felt that proof of them would be found, if anywhere, in the upper fort. However prudence demanded a concentration of work on the sandy plain below since this would go under water several years before the lake reached the cliff top and the upper fort.

Not until the beginning of 1964 were trial diggings made in the upper fort in an attempt to determine when the fort had been built. The logical starting point was the north-west corner where Lyons had unearthed the two stelae of Senusret III, but instead of chronological evidence what turned up was an Eighteenth Dynasty shrine dedicated to the goddess Hathor. It was poorly constructed of mud brick but in it were scores of small objects: amulets, beads, scarabs, basketry, broken pots and vases, fertility cult figures and stones of unusual shapes. The statue or stela of the goddess was missing but they did find four other small wooden stelae and these revealed that the inhabitants of Mirgissa during the New Kingdom worshipped a triad: Senusret I (or III), the falcon god Montu and the humanised form of Hathor. Further clearance revealed more votive objects, some bearing the name of Amenhotep III of the Eighteenth Dynasty, and another small wooden stela which had been miraculously overlooked by the termites. This tablet is about the most important single object discovered at Mirgissa (see Figure 4). It bore a text, "Hathor, Lady of Ikn". No more than that, but it confirmed what Vercoutter had long believed, that Mirgissa was nothing less than the long-sought Egyptian entrepot in Nubia. Several texts mention Ikn, notably the proclamation of Senusret III found at Semna which states that Ikn is the only place within the military zone of the Cataract district where Kushites are permitted to bring their produce for trade with the Egyptians.

With this discovery the elaborate fortifications in the plain bordering the river, the garrison town and the 'outer' town all

Fig. 4 Wooden Stela discovered at Mirgissa

fell into place, as did the location of the site. Mirgissa, at the southern end of the most hazardous of the Second Cataract rapids, was ideally situated to protect traffic to and from Egypt both by river and by land; from its fortifications high on the cliff sentries could survey the desert for miles around, as well as the river, while below the upper fort a smooth stretch of water offered a natural harbour. In short Mirgissa was ideal for commerce of the kind favoured by the Pharaohs of 1900 BC. Egyptologists had long disputed the whereabouts of Ikn and now one small wooden tablet had closed the argument for good. The next step was to locate the harbour, docks and warehouses and it was with high hopes that Vercoutter and his colleagues attacked the sand plain immediately below the upper fort and bordering the river. Frustrated by the thousands of tons of sand that had drifted in through the millennia they brought out from France a geophysicist equipped with apparatus capable of detecting solid objects or constructions below the surface. But even advanced electronics were defeated by the sand. Nothing short of a bulldozer would have served to slice away the top twenty feet or so to a reasonable working level. An army of labourers with baskets could have done it given time, but time was running out and to have hired a bulldozer and transported it to that inaccessible spot was far beyond the means of the French Mission. What the apparatus did locate was the line of the river bank at the time of the fort's occupation. It was considerably nearer the cliff than in 1964 which means that the river was that much wider and even better able, therefore, to accommodate harbour installations. The sandy plain south of the fort was never examined. Had the docks and warehouses been found they could have yielded invaluable information on the maritime and commercial activities of ancient Egypt in Nubia about which very little of fact is known.

Like Faras, another large site further north which is described in a later chapter, Mirgissa was a victim of the failure to coordinate the many field expeditions under a single direction and to draw up a cooperational plan for the whole area of excavation in Nubia. Had this been done the realisation would have come early on in the campaign that no single expedition would have the means or the funds necessary to clear so vast and important site. A division of the concession among several expeditions could have enabled Mirgissa to be cleared completely notwithstanding the short time available. As it was, Professor Vercoutter and his small band of colleagues were left to carry an impossible burden. They achieved wonders and made finds of outstanding significance but the melancholy fact remains that a unique opportunity to throw light on a critical and controversial period in the history of relations between Egypt and Kush has been irrevocably lost.

Arriving at Mirgissa in October 1962 Professor Jean Vercoutter and his party had installed themselves in Wheeler's old quarters. To Vercoutter who had been Commissioner for Archaeology in the Sudan until a year or so before that time, the site and working conditions were familiar and work started without delay. Accompanying him as Assistant Field Director was M André Vila and Mme Elisabeth Vila as Recorder. Digging started, as already described, in the sandy plain bordering the river and worked north from the fort. One of the first sites to be cleared was a small cemetery partly plundered. Nevertheless the mode of burial, the pottery and other objects found in the graves showed that they belonged to the Kerma culture. This cemetery was an important find for it marks the most northerly point of Kerma penetration from the South yet found, apart from a few individual graves. In addition to the native Kerma objects the graves yielded alabaster vases, a bronze mirror, beads and amulets of carnelian, blue faience, and silver and gold; all of Egyptian workmanship. Among them was a scarab inscribed with the name of a king of Egypt's Seventeenth Dynasty. Here was a discovery of great historical significance since it demonstrated that the Kerma culture was still very much alive at the end of that troubled era known as the Second Intermediate Period.

After clearance of the Kerma necropolis the survey proceeded in a northerly direction and in about 300 metres made a very rare find, nothing less than a cache of 'execration' texts. In a pit were lying some 3000 fragments of pottery bearing the names of many of the peoples regarded by the Egyptians as enemies. Nearby were fragments of four statuettes of prisoners deliberately broken, and a human skull laid on a dish. Alongside the skull was a flint knife and a broken pot. Here was a discovery of outstanding interest. Lists of foreign countries and peoples, of both Asia and Africa, would certainly be revealed by the texts, while the objects mixed with the ostraca–figurines of parts of human beings and animals–would enrich the study of the magical rites associated with the foundation of such deposits and enable comparison to be made with the few texts which refer to them.

Meanwhile the great girdle wall to the north of the upper fort cleared during the first season's work, turned out to be an extension of the lower fortifications which had been found under 15 feet of sand apparently unaffected by time, some walls and bastions standing to a height of 5 metres. By the following year when I next visited Mirgissa, further clearance had uncovered an array of fortified walls, towers and bastions all built of friable mud brick but so well preserved by the sand that some walls stood all of 8 metres high enclosing staircases and rooms with roofs intact. The girdle wall down in the plain was 5 metres thick and parallel to it ran another wall strengthened at intervals with semi-circular bastions. Running parallel with the Nile the two walls continued for close on a kilometre. Clearing the walls had been slow work since they were deeply buried in sand. The military township enclosed by the girdle wall proved to be so extensive that the excavators had to limit themselves to trial diggings here and there. The houses were of a rectangular plan and were enclosed by curious 'wavy' walls built, probably, to exclude encroaching sand. Several kilns came to light and scattered around them were many cylinders of burnt clay of the type found by hundreds in Middle Kingdom fortresses. Some were unbaked and the inference is that the kilns were furnaces for firing the cylinders. These cylinders have provoked much speculation. They are between 6 and 9 inches long, slightly wider at one end, and they appear to have been broken deliberately. The clue to the use of the "bodegas", as Vercoutter calls them, and a very practical use it was in the thirsty climate of Nubia, came from certain tomb paintings which illustrate the process of beer brewing as practised in ancient Egypt. Grain mash is shown being poured into a row of upright cylinders similar in shape to the "bodegas". Thereafter the cylinders would be sealed at the ends and then heated to the point of fermentation after which they were broken open to release what had now been transformed into malt. Soldiers have always been renowned for their addiction to beer and the Egyptian troops of 1900 BC were no exception, as is evidenced by the heaps of "bodegas" scattered around their quarters.

One construction in the fortified town defied explanation. The floors of several buildings had been carefully levelled and divided into neat squares measuring about 18 inches a side by rows of bricks laid lengthwise and crosswise. The effect was that of gigantic chessboards and the use to which the rooms were put is beyond imagining. They were, however, firmly dated to the New Kingdom because underneath one of the floors the excavators found a small cemetery of the Second Intermediate Period (Seventeenth Dynasty).

The 'outer town' beyond the girdle wall proved to be older than the adjacent fortified town. Among the mudbrick houses, each in its 'wavy' enclosure, were roughly built stone huts, some filled with pots, jars, bowls and plates, and all of a decorated type characteristic of the Egyptian Middle Kingdom. The site gave an impression of limited occupation and Vercoutter suggests it was a temporary settlement built to house the workmen and soldiers while the fortress and fortified town were being erected. Because of the shortage of time fully a quarter of the 'outer town' remained uncleared, which is unfortunate because only one other Middle Kingdom town site of this kind has been found and excavated–at el Lahun in the Fayum Province of Egypt. The el Lahun settlement offers remarkable parallels to the Mirgissa 'outer town' for it was put up to house the workmen who built Senusret II's pyramid, following the completion of which it was abandoned. There must have been many other towns of that period but all have long since been built over or carted away to spread on nearby fields as fertilizer.

The spur wall springing from the northern fortifications of the upper fort and so prominent a feature on the aerial photographs made no sense to the French excavators until they realised that the visible wall was a New Kingdom construction built exactly on top of an earlier Middle Kingdom wall already buried in sand. The older wall was found to turn towards the river then run down over the rocks to the plain to link up with the great girdle wall, thus adding yet another line of defence. Piercing this wall was a gateway wide enough for chariots to pass. As for the New Kingdom wall, this continued north in a more or less straight line for a full kilometre before losing itself in the sandhills.

In 1966 the waters had not yet covered Mirgissa's northern cataract and it was still possible to climb onto the rocks and look back across the sea of sand which so bedevilled the French Mission, to the ramparts of the massive fortress on the cliff with its triple line of defences and to follow in detail the complete system of defensive walls; here and there a darker filigree pattern denoted streets and houses of the two towns. Mirgissa could conjure up the past more than any other ancient site I know, but it is not a vision of the Egypt of solemn processions and priestly chanting, but of the bustle and activity of a great market. To the Nubians, Mirgissa in its heyday must have been an overwhelming demonstration of Egyptian wealth and power: the complex of military and commercial buildings sprawled along the plain below the cliffs, streets thronged with people, soldiers and Kushite traders mingling with sailors from the ships loading cargoes of produce from inner Africa down at the quays and warehouses, and dominating the scene the bastions and towers of the great citadel—here was a sight without parallel elsewhere in that vast continent, outside of Egypt itself.

Upstream of Mirgissa on the island fort of Uronarti, Senusret III left an inscription, found by Wheeler, which describes how bad the water was "because of the time of the year"—that is to say, the winter months of low water—and that his army had been forced to drag their ships through the rapids. This "dragging" of ships sounds improbable but is mentioned in a number of texts. The French Mission actually found a slipway which had been used for dragging ships and a remarkable example of the engineering prowess of the Egypt of 1900 BC it proved to be, and unique in Egyptian

(*above*) Mirgissa: fortifications unearthed by the French Expedition, led by Professor Jean Vercoutter, in the sand below the upper fortress, part of a chain of military constructions found spread along the Nile during six years of excavation. (*below*) Mirgissa: typical house of the Middle Kingdom military township unearthed from the sandy plain below the upper fortress. Note the curious 'wavy' enclosure wall.

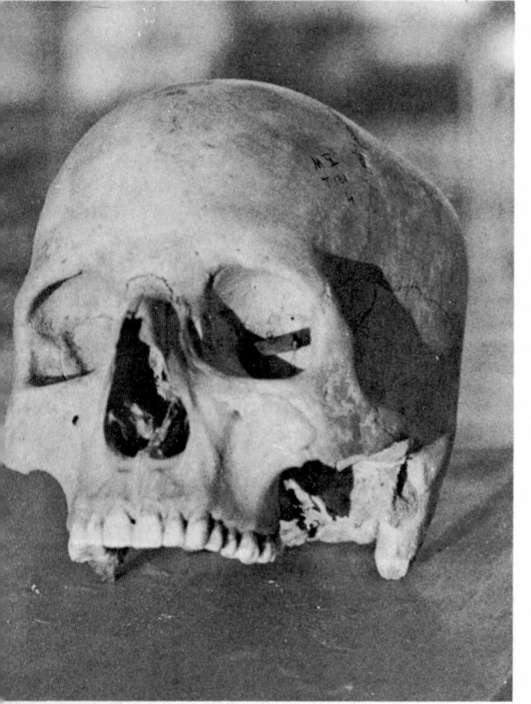

(*above*) Mirgissa: funerary masks from the Pharaonic cemetery found in the desert west of the fortress. (*left*) Mirgissa: skull of Middle Kingdom soldier with the shaft of the Kushite arrow that killed him still lodged in his eye socket.

archaeology. It took the form of a roadway laid with wooden poles rather like the sleepers of a railroad, each pole being slightly curved, with the lowest section in the middle, thus forming a shallow cradle. The whole roadway had been embedded in Nile silt. The poles had long since been eaten by termites but the dry mud had faithfully retained their imprints just as it retained the impressions of grooves made by the keels of the ships and the actual footprints of sailors who had pulled the vessels along the slippery surface some forty centuries ago. When I saw the slipway the sand was already drifting over it but still I was able to follow its course due north for three kilometres after which it lost itself in the dunes. The dangerous rapids nearby can be navigated in reasonable safety only during the period of high water between the end of July and November, and the slipway had been constructed to outflank them and make navigation possible throughout most of the year.

One other such slipway has been found, in the Fayum, where it was used to ease the movement of huge blocks of stone for Senusret II's pyramid. A famous wall-painting, also of Middle Kingdom date, shows a colossal statue some twenty feet high being pulled on a wooden sled by a gang of men. Ahead of it a man pours water on the ground; it used to be thought that he was pouring a libation—how curious it is that so many practical acts of the Egyptians are interpreted in our day in religious terms!—until the real explanation was grasped. Nile silt is a fine powder composed largely of colloidal clays and when water is added, it becomes as slippery as grease, as I discovered to my cost at Mirgissa when I stepped unsuspectingly on a patch of it and went head over heels to sprain a wrist. Professor Vercoutter describes an experiment made by an architect friend at Karnak. He laid down a track of silt and lowered on to it a block of stone weighing several tons. After he had wet the silt the problem was not how to move the stone but how to keep it under control and bring it to a standstill.

Over the long span of Mirgissa's occupation many people must have died there and not all of them would have been carried back to Egypt for burial. Extensive cemeteries, therefore, were to be expected. The first, located early in the campaign, was in the desert due west of the upper citadel and it dated from the end of the Middle Kingdom period (Thirteenth Dynasty) to the Second Intermediate or Hyksos period which immediately followed: the many scarabs found in the three hundred or so tombs excavated were all of these two periods. The graves were of two types; one, a shallow rectangular pit in which the body was laid with or without a coffin, the other a shaft cut down through the rock to terminate in one or more funerary chambers. Inexplicably none of the graves contained the customary stelae or offering tablets although the heavy coffins of wood, some of which were preserved, were typical of those used in Middle Kingdom Egypt, interiors overlaid with white stucco bearing funerary texts in black and red hieroglyphs. Most of the bodies in their linen shrouds had been broken up by robbers but several funerary masks of painted stucco had escaped their attentions. Other objects recovered were statuettes in stone, alabaster 'kohl' vases, pottery–including examples of the so-called 'Tel-el-Yahudiyeh' ware–and several Kerma vases. A vivid illustration of those violent days was provided by a skull with the shaft of an arrow still protruding from the left eye socket.

During six seasons of digging the French Mission cleared the interior of the upper fort leaving only a small section undug, roughly in the centre. Stone baths with elaborate drainage systems came to light and on the eastern side several very large houses with pillared rooms. A novel use for the geophysicist's detector was to map out the foundations of the entire fabric of the upper fortress, an experiment that was entirely successful. An unexpected find, made in the north western corner, was the armoury of the fort. In it were many javelin heads of flint and arrowheads of carnelian, and about three hundred bows. Objects for which there is no explanation were flat plaques of wood about the size and shape of the average book, pierced with rows of holes. Also in the armoury, when I saw it, were large wooden beams of rectangular section with no obvious purpose, but the most eye-catching objects were several slabs of worked stone standing upright like gravestones which, indeed, they resembled. They sloped inwards to their tops which were curved and through all of them a hole had been pierced through the 6-inch thickness of stone. At first they were assumed to be formers for leathern shields, an impression reinforced by the presence of several tanned hides of cattle lying nearby, but Vercoutter is doubtful. There are much simpler ways of making leather shields than by stretching them over cumbersome stone formers and the hole, big enough to thrust a hand through and drilled with considerable labour, would seem to be irrelevant for shield construction. Moreover he has since found a similar object at Sai Island 120 miles south of Mirgissa, in a site unconnected with military operations. Again, the explanation is probably simple. Other important finds made in the fort's interior were thousands of clay sealings many bearing the names of Thirteenth Dynasty kings, and in the south eastern corner was a deposit of Kerma pottery. The stratification of the sherds showed that they ante-dated the burning of the fort and its abandonment. These Kerma people, it would seem, were no more than squatters among the ruins.

At the very end of the Campaign the expanse of desert between the Middle Kingdom necropolis and the upper fort was found to contain an even larger cemetery. Time ran out before it was completely cleared although some three hundred graves were excavated. The necropolis, which was much disturbed and yielded little of interest, dated to the New Kingdom reoccupation and re-building of the fortress.

When the French Mission finished its work in 1968 it had clarified several outstanding problems of Egypt's relations with Nubia. On the other hand Vercoutter and his colleagues had raised new questions and among them the odd fact that so few of the finds made at Mirgissa could be dated to the Twelfth Dynasty, apart from its fortifications. The Hathor shrine with the Ikn tablet, the many clay sealings and the two Pharaonic cemeteries all belong to the Thirteenth Dynasty and later, when Egypt's Middle Kingdom was in eclipse. Yet if contemporary records are to be believed Mirgissa was at its most militarily active during the vigorous years of the Twelfth Dynasty when it was actually built. The soldiers killed in the fighting of that time or who died a natural death were possibly buried at Mirgissa but just where under those mountains of sand, we shall never know.

CHAPTER VI

Defenders of the Cataract

By far the most prominent features of the Nubian scene were the Pharaonic fortresses strung along sixty miles of the Second Cataract. The outcrops of granite along this section of the Nile Valley gave rise to dangerous rapids and so formed a series of natural barriers of which the military engineers of 1900 BC took full advantage. Wherever there was a perilous stretch of water there one would find a fortress. Some commanded the river from the peaks of islands. A group of three marked the southernmost limit of the line of forts where the Nile thrust through the granite barrier at Semna; it offered a natural strongpoint which the Egyptian engineers with customary ingenuity converted into a frontier post that was virtually impregnable. Moreover they constructed fortified walls on either bank of the river to link Semna with the next fort in line, three miles downstream on the island of Uronarti, thus enclosing a protected area several square miles in extent. The fortifications of Mirgissa have already been described but scarcely less impressive was the fortified town of Buhen excavated by the late Professor W. B. Emery on behalf of the Egypt Exploration Society. An architect himself, Emery was convinced that all the forts bore the imprint of a single directing intelligence, an architect of genius. They represented military engineering on a scale never before attempted in the ancient world and never to be equalled. It is a great misfortune that not one of the forts has been preserved; unlike the temples of Nubia which were built of stone and consequently transportable, the forts were of mud brick construction too friable to be moved. Several have already gone to swell the mud at the bottom of the new reservoir and those that remain above water will join them within a few years.

Now comes the vexed question of the builders. Undoubtedly all the forts were a single tactical conception but so gigantic was the task of building them that it cannot have been completed in a single reign. Construction was probably started by Senusret I and completed by Senusret III which thus covers the reigns of four pharaohs. Here we are at a turning point in Egypt's history. The two centuries of lawlessness and despair that had followed the collapse of the golden age of the Old Kingdom–the First Intermediate Period–had ended. The lost virtues of righteousness, justice and moderation were again in the ascendant and the re-unifying agent was a nobleman of Upper Egypt, Amenemhet by name. It was he who founded the Twelfth Dynasty, probably the most able and vigorous in the long succession of dynasties that ruled the Two Lands. Having re-established law and order in Egypt itself and put to rights the country's irrigation system long since fallen into disrepair, Amenemhet and his immediate successors of the Middle Kingdom turned their attention to the territories south of Egypt. Contact with Nubia had been lost during the unhappy days of the First Intermediate Period and the re-organised economy of Egypt demanded a speedy resumption of the flow of essential commodities from up the Nile. However, the dwellers along the upper reaches of the river with two centuries of independence to strengthen them and probably reinforced by newcomers from the south, were in no mood to accept Egyptian exploitation; a century was to pass involving military campaign after campaign before Senusret III, the fourth king of the Dynasty, was able to bring Nubian resistance under control. However, the Nubians were far from cowed and had the fortresses not been built it is doubtful whether the Egyptians would have been able to maintain their continued presence in the southern lands, which harboured the intractable people invariably described in the Egyptian records as "Kush the Vile." What kind of fighting men did the Nubians have to face?

Cavalry and chariots were not introduced into Egypt until

the Eighteenth Dynasty. The Middle Kingdom soldier was an infantryman and he fought with arrows, slings, spears and axes. He wore a minimum of body armour, relying on shields of hide for his protection. On campaigns up-river the army would be transported by naval vessels and this was a limiting factor that probably restricted the fighting season to about six months of the year, when the rapids could be negotiated in reasonable safety, although as I shall describe in the next chapter, Vercoutter considers that towards the end of the Middle Kingdom the period for navigation was greatly extended by the introduction of an ingenious system of flood control. The Egyptians could, however, move up and down stream at periods of low water, as the slipway discovered at Mirgissa has revealed. There can be little doubt that similar slipways would have been found in other dangerous reaches of the Cataract had the archaeologists conducting the Survey known what to look for. All the fortresses must have had quays or even harbours for sheltering the vessels and at Buhen and Serra forts the quays were *in situ,* massive constructions of masonry.

But to return to the forts. The earliest known reference to them comes from a collection of papyri found in a tomb below the Ramasseum at Thebes. Seventeen are listed, all with highly descriptive names which mostly refer to the conquest of southern lands: "Khakoure (Senusret III) is Powerful", "Warding off the Hostile Bows", "Curbing the Countries", and so on. Of the 14 in the Second Cataract region, 12 have been located, 2 were further north and the remaining fort may have been on the Island of Elephantine at modern Assuan.

All the Second Cataract forts have been at least partly cleared but only one, Buhen, was completely excavated, being literally taken apart and recorded in detail; it took Emery and his colleagues seven years to do it, a measure of the fort's size and the complexity of its construction.

The abrasive winds of the Sudan are a powerful agent of destruction and many ancient buildings have been eroded away by wind and flying sand. Buhen escaped because over the millennia the configuration of the land caused the wind to deposit sand on the site: moreover the Middle Kingdom fortress had unwittingly been given further protection when much of it was covered over by the New Kingdom armies who re-occupied the fort and rebuilt it. After reconstruction, the original fortified town, which had been stormed and partly destroyed at the end of the Middle Kingdom or in the troubled times that followed it, became a citadel around which grew a much larger town with perimeter fortifications extending for more than a mile. The New Kingdom reconstructions were examined by Emery and recorded after which they were dismantled in order to expose the original Middle Kingdom fortress beneath. Inside its protective walls were paved arterial roads that divided the town symmetrically into three equal parts. Down the centre of each road ran a stone drain presumably to carry away rain. Such drains would be superfluous today so here was yet one more indication of an appreciable rainfall in the Nubia of 1900 BC. The design and decoration of the palace of the Governor or Commandant showed that high ranking Egyptians stationed in frontier outposts saw no reason to depart from the standard of luxury they enjoyed at home in Egypt. A temple and domestic habitations, a barracks, workshops and storerooms all testified to a high degree of organisational skill in the Egyptian army of that day. According to Emery, Buhen at its peak could have supported 2000 combat troops, and one must bear in mind that Buhen was only one of twelve strongholds. The main defensive wall with rectangular towers projecting from it at regular intervals was 5 metres thick and 11 metres high and was strengthened with wooden beams and halfa mats in the manner already described at Mirgissa. Emery's estimate of the number of bricks that went into its construction reached the staggering figure of ten millions.

On one of my visits to Buhen Emery conjured up a vivid picture of how the defences were manned and the hazards facing any attacker rash enough to try forcing them. We were standing at the foot of the outer face of the great wall, on a sentry walk or firestep protected by a rampart which opened out at intervals into round bastions. The rampart descended by a steep scarp to a ditch hewn from the rock to a depth of 6 metres. Across the ditch the counter-scarp was heightened by brickwork surmounted in turn by a narrow covered way;

beyond this again was an outer glacis. An attacking force would first have to scale the outer glacis then force a passage through the defences of the covered way while under constant fire from the top of the great wall. Then would come the descent of the steep counter-scarp to the bottom of the ditch 6 metres below, fully exposed to fire from ramparts, bastions and inner walls. It is doubtful whether any force could survive the intense cross fire directed at point blank range by archers shooting from behind the round bastions and the parapet of the firestep. Piercing the bastions were double rows of loopholes, one for standing and the other for kneeling archers. The loopholes had a single opening on the defender's side opening out into three slits on the outside, an ingenious arrangement which enabled an archer to shoot straight ahead or at angles to left or right (see Figure 5). The resulting fire from kneeling and standing archers simultaneously would cover every inch of the counterscarp and ditch below. This triple loophole and embrasure is unique, a military invention which not even the Crusaders or their Saracen opponents developed; indeed other features including baffle walls showed that the military architects of 1900 BC were every bit as imaginative and in some ways more advanced than the designers of the fortresses of our Middle Ages. But to continue our reconstruction of the storming of Buhen. Survivors from the hail of crossfire would be forced to climb the steep scarp in order to storm the ramparts, thus coming under a rain of missiles hurled or shot from the top of the wall towering ten metres above. In the meantime those attacking the West Gate would face the most strongly fortified of Buhen's defences (see Figure 6). The gate was closed by double doors beyond which was a drawbridge which could be pulled back on rollers from across the ditch. Gate and bridge were protected by spur walls forming a corridor through which the attackers would have to fight their way, again exposed to a hail of missiles from battlements on three sides. Having broken through the gate, instead of finding the interior of the fort open and exposed, the attackers would find themselves in a small square and facing a wall with exits only to left and to right. Forced once more into a narrow corridor under the walls they would be

Fig. 5 Constructional details of the loophole system.

Fig. 6. Reconstruction of the west gate of Buhen.

exposed to every kind of missile and boiling liquid hurled down on them by defenders on the inner side of the main wall.

The foregoing reconstruction shows that Buhen was virtually impregnable and that nothing short of artillery could have breached its defences. Yet captured it was and burned. Around the formidable West Gate evidence of fierce fighting came to light and much of the brickwork had been burnt by fire. When subjected to great heat the dun colour of mud brick turns to the bright red of burnt brick and the resulting change can be spectacular. In Semna West for example an entire wall of the inner defences was burnt bright red. So it was at Buhen. Perhaps the defences were undermanned. Perhaps the attackers stormed the West Gate under a kind of canopy to protect them from the defenders above; Egyptian soldiers of the Middle Kingdom certainly used such devices as is demonstrated by a tomb painting in Beni Hassan which shows a group of them battering the wall of a fortress with a beam under the protection of a kind of canopy. Or perhaps, as Emery suggested, the fortress may have been taken through treachery among the defenders. Whatever the cause, Buhen shared the fate of all the fortresses of the Second Cataract. One could speculate endlessly on the nature of the enemy who could overcome those mighty citadels and the seasoned troops who manned them. The Egyptian records of the time are silent and their opponents had no written language. Nevertheless certain theories have been put forward and these will be discussed in a following chapter.

A most surprising discovery at Buhen was the skeleton of a horse. It had been buried beneath a well-stratified deposit below the New Kingdom brickwork. The horse was known in Mesopotamia in 2000 BC but did not appear in the Nile Valley much before the Eighteenth Dynasty having been introduced, it is believed, by the Hyksos invaders from Asia who occupied northern Egypt during the Second Intermediate Period. Now it appears that at least one horse had arrived in Nubia some two centuries before that time.

Before leaving Buhen, Professor Emery had one additional responsibility to fulfil on behalf of the Egypt Exploration

Society: the dismantling of the Eighteenth Dynasty temple and its removal to Khartoum. Buhen temple, built by Queen Hatshepsut, *c.*1500 BC, was added to but certainly not improved by her husband and successor Thutmose III who, following his usual policy of vengeful spite against the former Queen, obliterated every mention of her name from the walls. It is the largest of the temples of Sudanese Nubia and its walls are carved with painted reliefs as fine as any to be seen in Egypt of the same period. Many inscriptions needed to be recorded before dismantling began and this task was undertaken by Dr Ricardo Caminos, the epigraphist from Brown University in the USA. Work on the preservation of the painted reliefs and the strenthening of the stone-work by chemical and other means was supervised by Dr H. J. Plenderleith, Director of the International Centre for the Preservation of Cultural Property, Rome, and here is an outline of the procedure he followed:

1 Encrustations of hornets' nests, bird lime, modern cement and other deposits on the wall surfaces were carefully removed with sharp knives, and the joints between the blocks were cleaned out as far as possible.
2 All carved and painted surfaces were covered with a five per cent solution of white flake shellac in alcohol. This solution was just brushed on.
3 Cotton voile was then applied to all weak plastered and painted wall surfaces. The adhesive used was 'Cellofas B', which was applied by brush in a fairly thick solution. The shellac was allowed 24 hours to harden before the application of the cloth.
4 When the cloth was dry, the joints between each block were cut with a sharp knife and the edges were stuck down with a further light application of shellac.

The masonry was found to be in better condition than had been expected so the work of dismantling and packing the walls, columns and pillars of the temple, which when broken down consisted of 281 blocks of stone of 2 tons' weight on average, was accomplished in the remarkably short space of 59 working days. The operation was directed by Dr F. Hinkel, a German architect working with the Sudan Department of Antiquities. To dismantle the temple he reversed the process used by the Egyptians to build it. The temple area was completely filled with sand and the top course of stones removed, the sand acting as a cushion to support the blocks.

As each course of stones was lifted off, the level of sand was accordingly lowered. Using this method the dismantling was completed without damage. Each block after numbering, was packed in a hardwood frame lined with cotton wool and transported across the Nile to Wadi Halfa, terminal point of Sudan Railways. The 59 cases weighing 600 tons in all were carried to Khartoum in 28 wagons where they arrived in good condition. Today Buhen Temple, reconstructed by Dr Hinkel, stands in the grounds of the new Museum while 700 miles to the north the place that saw its creation lies at the bottom of a lake. As a footnote, Hinkel noted in his report that the cost of dismantling and transporting the temple, including Sudan Railways charges, came to 25,150 Sudanese pounds, which was borne by the United Kingdom's Egypt Exploration Society as part of their contribution to the Nubian Campaign.

Emery had been awaiting the removal of Hatshepsut's temple with impatience, having long expected that beneath it would be found a temple of the Middle Kingdom period. And so it proved. Unfortunately, to provide foundations for Hatshepsut's temple the builders had driven so many huge stone pillars down into the edifice beneath that they had largely destroyed it. However, there were compensations because clearance did reveal in detail exactly how the Eighteenth Dynasty architects and masons constructed the new temple. The original Middle Kingdom structure had been a simple affair. Emery took me down into the foundations and pointed out the passages and alleyways of a series of domestic buildings, all of mud brick, probably the priestly quarters. The newcomers finding the edifice in ruins filled in the whole area with debris until they had an earthen platform and on this the architects marked out the plan of the new temple. Where there were to be columns they dug pits down to the original floor level and where there were to be walls they dug trenches. Both pits and trenches were then filled with soft sand and the various blocks of masonry for the foundations were brought into position so that, for example, a block which was to support a column was laid on top of a sandfilled pit. The sand was then removed and the block weighing perhaps two tons sank into position. These became the lowest foundations. More sand was poured into the pits and trenches, the next layer of blocks placed in position and the process repeated until the required new floor level was reached. After this the whole area was covered with sand and the next layer of blocks above ground level moved into place, and so on, using sand to cushion the blocks until the roof level was reached. An interesting discovery was that the blocks were placed one above the other in a rough state, that is to say, unfaced. They were then marked out to the prepared design–the excavators found the markings–after which the masons faced the surfaces of the walls and pillars. Here is the explanation for the wonderfully close fitting of Egyptian masonry. Finally in came the sculptors and painters to carve and colour the interior. When Emery and his colleagues removed the blocks of Hatshepsut's temple they found between them the grains of sand left there from the original building process.

All in all, Professor Emery's excavations at Buhen, notably the Middle Kingdom fortified town and the Old Kingdom copper smelting settlement, have revolutionised our knowledge of ancient military architecture and have added new pages to Nubian and Egyptian history. His was by far the longest sustained single excavation made in Nubia, and one of the most exhaustive.

About three miles south of Buhen and within shouting distance of Gebel Sheikh Suleiman with its King Djer inscription, lay the large fortified town of Kor. It spread along the west bank of the river for a considerable distance, a long, narrow rectangle of a site covering a large area. Kor had been examined by Somers Clarke as far back as 1899 when he cleared parts of the two visible lines of fortifications. When Professor Vercoutter arrived at Kor for the season of 1953-54 he found that since Somers Clarke's day the town and cemeteries had been systematically looted by illicit diggers. In the short time at his disposal he was able to clear only a part of the site but he found what appeared to be a harbour, laid bare four mud-brick buildings large enough to be administrative offices and exposed an inner line of fortifications not noted by Somers Clarke. He also tested three cemeteries. In 1965, when H. H. Smith, working on behalf of the Egypt Exploration Society, undertook further clearance of the site, some of it had already gone under water. Everything was denuded almost to desert level yet he was able to trace the plan of the walls with semi-circular bastions projecting from them at intervals. Among them was a serpentine wall one brick thick, similar to the 'wavy' walls cleared by Vercoutter in the fortified town at Mirgissa. By the end of his mission Smith had worked out the building history and chronology of Kor. An unexpected finding was that Kor with its weak defences seems to have been attacked and its fortifications razed late in the Twelfth Dynasty or early in the Thirteenth at a time when the other fortresses, including Buhen nearby, were still held by Egyptian forces. It was then hurriedly refortified only to be destroyed again when all the Second Cataract fortresses were finally stormed and burned. Like the other forts, Kor was re-occupied in the Eighteenth Dynasty but without serious restoration of the fortifications.

About twenty five miles upstream from Buhen lay Askut, a long and narrow island with another fort of the Middle Kingdom crowning its summit at the north west corner. Askut was the only fortress of the chain that had never been examined by earlier excavators and its clearance was undertaken in 1968 by Dr Alexander M. Badawy of the University of California, Los Angeles. The girdle wall, nearly seven metres thick, suggested the outline of a kite with the usual strengthening device of wooden beams and halfa grass matting. The bricks, too, were the standard size of 32 x 15 x 8 centimetres. The street system within the body of the fort radiated from a small square behind the main gateway. Main Street divided a series of magazines on the east side from, on the west side, dwelling houses and the Commandant's palace. This was a splendid affair, its walls bearing the same kind of coloured decorative patterns as those found by Vercoutter and Emery in the commandants' quarters at Mirgissa and Buhen, respectively; six octagonal wooden columns painted red had once stood in a broad hall supporting a ribbed ceiling of plaster. Near the Commandant's quarters a large area had been transformed into red brick by fierce fire, mute evidence that Askut had shared the fate of the other forts. A burnt wooden lintel still hanging loosely from the west wall indicated a doorway and clearance of this revealed a flight of beautifully cut stone steps leading down the cliff towards the river. It was the 'water-stairway' and as with all the forts this vital feature was originally covered over to protect access to the water supply in time of siege.

Down near the water's edge Dr Badawy made the important discovery of an inscription registering a Nile flood level in the reign of Sekhemkaré, who was the second king of the Thirteenth Dynasty. Another find, and a very curious one, was a collection of broken jars, seven of which contained still-born infants. Similar jar burials have been found in other forts–I saw some myself just outside the Armoury at Mirgissa. Their meaning may be connected with the custom, still followed in Egyptian villages, of burying still-born children with great care to ward off the possibility of a recurrence at the next birth. These were, in fact, the only contemporary burials found at Askut. No garrison cemetery came to light and indeed so small and so rocky an island offered little enough space for the living let alone the dead. Yet buried they must have been and it was Mills who found them on an island immediately south of Askut. The island was literally stuffed with burials under rocks and ledges and in every possible nook and cranny and it is reasonable to assume that they were soldiers from nearby Askut since the burials were all Egyptian in character. A number of the controversial egg-shaped objects in burnt clay turned up in the debris of the fort. They are flattened, grooved along one edge and pierced by one and sometimes two holes. Only in forts have they been found which points to their use as weapons. Emery suggested that bound to a stick with a thong such an object would make a very effective mace, fully capable of cracking a skull–the objects weigh about a pound–while Vercoutter's idea is that reinforced in this way they could be thrown considerable distances, after the fashion of stick bombs. Badawy's thoughts run along more peaceful lines and he believes them to be loom weights. If so a great deal of weaving must have gone on up and down the Cataract between sorties! Yet another suggestion is that (*left*) Mirgissa: a unique discovery – the slipway used for dragging ships round the cataract rocks. Note the imprints of the wooden 'sleepers' and foot prints (top left) of the sailors of forty centuries ago. (*right*) Semna: the natural rock barrier where Professor Vercoutter discovered traces of a barrage constructed by Egyptian engineers some 39 centuries ago to form a lake. A fort is on either side of the barrier and a third fort above right (to the south).

(*above*) Mirgissa: the armoury discovered during clearance of the upper fortress. Among the many weapons were several slabs of worked stone, seen above. Their purpose is doubtful though they could be leather shield formers. (*left*) Mirgissa: removing a Pharaonic mummy from the western cemetery.

they were weights for fishing nets. To me any of these possibilities seemed reasonable until one day in Kumma fort my foot kicked against one of the objects. It was tiny, small enough to fit into a matchbox and useless either for looms, fishing or head cracking. So the mystery remains.

By chance I had arrived at Askut on the final day of Dr Badawy's work there, in fact he was about to pay off his labourers at the end of two seasons of digging. Wind and sand, therefore, had not had time to blur the sharp outlines of the site lying exposed in its entirety, completely cleared and all debris removed. It was an odd experience thus to see the bare bones of a town scraped clean of all flesh. All around me the walls of the Middle Kingdom buildings stood to a height of nearly two metres. At my feet was the inspection pit which discharged water from the two bathrooms in the Commandant's residence into a pottery drain of startlingly modern appearance running along Main Street where Badawy had found a large deposit of several species of fruit, part of the garrison's menu perhaps. Unbroken pots piled on all sides, over to my right the stone staircase to the river looking as if it had been laid only yesterday, the fiery red of the burnt bricks–grim evidence of the final battle, all these conjured up a vivid picture of Askut in its last hours. And to round it off, in a room nearby Badawy had found a flint blade, a copper razor and abundant lumps of curly black hair–the garrison barber's shop. No Egyptian, with his addiction to sympathetic magic, would have left such potent stuff as hair lying around except in extreme exergency. In another room two grindstones daubed with vivid colours together with cakes of yellow pigment and haematite, pointed to the activities of painters. Pounding balls and grindstones similar to those found in the Duweishat mines twenty-five miles up river, were convincing evidence to Dr Badawy that the processing of gold-bearing quartz had been included in the duties of the Askut garrison.

Here perhaps I can digress to discuss Egypt's gold mining activities in the southern lands. In 1963 the Epigraphic Mission to Sudanese Nubia led by Dr Fritz Hintze found a group of rock inscriptions at Kulb some fifty miles up-stream from Semna. They are the most southerly Old Kingdom inscriptions yet discovered and they were made by a "scribe of the prospectors" and two "overseers of the prospectors". Here was new evidence that Egyptians were prospecting for minerals well inside Kush even at that early date. That they found copper is clear from Emery's discovery of the Egyptian Old Kingdom copper-smelting settlement at Buhen. However, in Old Kingdom records gold is never mentioned in relation to Nubia. Only with the penetration of the Middle Kingdom Pharaohs around 1900 BC does the extraction of gold from Wawat and Kush begin to appear in the records. Possibly the mines in Egypt were becoming exhausted or else the demands of the Twelfth Dynasty Pharaohs for gold were on the increase. Whatever the reason, Nubia from now on became Egypt's main source of the precious metal and by the end of the Eighteenth Dynasty gold had become the most important item in the annual tribute sent to Egypt by Kush, as is shown in the tomb paintings of Huy, Viceroy of Kush under the Pharaoh Tutankhamun (see Figures 7–10). Egypt's dominant position in the world of that time was probably due very largely to the gold she took out of Nubia; certainly her neighbours regarded Egypt as an El Dorado: "Send me much gold, more gold," writes an Asiatic king to the Pharaoh Akhenaton, "for in my brother's land gold is as common as dust". The Egyptian word for gold was, in fact, *nub*, the derivation so some say of "Nubia".

One of the richest of the mines in Lower Nubia (Wawat) was in Wadi Allaqi where the Middle Kingdom fortress of Kuban excavated by Emery in 1930, was built to protect the workings. A document which lists the mining areas known to the Egyptians shows that gold was collected from as far south as Gebel Barkal near the Fourth Cataract; that, however, was much later than the period of the Middle Kingdom forts. In 1928, in a room of the western fort at Semna Reisner found a pair of scales for weighing gold; it consisted of a small wooden pillar carved in the form of a palm tree, a wooden cross-beam and two copper pans, while later he obtained from farmers in the vicinity three inscribed and graduated weights for use in such scales.

Professor Jean Vercoutter has produced a fascinating study of gold production in ancient Egypt and the Sudan and this is his conclusion:

Fig. 7. Weighing of gold (tomb of *Huy*).

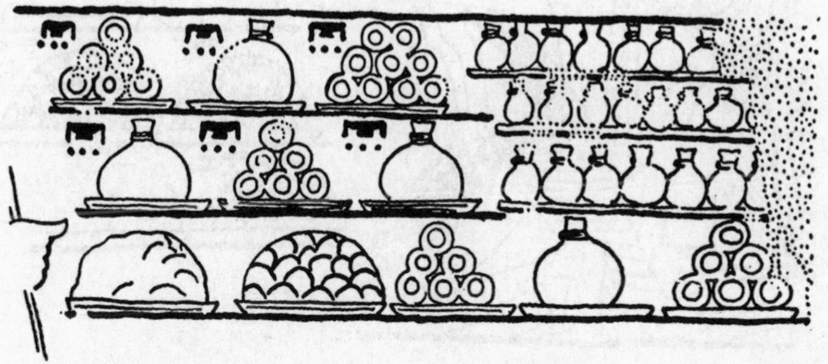

Fig. 8. Tribute of gold (tomb of *Huy*).

Fig. 9. Bearers of gold tribute (tomb of *Huy*).

Fig. 10. Negroes bringing gold tribute (tomb of *Huy*).

> Kush, contrary to the hopes of Mohammed Aly, had never been the El Dorado he dreamed of. The relative wealth of the Sudan, in gold, was based on gathering together the output of a number of small mines; on the ruthless exploitation of men condemned to the mines; and, above all, on military power which enabled the rulers of the country to raid the tribes where gold washing was practised. Each time there was a diminution in the strength of the ruling power, there was a subsequent drop in gold production, and the peak reached during the Eighteenth Dynasty seems never to have been attained again.

Vercoutter himself found in 1955 two strange structures at Faras East on the border with Egypt, which he tentatively suggested were gold washing basins. A shallow rectangular basin led into a small square receptacle hewn from the rock and below that again into a deep square basin. Similar structures had been found elsewhere in Lower Nubia by Emery and Kirwan who described them as wine presses although they do not at all resemble the wine presses portrayed in Egyptian tombs. The Scandinavians while conducting their Survey, came across in 1962, three of the so-called "gold washing basins". So a controversy was born.

There was, however, nothing controversial about the discovery made by Anthony Mills in the course of the Survey of the Sudan Antiquities Service. At Sarras three miles from Askut, on the east bank of the Nile, Mills identified a gold processing workshop of Middle Kingdom date. He cleared a series of small rooms, roughly rectangular, with packed mud floors and walls made of boulders held together with mud mortar. Some thirty more rooms he left untouched. It turned out to be a workshop, quite as primitive in construction as the granite 'apparatus' it contained for crushing quartz and separating out the gold. The process could hardly have been simpler. Two large stones set on edge supported a flat stone with a highly polished depression in its centre. This depression was scored with lines. Mills pointed to a parallel with the Nubians of our day who use exactly the same kind of stones supported in the same way for the grinding of grain; it is a method that avoids kneeling, which bears hard on the back while with the grindstone a foot or so above floor level it is possible to bear down on it for better purchase. Fitting into the grindstone was a rubbing stone. A second type was more massive with the depression both smaller and deeper; with a heavy crushing stone cut to an exact fit, the two stones combined to form a pestle and mortar. Mills gave a demonstration of the process using quartz left nearby by the ancient workers. A lump of quartz laid in the mortar was pounded to coarse powder by the heavy pestle in a matter of seconds. He then laid the powder in the depression along with a handful of sand and whisked a rubbing stone back and forth across the scored lines. Soon the quartz had become fine powder and in it I could see the glitter of several grains of gold. Had we had any water handy the next step would have been to pour it into the depression and the powder would have floated away leaving the heavy gold lying at the bottom. I tried it myself and nothing could have been easier. The fine quartz powder is known as 'tailings' and Mills pointed out large deposits of it outside the workshop. Dozens of grindstones and pestles lay scattered in the huddle of rooms. The process is much the same as that described by Diodorus of Sicily writing in Egypt around the year 50 BC. He tells how the miners spread the crushed ore

> upon a broad table a little inclined, and pouring water upon it rub the pulverised stone until all the earthy matter is separated, which flowing away with the water leaves the heavier particles behind on the board. This operation is often repeated, the stone being rubbed lightly with the hand: they then draw up the useless and earthy substance with fine sponges—gently applied until the gold comes out quite pure.

Evidently the method of separating out the gold had changed little in nineteen centuries. As for the mines which kept the workshops busy Mills located them by the simple expedient of searching for a road. He found one, wide and well constructed, running back from the river into the interior. We followed it over the tops of the stony hills noting the quartz pebbles that littered its length and speculating whether they had fallen from donkey panniers or from baskets carried on human backs. In about two miles white patches of quartz appeared on the surface, scarring the brown flanks of the hills and soon I was staring into the first gold mine I had ever seen. A narrow shaft not 2 feet wide sloped down into darkness at an incredible angle of 50 degrees. It seemed impossible that human beings could ever have worked in it and it seemed even less likely when Mills explained the method of extraction. Wherever the prospectors found a vein of quartz at the surface they followed it in all its twists and turns down through the bedrock until the quartz ran out. Extraction was done by heating the quartz with fires and sousing with cold water when a critical temperature was reached. It had the effect of cracking the quartz and causing it to break away cleanly from the matrix. The mortality from collapsing galleries and heat exhaustion must have been appalling. Mills had located many such mines in the hills round about, and four workshop sites down by the river.

Walking back from the mines I became aware of a sharp increase in temperature. The wind had dropped and very soon the air was stifling. How could human beings, I wondered, have endured such working conditions in the heat of a Nubian summer smothered in quartz dust and crouched among blistering fires? Were they native Egyptians? Probably not. The overseers would be Egyptians from the nearby forts of Askut or Shelfak but the poor devils sweating it out down in that choking inferno must have been Nubians pressed into servitude by the military occupiers of their land. And suddenly I had a vision of the treasures of the Pharaoh Tutankhamun, those magnificent examples of the goldsmith's art now in the Cairo Museum and gazed at in awe by thousands every year. All that mass of gleaming gold: how many unnamed men had suffered here in Nubia to get it? How many lives were sacrificed to make such beauty possible?

About 25 miles south of the Sarras gold workshops was Duweishat in the heart of the Belly of Stone. Here in a landscape as bleak and harsh as anything on this planet is Africa's richest gold mine this side of the equator. I went to Duweishat to see the modern workings, abandoned now to the rising waters of the Nile. The Egyptians had, of course, worked the mines extensively, as the European miners discovered when they arrived with their machinery. Gallery after gallery of the twentieth-century mining operation had broken through into the ancient workings so that I found it hard to distinguish which was ancient and which modern. Later, in Khartoum, the former manager of the Duweishat mine told me there was nothing his people could have taught the Egyptians about gold prospecting. He had many things to say about the ancient miners—evidently they had fired his enthusiasm—but one of the most interesting of his observations and the most chilling was that the method of extraction had been shockingly dangerous and that in some of the galleries less than 2 feet across only very small humans could have worked—in other words children. From the foregoing it becomes clear that the fortresses were a key factor in Egypt's hunger for gold and the probability is that the garrisons of them all were to some extent concerned in the collection and processing of the metal, as in Askut.

Six miles south of Askut one came to Shelfak fort, another kite-shaped structure which at first sight appeared to be on an island but in reality crowned a high cliff projecting from the west bank of the Nile. Upstream again and almost within sight of the fort, was Uronarti called by the Nubians *Gezirat-al-Malik* (Island of the King); it was a haunting place surmounted by yet another fort also built in the shape of a kite to conform to the topography of the island. To stand on the battlements of Uronarti and look south towards Semna was to see the finest spectacle in the whole 100-mile length of the Cataract and Belly of Stone. Three miles off, the barrier of crystalline rock stretched clear across the Nile and through the narrow gap the whole weight of the great river surged with a roar that could be clearly heard. On either side of the gap stood a fortress, each with its stone temple, and so dramatic was their siting that they appeared to stand above the torrent on towering cliffs, indeed one writer has described the Semna forts as being 600 feet above the river whereas the actual height was only 60 feet. To my mind the view of Semna from Uronarti was unmatched in the Nile Valley although I doubt whether the Nubians of 39 centuries ago would have appreciated it.

Before the Nubian Campaign few people in the world had ever heard of Nubia, yet this remote corner of the Nile Valley held a collection of defensive constructions unmatched anywhere from the beginning of history up to the advent of the military engineers of fifteenth-century Venice. Apart from Buhen near Wadi Halfa, the Second Cataract forts had been visited by a mere handful of archaeologists and travellers. For close on four thousand years they resisted the abrasive winds of Nubia and it is hard to credit that now in the year of 1974 not one of these absolutely unique structures survives. All that remains of them is locked up in drawings and sections, photographs and reports.

CHAPTER VII

The Southern Frontier

This chapter is devoted in the main to the group of four forts that together formed Egypt's southern frontier in the Middle Kingdom period: Semna East, West and South, plus Uronarti. All were dug by Reisner, except Semna South, which was left undisturbed for an odd reason which I shall describe later. Until the 1960s most of what we knew of the Middle Kingdom's military operation in Nubia stemmed from the material uncovered by Reisner between the years 1924 and 1932. It was he who established the history of the Second Cataract forts as accepted until now. Started in the reign of Senusret I and completed by Senusret III they were in continuous use as strongholds for close on two hundred years until stormed and burned sometime after the Thirteenth Dynasty. Thereafter, abandoned to the ravages of wind and sand they fell into ruin and generations were to pass before the Eighteenth Dynasty Pharaohs, pursuing their policy of outright annexation of Nubia, re-built and reoccupied them. Now, however, with Egypt in the new expansionist mood which was to lead her to the glittering pinnacle of Empire and domination of the ancient world, the function of the forts shifted from that of military oppression to the more peaceable role of trading posts, after the manner of the fortified posts of the Hudson's Bay Company. Before long Egypt's southern frontier had been extended even further up-river until it was established almost at the Fourth Cataract four hundred miles south of Semna. Under the long reign of successive Viceroys of Kush the forts continued to function for close on five hundred years after which, with the collapse of the central power in Egypt, they were finally abandoned.

While clearing the fortresses of Uronarti and Shelfak Reisner found a large number of clay sealings with seal impressions of the kind found in all the forts, without exception. About five thousand turned up in Uronarti alone. Classified and published by Reisner, they are of great importance in dating and indicating connections with the Egyptian royal house because they were used to seal letters and packages, boxes, sacks and other containers and were even used to seal door locks (see Figure 11).

Of the Uronarti seals 3,473 had been the property of private individuals and were used presumably in the exchange of letters. Of the official seals, Reisner makes particular mention of a series made in Uronarti itself, and of these 503 were overstamped. This seems to have been an administrative precaution of the kind we are all too familiar with today when a letter has to be visaed by one or more people other than the original writer. In UNESCO, I remember, certain categories of letters needed as many as five visas. The Treasury and storehouse officials concerned with receipts and payments would apply their private seals over the official sealing as a safeguard against mis-use of the official seal. The seals of 47 Uronarti officials were thus identified. The custom of overstamping, occasionally several times, was so widespread that one can only conclude that pilfering and 'fiddling' in the Nubian forts of 39 centuries ago was as prevalent as it is in our day. Reisner estimated that over five hundred different seals were in use by the occupants of Uronarti fort and their correspondents in other forts and in Egypt. Incidentally, the practice indicates a high level of literacy at that remote time. From his studies of the sealings Reisner came to the conclusion that the system of seal registration used in ancient Egypt was superior to the modern Egyptian method whereby seal-engravers are licensed by the provincial authorities and are required to keep a register of all seals cut, together with particulars of their owners. There is certainly some significance in the fact that most of the sealings that came to light during Reisner's excavations date from the Thirteenth Dynasty, and this is true of all collections of fortress seals found elsewhere in the course of the Nubian Campaign.

Fig. 11. Selection of sealings found by Reisner in Uronarti Fort.

The Semna forts contained temples which, after Buhen, were the most important in Sudanese Nubia. They had, therefore, to be removed out of reach of the waters that otherwise would engulf them. Both temples, though small, were well preserved. The temple of Semna West had its roof in place and on many nights I have slept in it alone and undisturbed except for mice scuttling among the stones. Both temples were embellished with finely executed reliefs and historically important hieroglyphic texts. Many of these texts had been copied by Lepsius but since 1844 the study of the Egyptian language has moved forward so it was felt advisable to have them re-examined in the light of modern scholarship before removal. The work was undertaken by the joint expedition of the Egypt Exploration Society and Brown University in the USA. The epigraphist was Dr Ricardo A. Caminos who had recorded Buhen temple. He confesses that his mouth watered when he first visited the site and saw the rock inscriptions which, aside from the temples, were an outstanding feature of Semna. However, those were to be dealt with by a German expedition under the leadership of Professor Fritz Hinze so Caminos concentrated on the two Eighteenth Dynasty sandstone temples. Despite their small size–Semna West is only about 9 metres by 5 metres–both are so rich in inscriptions that cover much of Egypt's history that Caminos needed two seasons of work to copy them and make detailed plans, sections and elevations. His completion of the work in the winter of 1963 was the signal for Fritz Hinkel to move in.

By this time Hinkel was becoming adept at moving temples and cutting away rock inscriptions, and he went to work with characteristic ingenuity and energy (see Figure 12). My arrival at Semna to see him coincided with a choking sandstorm such as only Nubia could produce. Semna was inaccessible to all but the most determined of travellers and never before had I seen it other than deserted, but now it was like a scene from the Inferno with dozens of white-clad figures looming through the haze, heads shrouded to protect them from flying dirt and sand. Across the river on the east bank stood a heavy lorry awaiting the arrival of a pontoon ferry. Impossibly small and frail it looked as it strained

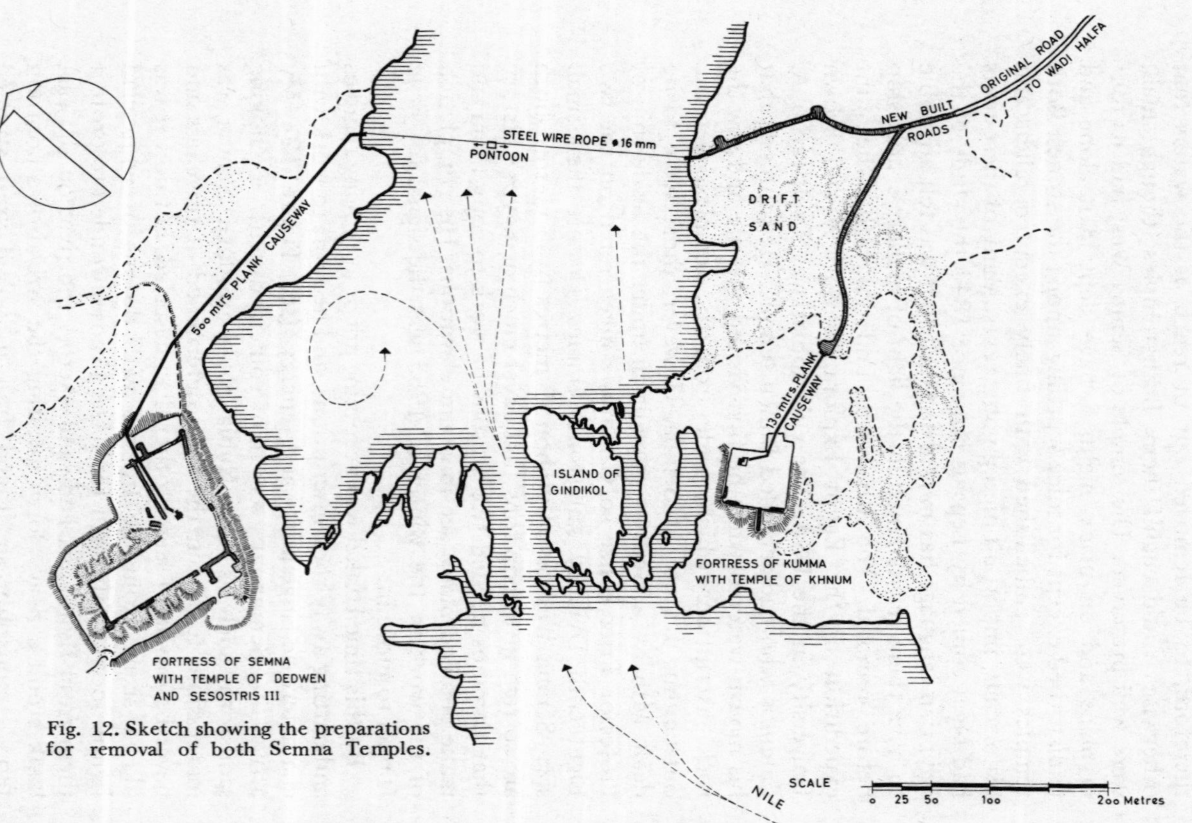

Fig. 12. Sketch showing the preparations for removal of both Semna Temples.

against the surging current—we were only two hundred yards below the rock barrier and the force and tumult of the Nile plunging through the gap was awe-inspiring. The pontoon, an ingenious construction of mahogany planks supported on empty oil drums, was secured to a wire hauser that stretched from bank to bank. Several sandstone blocks embellished with carvings had been lashed to the planking while half a dozen Nubians heaved and strained against the wire using ingenious wooden levers to drag the contraption and themselves across the river, at this point fully a third of a mile wide. That slender cable was all that stood between them and destruction in the swirling currents of a rapid three hundred yards downstream.

From the wire hauser secured to a rock at my feet, a railroad constructed like the pontoon of mahogany planks, climbed the river bank, crossed a quarter of a mile of vicious granite outcrops, to pass in through the walls of the fortress. Beyond the walls it mounted a hillock of rubble to terminate on the roof of Hatshepsut's temple. Following the method used at Buhen, Hinkel had buried the temple in sand and rubble to roof level and was about to remove the roof blocks after which the level of the filling would be lowered with the removal of each successive course of masonry until the foundations were reached. I watched a roof block weighing two tons being levered onto a mahogany sled at the top of the mound while at the bottom a gang of 40 labourers took the strain on a rope that would pull the sled down the wooden slipway; on the roof of the temple stood more men who grasped a second rope to prevent the stone running out of control. With them on the roof was the chanty-man, skinny legs outlined through his *galabieh* by the tearing wind, in his hands a drum contrived from a petrol tin. At a word from Hinkel his wailing voice rang out, the men took the strain and amid much laughter and cries of encouragement the great stone groaned its way down the mahogany slipway just 3500 years after Hatshepsut's builders had placed it in position.

Below, among the fortifications, a workshop was in full swing with carpenters cutting and planing baulks of mahogany and hammering them into sleds and packing cases.

Not for several thousand years had the Semna forts witnessed so much human activity.

After 35 centuries of exposure to the near-freezing cold of Nubian winters and the great heat of summer many of the sandstone blocks were in poor condition and had to be reinforced before removal. Chemical treatment was used to fix the wall paintings and the stones themselves were wrapped in textile bandages and padded with cotton wool. To transport the 146 blocks totalling 130 tons to the waiting lorries on the first stage of their long journey south to Khartoum 53 crossings of the loaded pontoon were necessary. A few weeks later Hinkel had dismantled the eastern temple at Kumma (Semna East) and all 185 tons of it (480 pieces) were also on their way to Khartoum. So ended a remarkable feat of improvisation in civil engineering, successfully concluded with none of the mechanical aids of modern technology.

When, at Kumma on the eastern side of the gap Hinkel removed the lowest course of stone and exposed the foundations, he discovered that Amenhotep II had used a number of inscribed and decorated blocks from the temple erected on the same site by his mother Queen Hatshepsut and her husband Thutmose III. Foundation deposits were found beneath both temples. These took the form of miniature pots, vases, saucers and bottles—about five hundred in all—together with models of all the tools used in constructing the buildings; there were samples of all the materials employed and animal bones and seeds from surrounding plantations. Among the deposits from the Semna West temple were tiny plaques of gold bearing inscriptions recording that this was a temple of Seshat, the goddess of history and architecture. It was a fascinating collection to see and examine in Hinkel's workshop at Khartoum. When studied in relation to the re-used blocks the many objects found at Kumma will be extremely helpful in reconstructing the history of the temple there.

The cost of moving the Semna temples was borne by the governments of Belgium and the Netherlands, while the British Government through the Egypt Exploration Society, assumed financial responsibility for Buhen temple. Those sections of the Rameses II temple at Aksha that could be moved were taken to Khartoum at the expense of the Government of France. One wall is of particular importance because engraved on it is a list of all the countries and tribes that were subject to Rameses II. The temples have now been re-erected by Hinkel in the grounds of the new Museum at Khartoum. There the sixty miles of the Second Cataract has been compressed into a few hundred yards of pseudo-Nile and along its banks are the re-erected temples, tombs, fragments of monuments and rock carvings and inscriptions, all in the same physical relationship to each other as they had in Nubia. The concept is a bold one but the effect is somewhat marred by the concrete bulk of the Museum fronting the waterway and the movable structures of glass and steel designed to cover and protect the three temples during Khartoum's rainy season. But at least they have been preserved to remind the Sudanese of the long shadow cast across their country by Egypt throughout history.

Kumma fort became Anthony Mills's headquarters in 1966 while he was surveying the surrounding district. His usual method of working was for him, his assistant and the half dozen Quftis (Egyptian foremen trained in archaeological digging) to walk over the ground in extended line from the river bank to the limit of the alluvium deposit. It was in this deposit or on its verge that the cemeteries and settlements were to be found, for it was there close to the water that people settled. To survey the hills behind would have been a profitless exercise. However a good archaeologist keeps his eyes open and Mills happened to notice what appeared to be a road on the summit of a hill well back from the river. He clambered up the slope and there sure enough was a road about six feet wide, its surface flattened and swept clear of stones. He followed it down into ravines and over hilltops for five miles to where it ended in a granite quarry. Then Nubia produced another of the mysteries thrown up from time to time during the nine years of the campaign. On the flanks of a valley stood some thirty structures such as Mills had never seen before, drystone cairns carefully put together in the form of truncated cones. Each was surmounted by an upright slab of stone and built into the south face was a niche some

12 inches square. The average height was 2½ metres and the base about 1½ metres in diameter. Mills demolished two down to bedrock only to find them solid right through. A few potsherds scattered around were all of Middle Kingdom type and this dated the cairns to about 1900 BC and linked them with the builders of the forts. This valley is well above the flooded area, in the heart of the Belly of Stone. It is one of nature's rubbish heaps, a landscape that early Christian ascetics suffering zealously in their caves would have relished. Not so the Egyptians with their devotion to the good things of life. Why then did they build their cairns in this hidden valley so far from the Nile and what did they signify? Perhaps they were put up as offerings to a god or to commemmorate each year of a Pharaoh's life, or even the accession of a series of Pharaohs. In the absence of a single clue the puzzle is insoluble. In Nubia one was seldom out of earshot of tumbling water, while the singing of many birds and the sighing of the wind were as inescapable as they were delightful. But down among the cairns there were none of those familiar sounds. The silence was absolute, uncanny. I could hear the beating of my heart. Even the usually talkative Mills was silent. The valley of cairns is one of those places with a definite presence, a haunting spot—perhaps haunted even—and very disturbing. Only once before had I experienced a similar feeling of unease and that was in a wadi of Egypt's Eastern desert. Climbing up to the ancient road I looked back to those strange relics of the past and the thought crossed my mind that in all probability they would never again be seen by human eyes.

In all, Mills located some fifty hitherto unrecorded sites in and around Semna ranging from A-Group cemeteries to Christian settlements. His routine in Nubia never varied: up at dawn and off to the site, back to breakfast at around 9 o'clock, then return to the site until 2 when work ended as far as the labourers were concerned. After lunch at 3 o'clock the rest of the day would be devoted to writing up the day's work, examining and recording any objects discovered, sorting and classifying sherds, drawing plans and elevations of structures and so on. A healthy life but strenuous and demanding. On our way back to breakfast one day Mills pointed to a rectangle of mud brick walls. Following the rule of "if it's man-made, dig it", he had started excavation but when the first body was exposed hastily stopped; he had found a cemetery of British troops killed in the River War. With 5000 years of history thick in the ground one never knew what would turn up. In Nubia most mud-brick structures looked alike and the only way to date them was to excavate. Mills once spent several days at Serras clearing a building which produced neither pottery nor artifacts and which seemed to have no connection with any of the recognised historical periods. The riddle was solved when an aged Nubian revealed that it had been a workshop of a long-defunct light railway built by General Gordon back in the '80s.

One of the more spectacular of Mills's discoveries at Semna was associated with the forts. On the west bank three hundred metres back from the river he came across a length of wall and traced it from the southern fort, running north behind the Semna West fort and keeping always parallel with the river, almost to the southern end of Uronarti island—a distance of about three miles. Fragments of pottery, the method of construction and the dimensions of the bricks made the wall contemporary with the Middle Kingdom. I was able to walk on top of it easily enough since it was denuded down to desert level, in fact it looked more like a brick road than a wall. It bore a strong resemblance to the great girdle wall at Mirgissa. In the absence of excavation the original height was difficult to estimate but it was probably around 3 to 4 metres. Wherever it crested a hill or a rise in ground level, towers 4½ metres square were built into it, and at points where it crossed a wadi or ravine the mud-brick structure was reinforced with massive stone foundations to withstand the 'flash' floods of rainstorms. Almost certainly it formed part of the defensive enclave that embraced the Uronarti and Semna forts. As at Mirgissa I was struck by the labour that had gone into its construction. Originally it was painted white, in places traces of the paint remained, and seen from the river the wall and its many towers must have been an impressive feature of the landscape 39 centuries ago. Thinking it might have been built to defend a slipway for "dragging the ships" similar to that found at Mirgissa, I persuaded Mills to look for one down by the northern rapid. We dug a series of trial pits but with the handful of men at our disposal and time, as usual, in short supply, the accumulation of sand defeated us. Was there ever a slipway? Alas, the wall has now gone under water.

Whilst walking along the wall I noticed several large enclosures between it and the river. Some were very large, fully 300 metres by 100, and the surrounding walls were built of boulders roughly laid. I was trying to work out a possible connection between these odd structures and the fortified wall when from out of the setting sun behind the fortress came a line of camels. In that empty desert it was an astonishing sight. Hundreds came into view, driven by a handful of ragged men, until the whole space between fort and river was crowded with them and the noise of their bellowing as they stooped to drink drowned even the roar of the cataract. They came I surmised from the grazing lands of Kordofan in Central Sudan and were taking the ancient camel track to Egypt where they would be sold for food. Their flesh could hardly have made tender eating after 1800 or so miles of desert travel! I had seen a similar caravan some years before, behind Buhen, and had counted over 3000 animals padding through the sand. Watching them now gave me the idea that perhaps the enclosures had been built for corralling cattle. The C-Group people of Nubia who were contemporary with the forts, were cattle breeders above all and we know from the lists of tribute gathered in Bubia that cattle were taken to Egypt in large numbers. Semna, the southern frontier, controlling with Uronarti a considerable fortified zone, would be ideally placed for the collection and herding of cattle seized from the surrounding tribes. Mills was attracted to the idea but rightly pointed out that any evidence could only be found in or around the enclosures and who would excavate them?

So far I have made only the briefest of references to the third of the Semna forts, Semna South. Reisner records that his reason for not clearing it lay with the local people who had a superstitious fear of the place, refusing to go near it, and this fear was transmitted to his Egyptian workmen.

Twenty years later the superstition must have evaporated so that when Vercoutter arrived to excavate the site in 1957 he had no trouble on that score.

The fort was built on an ancient alluvial terrace of the Nile about a mile south of Semna West fort and some two hundred metres inland from the river. It was a small structure much denuded by sand and wind erosion. The inner courtyard, approximately 34 metres square, was enclosed by a main wall 12 metres wide at its base with projecting square bastions at each corner. Then came a ditch 7½ metres wide and beyond that an outer girdle wall 4 metres thick. Finally, surrounding the whole structure, was a glacis faced with stone some 10 metres wide (see Figure 13). Despite its small size the fort was a heavily protected affair; nevertheless all indications showed that Semna South, like the fort on Dabnarti island opposite Mirgisa, was never inhabited permanently and was probably manned from the garrison of Semna West in the emergency of a sudden attack or when the arrival of a fleet from north or south called for special guard duties. At the inner north-eastern corner was the entrance to a subterranean stairway, no doubt the water-gate, built of large slabs of granite. Vercoutter cleared it below ground for a length of 50 metres beyond which he was unable to go for lack of air. He tried to find the termination of the stairway by digging but was baulked by the presence of a moslem cemetery, which he could not, of course, disturb. However, trial trenching did reveal a heavy deposit of Nile silt lying on top of the glacis, a discovery that set in motion an investigation and chain of deduction which reads like a detective story. How could Nile silt have been deposited to a height of 8 metres *above* the glacis wall? Vercoutter noted that the deposit could not be the debris of a disintegrated section of girdle wall since it was in horizontal layers and was obviously the result of regular Nile flood deposits over a considerable number of years (see Figure 14). I should perhaps explain that in 1957 the southern fort stood on ground about 8 metres above Nile level. There could be only one possible explanation: a series of exceptionally heavy floods *after* the construction of the glacis, around 1870 BC. Now came the first link in the chain of deduction. Less than a mile downstream from Semna South was the natural granite barrier already described and on the rocks of the barrier below Kumma fort (Semna East) the occupants had recorded Nile flood levels over a span of some seventy years, from the Twelfth Dynasty well into the Thirteenth; all these levels recorded floods averaging 8 metres higher than the floods of our day. Surely, Vercoutter reasoned, there must be a connection between this phenomenon and the 8 metres of silt deposited after the construction of Semna South fort.

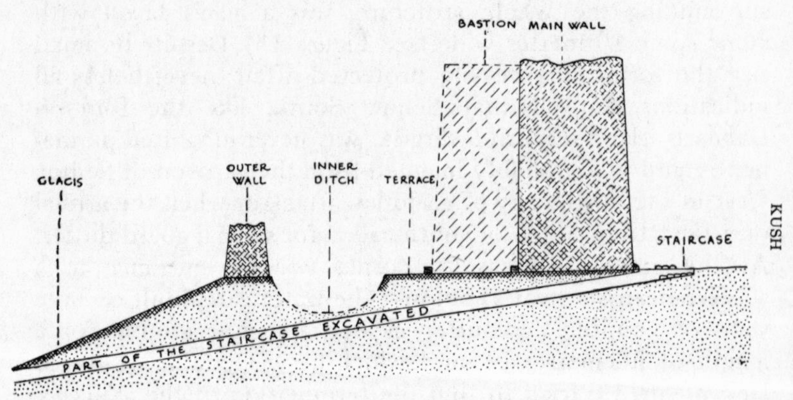

Fig. 13. Cross-section of the fortifications at Semna South Fort.

Scholars have long disputed the significance of the Semna flood inscriptions, some gong so far as to doubt their accuracy, maintaining that the Egyptians did not intend them to be true indicators of the Nile levels. If this were so the Egyptians stationed at Semna were acting out of character. Egypt has scores of instances to show what accurate recorders her people were, particularly in relation to irrigation and flood control; the Nilometers are examples. The Egyptians were obliged to keep accurate records since the periodic oscillations in Nile flooding determined the volume of water available annually for irrigation distribution and this in turn affected the pattern of taxation. Such records would have been useful, too, in estimating the navigability of the river as the flood waters receded. Vercoutter rejects this negative interpretation and has gone on to show, using epigraphical analysis, that the inscriptions are true recordings. Another explanation could be that the climate of 1900 BC was more clement than today's and the discharge of the Nile much greater in consequence. However, climatologists and palaeo-botanists working in Nubia during the campaign do not think so, their investigations having shown that the climate then was not much different from today's. Geologists in their turn have dismissed a third explanation which saw the rock barrier at Semna as a natural dam that collapsed or eroded progressively after the Semna recordings were made.

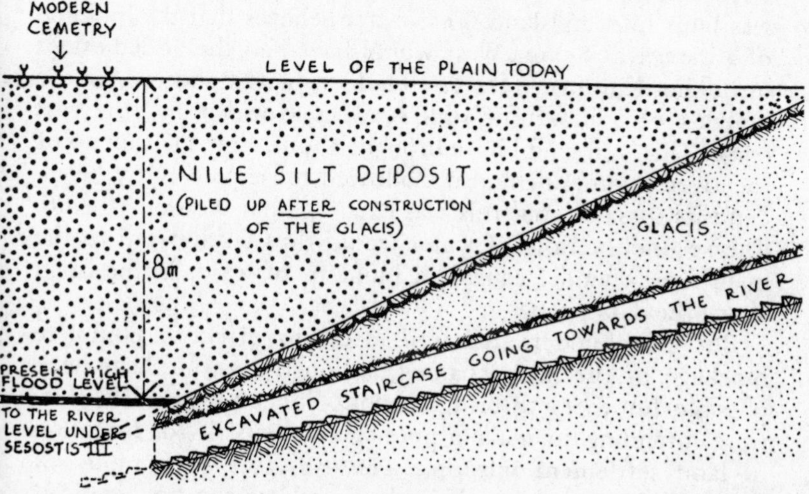

Fig. 14. Cross-section of the lower edge of the Glacis at Semna South, showing overlying Nile silt.

Thus Vercoutter was left with the possibility of an *artificial* dam at Semna built by Egyptians around 1850 BC. Certainly such a construction would have been well within the range of their technology. Dykes, channels, embankments, all these had been built by Egyptians since the beginning of their history. According to tradition Memphis, the first capital, was built on land reclaimed by the construction of a dam which seems to have been fully 500 metres long and 10 metres high. To this day one can see a dam which closes the neck of the Fayum Depression leading to the Nile Valley; it was built by the Middle Kingdom Pharaoh Senusret II. Old Kingdom engineers erected a masonry dam of sizeable proportions across the Wadi Garawi 500 years earlier.

While building the Semna dam the Egyptians would have had to provide a by-pass to divert temporarily the main flow of the Nile, but this they could have done easily since a natural channel already existed behind Kumma fort; it had obviously carried part of the Nile flow at some period though whether during historic times it is impossible to say. The effect would have been to make the rock on which Kumma was built into an island. Vercoutter believes that the building of a barrier at Semna West would have had the added effect of linking Kumma to the east bank; in fact he showed me the remains of a dry-stone wall between Kumma and the east bank. This wall could have brought about, first a silting up of the river channel behind it, followed subsequently by heavy deposits of sand, and this was exactly what we saw in 1966. The secondary flow of water would thus be diverted to the main river channel causing a build-up of water in the basin above the dam proper.

But the builders did not need to effect a complete blockage of the main channel, although it would have been possible for them to bring it about–indeed essential if they were intending to make a permanent reservoir for irrigation or land settlement purposes. However, the topography of Semna did not lend itself to land reclamation nor would it have been practical to maintain such schemes in what was, in effect, hostile territory. Probably the intention was to establish a habour for shipping in the form of a basin which would build up to its maximum area at times of high Nile and while shrinking as the flow of the river diminished, would yet retain a reasonable depth of water during the dry months.

To meet this requirement strong spur walls built out into the river so as to link already existing rocks and islets would have sufficed. The work, of course, would have to be done at times of low Nile. A series of spur walls would impede the flow and build up a considerable head of water at times of flood. Evidently such spurs would have to be immediately down-stream of the gap in the natural barrier and that is exactly where Vercoutter found what he considers to be traces of them. Below Semna West fort and just north of the rock barrier lay a great number of large stones, some weighing many tons. Among them were a number of flood-level inscriptions but unlike the horizontal inscriptions at Kumma those at Semna West were all higgledy-piggledy, some even upside down. Moreover there were only 24 as compared with 130 at Kumma although Semna West was the more important fortress of the two. The supposition is that in the Twelfth and Thirteenth Dynasties there were many more inscriptions lining the face of a dam or spur walls and that at some time after the Thirteenth Dynasty an unusually violent flood caused the structure or structures to collapse suddenly and carry with it downstream many of the inscribed blocks. The force of the current that carried them away can be gauged by the masses of granite bearing inscriptions and weighing hundreds of tons that have been rolled over like pebbles. Another pointer to the violent flood theory is that the lower part of Semna West's water stairway has obviously been washed away to a point some 8 metres above the low Nile level of 1966.

A close examination of the confusion of stones lying below Semna West fort convinced Vercoutter that this is exactly what had occurred and that the spurs or dam had been mixed structures of natural rocks and building stones. These latter implied the proximity of a quarry and, sure enough, he found one at the foot of the hill that overlooked Kumma. There is no proof that stone cut from the quarry was used for the barrier but the probability is strong; the forts themselves were built of mud-brick, granite slabs being used only for foundations and the paving of streets, while the stone temples were of course built after the period under discussion. The puzzling Kumma inscriptions now fell neatly into place as did the deposit of Nile silt on top of the glacis at Semna South. Evidently the waters of the flooded basin came right up to the walls of the southern fort as far as the outlet of the subterranean river stairway.

Vercoutter's elegant edifice compounded of close observation, research and deduction, to which I fear I have done scant justice, was abruptly shaken by Badawy's discovery of the Thirteenth Dynasty inscription below Askut fort, 15 miles downstream from Semna. The inscription shows that at the beginning of the Thirteenth Dynasty the flood level at Askut differed little from that of 1962 which means it was 8 metres lower than the Kumma inscriptions upstream.

This discovery gave rise to yet another explanation for the Kumma inscriptions, that a series of exceptionally high floods happened to coincide with the period spanned by the Twelfth and Thirteenth Dynasties. However, such high levels would certainly have inundated the fortresses lower down the Cataract, notably the lower fortifications at Mirgissa on the plain plus Kor, Buhen and Serra, and all those mud-brick constructions would certainly have disintegrated. None of them have revealed any signs of damage by water and all the indications they provided showed little difference in the flood levels of 1900 BC and AD 1960. The *coup de grace* for the high floods hypothesis was provided by the UNESCO team. In the very last days of the Survey, at the Dal Cataract, Mills's colleague James Knudstad, as he described the incident to me, was approached by a boatman who asked whether he would like to see some "English writing" on an island opposite. Having nothing better to do Knudstad let himself be guided to a long black stone and on it to his surprise was an inscription in Egyptian hieroglyphs. Mills copied the inscription and it turned out to be a Nile level recorded in the reign of Senusret III. It is 55 miles upstream from Semna, it pre-dates by several years the alleged construction of the Semna barrier, and it shows little change from the flood levels of today.

Askut might have been selected as suitable for the building of a dam rather than Semna; the topography would have made it possible but for other reasons Askut was less well-favoured than Semna. So we fall back on spur walls. If such walls could be constructed at Semna why not at Askut where the rapids were well placed for flood control of this nature? The linking of natural spurs to islets and rocky outcrops by means of stone walls is an ancient technique. Silt building up behind the barrier can be used for cultivation, while the blocked channel forces the river to seek deeper channels. At Mirgissa Vercoutter found such a wall buried in sand and so effective had it been that the channel it blocked had long since become a part of the mainland. Meanwhile, a careful study of aerial photographs of the Second Cataract had revealed artificial spurs among several rapids and it is entirely conceivable that had Mills and his colleagues known of the existence of such spurs, which are difficult to spot on the ground, they could well have located and mapped others during their survey of the river and its islands. It is an opportunity lost which can never recur since the whole region is now submerged.

To sum up then: Professor Vercoutter believes that in the reign of Amenemhet III who succeeded Senusret III, two massive spur walls were built over the natural barrier at Semna leaving open only the narrow middle channel. At high Nile these constructions caused a build-up of water on both sides of the barrier to an average of 8 metres and a high level of water was maintained by other spur walls at Uronarti and Askut, and so on down the length of the Cataract. This implies a systematic control of flooding along this entire reach of the Nile but it was an enterprise well within the capacity and experience of the Egyptians of that time. It would make for the easier passage of fleets during high Nile by virtue of the raising of water levels wherever there were dangerous rapids to traverse. Moreover, the blocking of subsidiary channels would tend to deepen the main channel and make it possible for expeditions to navigate well into the period of low Nile, thus lengthening the season for military operations. In short, the main reason for these hydraulic works was strategic. If Vercoutter's hypothesis is valid, and there is little reason to doubt it, then we are drawn to the remarkable conclusion that one of the great rivers of the world was effectively brought under control nearly forty centuries ago.

New evidence brought to light during the campaign, combined with data already known, makes it possible to conjecture how the Egyptians of, say 1800 BC maintained control of the Second Cataract. Clearly the forts themselves were the backbone of a well-organised military machine; they were in constant touch with one another and with Egypt through a system of couriers, and via look-out posts and signalling towers were made aware of the movement of strangers on both banks of the river. The river itself carried considerable traffic in military personnel, officials and merchandise between Egypt and Nubia during much of the year. The picture is one of considerable activity up and down the length of the Cataract except at those times when fighting broke out. Drawing a little further on recent archaeological evidence one can get a fair idea of how individual forts fitted the overall pattern. Starting at Semna we see four forts, if we include Uronarti, holding the southern frontier, keeping the surrounding tribes out of the fortified zone, and protecting ships bearing expeditions and commerce from north and from south and seeking shelter in the basin behind the artificial barrier. The garrisons may well have had the additional duty of guarding the many head of cattle collected as tribute from the surrounding tribes while awaiting a convoy for on-carriage to Egypt by ship, or on the hoof via the ancient highway; an appropriate number, no doubt, would be reserved as food for the officers and men of the forts. Next down the line, the smaller forts of Askut and Shelfak could be largely concerned with supervising the mining and processing of the gold found in the hills nearby. Moving further north we reach Mirgissa–Ikn–Egypt's main entrepot in Nubia, with its docks and warehouses. We then pass Dogonarti Island on which two centuries later an Eighteenth Dynasty fortress will be built, to reach Kor and Buhen. Here at Buhen is the residence of the Governor, for Buhen is the nerve centre of Egyptian hegemony in Nubia. Yet for so important a town it is small, and herein may be the reason for nearby Kor with its lightly constructed defences but much greater size. Serving officers and civil and temple officials would live at Buhen and accommodation would have to be available at all times for important visitors arriving from Egypt, even the Pharaoh himself with his retinue. Craftsmen and labourers, servants and soldiers would need to be housed somewhere and Kor would be the obvious place. Kor could also take care of the pack animals used to carry the smaller

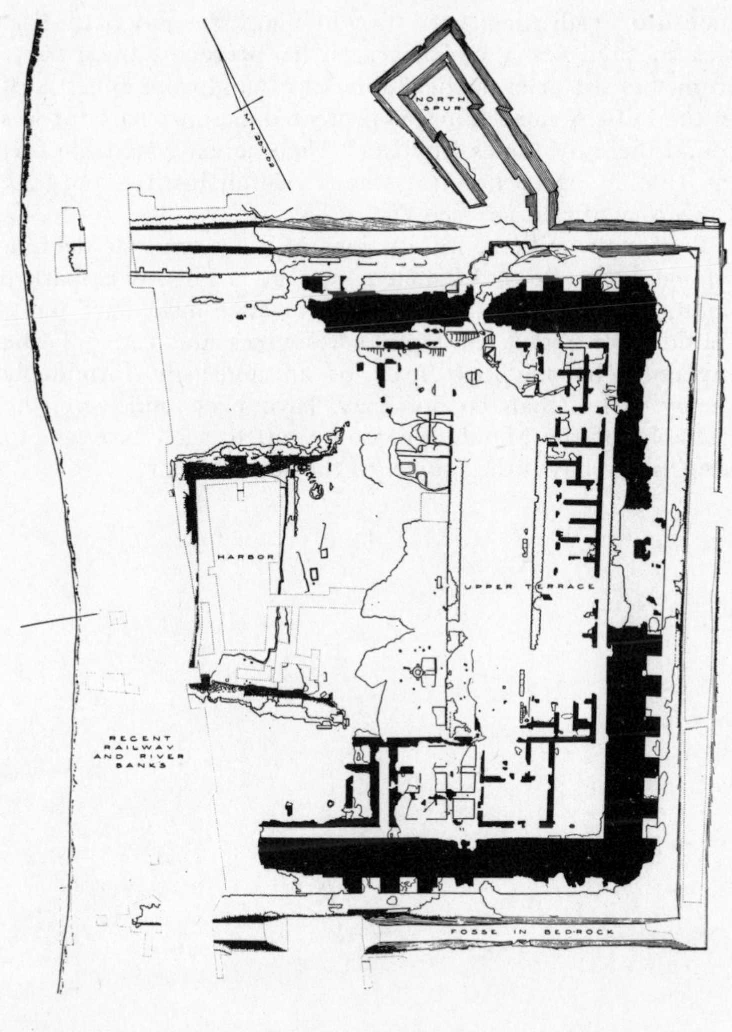

Fig. 15. Plan of the Fortress of Serra East, Middle Kingdom level.

items of foreign trade. In short, Kor could be the overflow for Buhen. Only one fortress is left to be accounted for: Serra East, some twenty miles downstream from Buhen. It is the only fort built on the east bank, apart from Kuban fortress in Lower Nubia. But Kuban was built to guard the mouth of Wadi Alaqi with its gold mines. Possibly Serra East was so sited for a similar reason, to protect a trade route from the east or even the shipment of gold from mines back in the hills. A small but well protected masonry harbour was found there by James Knudstad when he excavated the fort in 1962-3 on behalf of the Oriental Institute of the University of Chicago (see Figure 15).

Permanent military installations of the magnitude demonstrated by the Second Cataract forts are not lightly embarked upon; their construction and maintenance must have put a considerable strain on Egypt's resources and can only be explained by Egyptian fears of an unusually formidable enemy. Who that enemy may have been and why the Pharaohs of the Middle Kingdom went to such extremes to keep him at bay is the subject of the next chapter.

CHAPTER VIII

The Nameless Enemy

From earliest times the Egyptians seem to have understood that the peoples of the Middle Nile Valley south of Elephantine were a potential danger to Egypt's interests. As far back as the First Dynasty, around 3000 BC, we see King Djer sending a punitive expedition to the Second Cataract region and four hundred years later Sneferu's devastating campaign at the beginning of the Fourth Dynasty. Yet within a few years of Sneferu's death Egypt had managed to achieve relations with the Nubians amicable enough to be allowed to build a town inside Nubian territory at Buhen and there operate a copper smelting industry for the best part of two hundred years. It is, of course, conceivable that Sneferu's act of frightfulness had so weakened the Nubians that they were forced to submit to the Buhen occupation, as has been discussed in an earlier chapter. Whatever the reason, relations appear to have remained reasonably friendly and Egypt's Sixth Dynasty was notable for the trading expeditions to the south organised by the Princes of Elephantine, the "Keepers of the Door of the South." Most celebrated of these was Herkhuf (*c.* 2300 BC) whose adventures in the southern lands have been described briefly elsewhere in this book. He was one of a long line of "Caravan Captains" and on the whole their journeys up-river seem to have been peaceable enough and no doubt profitable to both sides. Yet towards the end of the Sixth Dynasty relations seem to have deteriorated since Pepinakht, another of the Elephantine Princes, was sent to crush a rebellion in Nubia:

> The Majesty of my Lord sent me to harry the lands of Wawat and Irthet. I acted to the approval of my Lord and slew a great number there, the children of the chieftain and doughty army captains. And I brought thence to the Residence a large number of prisoners, I being at the head of many strong and bold soldiers.

Uni was another noble who was detailed to pacify the troublesome people up-river. Thereafter, over the centuries, dynasty after dynasty found it necessary to send troops up the Nile to show the Egyptian equivalent of the flag by destroying villages and bringing back captives as slaves. Thutmose I, the Eighteenth Dynasty Pharaoh who with his son Thutmose II finally subdued and annexed Nubia, did exactly that, sailing back to Elephantine with the body of a Nubian chief hung head downwards at the prow of the royal barge. It has even been suggested that the battle scenes so vividly portrayed in Rameses II's temple at Abu Simbel—among them rows of Nubian prisoners bound and submissive—were intended as a warning to the surrounding tribes of the inescapable consequences of resistance to the might of the Pharaoh. Some of those scenes were repeated on the walls of Rameses II temple at Aksha near Buhen which was excavated in 1961 by Professors A. Rosenwasser and J. Vercoutter of the Franco-Argentine Expedition to Nubia.

However, by Rameses' day organised revolt was no longer possible, certainly not of the magnitude so feared by the Pharaohs of the Middle Kingdom some seven centuries earlier and which had moved Senusret III on one of his military campaigns up-river to infuse courage into his troops, by setting up a stela to proclaim Semna as his kingdom's new southern frontier, with a duplicate proclamation on Uronarti. In it he admonished them to show no fear:

> Stela made in year sixteen—third month of winter when the fortress "Repelling the Iunu" was built . . . to desist after being attacked boldens the heart of the enemy. To be agressive is to be brave, to retreat is timidity. . . The answering of him (the Nubian) causes him to retire. If one is aggressive against him he turns his back; if one retreats he falls into aggression. They are not people one must fear; they are wretches, broken of heart. My Majesty has seen them, there is no untruth. I have captured their wives and I have brought back their inhabitants, ascended to their wells and slain their bulls. I have pulled up their barley and set the flame in it. As

(*above*) A company of Egyptian spearmen found in a tomb *c.* 2100 BC. Such men formed the garrisons of the Second Cataract forts.

(*below*) Buhen: artist's reconstruction of the Pharaonic fortress excavated by Professor W. B. Emery during eight seasons. One of twelve along the Second Cataract, it shows the advanced military architecture of *c.* 2000 BC.

(*left*) Buhen: a section of the ramparts, scarp, ditch and counterscarp after excavation. Emery estimated ten million bricks were used in building the fort. (*below*) Buhen: foundations exposed when Queen Hatshepsut's New Kingdom temple was dismantled for removal to Khartoum. Beneath it Emery found remains of an earlier Twelfth-Dynasty temple, *c.* 1900 BC.

> my father lives for me; I speak in truth, without a word of boasting issuing from my mouth.
>
> Now as for every son of mine who shall strengthen this boundary which my Majesty (life, prosperity, health) has made, he is my son and he is born to my Majesty. Good is a son, the helper of his father, and who strengthens the boundary of him that begat him. Now as for him who shall lose it and shall not fight on behalf of it, he is not my son and he is not born to me.
>
> Now My Majesty has caused the erection of a statue of My Majesty on this frontier in order that you might persevere in it and that you might fight on behalf of it. . .

Obviously the Egyptians of that time were very much afraid of the Southern peoples. Indeed they somewhat overdid it in always referring to them as "Kush the Wretched" or "Kush the Vile." Also there were undoubtedly maurauders of another kind, nomadic peoples from the surrounding deserts ever ready to raid passing caravans or expeditions. It is known from the Semna Despatches that all movements of strangers were recorded by Egyptian patrols. Here is an example:

> This is a communication to your scribe about the fact that those two guardsmen and the seventy Medjay people who went following that track in month four of Proyet, day four, came to report to me on this day at the time of evening having brought three Medjay men, saying, "We found them on the south of the desert edge below the inscription of Shomu, likewise three women." So said they. Then I questioned these Medjay people saying, "Whence do you come?" Then they said, "We have come from the Well of Yebheyet.". . .

Trivial stuff, but indicative of a good intelligence service.

However, the suppression of local rebellions and the protection of the trade route to inner Africa could hardly justify the labour and expense of fortifying the Second Cataract to the extent that we have seen. The lengths to which the Egyptians went demonstrates an almost pathological fear and it points to only one possibility: the threat of an invasion of Egypt from the south. The innumerable rock drawings and the many cemeteries make it reasonable to suppose that the Nubia of 2000 BC with a climate less harsh than today's would have supported at least as many people as the Nubia of our day, that is to say about 120,000, probably more. Even half this number of armed men, legendary for their prowess as warriors and envious of the fertility and wealth of the land of the Pharaohs, would have been regarded as an ever-present threat to the security of Upper Egypt. At that time, Egypt's population was relatively small, and then as now, most of her people were concentrated in the Delta, leaving the upper valley sparsely peopled. No wonder the Nubians so worried the Egyptians and, as so often happens when fear is uppermost, Pharaoh's advisors seem to have over-reacted. Hence the vast defence works. They have led some historians to believe in an enemy of exceptional strength and military prowess concentrated in the country south of the Semna frontier and held at bay only by the impregnability of the fortress chain. There were those who expected that as the campaign advanced the sands of Nubia would reveal traces of a hitherto unknown culture with warlike tendencies thus providing a neat solution to the enigma of Egypt's most feared enemy of Middle Kingdom times. Of course nothing of the kind emerged and the two original contenders remained unchallenged. It was either the Kerma people or the C-Group, both of whom will be discussed later in the chapter.

The fighting prowess of the Nubians had long been exploited by the Egyptians themselves. The *Medjay,* as they called the southerners, fought in Egypt's armies throughout much of her history. Medjay troops are often referred to in the texts and there is even a model in the Cairo Museum of a company of them fully armed and in marching order; it was found in a Twelfth Dynasty tomb contemporary with Senusret's campaigns in Nubia and the building of the forts. And if anyone should think it strange that Nubians could fight in the ranks of their erstwhile enemies, let him recall the long record of Irish soldiers who have served with distinction in England's armies in the field as far back as Marlborough. Yet Ireland's relations with England over the same period can hardly be described as continuously amicable. The two loyalties are not incompatible—between rebellions!

So we come to the Kerma and C-Group cultures. First let it be said that neither had a written language and that all that is known of them is derived from burials and funerary objects with, in the case of the C-Group, a few nondescript dwellings.

First then, the Kerma culture. It is the first truly African culture to emerge from the shadows and enter the pages of history, and herein lies its importance. Virtually all the data that we have emerged in three short seasons of digging from 1913 to 1915. Since that time the Kerma mounds covering acres of alluvium bordering the river have lain untouched and unheeded. Kerma is near the Third Cataract, some two hundred miles south of Semna. Rising above the mounds are two puzzling buildings known locally as the Eastern and Western Defufas. Separated by what must have been an eastern branch of the Nile 4000 years ago but long since silted up, these two constructions of solid mud-brick, typical in style of the Middle Kingdom period, are fully two miles apart which gives an indication of the size of the site. The excavations were conducted by The Harvard-Boston Expedition, led by G. A. Reisner. He described the Western Defufa as a fortified trading post by reason of the discovery in it of a series of "storerooms", so called because they contained many objects made in Egypt, together with a great quantity of unfinished articles, pottery beads and faience and the raw materials for producing such things. The Eastern Defufa seems to have been a funerary chapel because near it fragments of an inscribed stone told of how one Anhef had been sent by Amenemhet III (*c.* 1800 BC) to repair a building known as "The Walls of Amenemhet of Blessed Memory". This then must have been the name of the trading post and implies that it was built either by Amenemhet I or II. Here was proof of a large Egyptian commercial establishment flourishing far south of the hostile region so feared by the Middle Kingdom Pharaohs and which, if the archaeological evidence is accepted, continued to flourish right through the Twelfth and Thirteenth Dynasties and into the troubled times of the Second Intermediate Period when the indications are that it suffered the same fate as the Second Cataract forts: destruction by burning. Obviously, all trading caravans and fleets moving between Egypt and Kerma would have to run the gauntlet of the Second Cataract, under the protection of the forts, in enemy territory. To equate this enemy with people so friendly with the Egyptians as to permit them to maintain a trading post in their capital for close on two centuries is to stretch credulity too far. Moreover the dates do not fit. Professor T. Säve-Söderbergh, leader of the Scandinavian Joint Expedition to Nubia, has shown that the Kerma people arrived in Nubia some two centuries later, and remained there two centuries longer, than has been hitherto accepted by most Egyptologists, and his findings are supported by evidence from Professor Vercoutter's excavations at Mirgissa. This revised dating does not conflict with the dates of the "trading post" at Kerma; it simply means that the period of expansion from Kerma to the north does not begin until *c.* 1650 BC and ends with the close of the Seventeenth Dynasty or beginning of the Eighteenth Dynasty, *c.* 1570 BC. The furthest north the Kerma people seem to have reached was Mirgissa, as Vercoutter showed with his discovery there of a partly plundered Kerma cemetery in the plain below the upper fort. Up-river of Mirgissa one would expect to find Kerma traces increasing as one moved further south and that is exactly what the Sudan Archaeological Survey has confirmed. In 1969 at Akasha 45 miles upstream from Semna, I found Mills sampling a very large Kerma cemetery estimated to contain about five hundred graves, unfortunately plundered. A few months later this cemetery was completely cleared by the Joint Expedition of the University of Geneva and Blackmer Foundation of America, the last expedition to work in the threatened area of Nubia. In 1955 on Sai Island, roughly halfway between Semna and Kerma, Vercoutter had partly cleared a Kerma site second only in size to Kerma itself. There can be little doubt that if the survey had continued up-river beyond the Dal Cataract, where it terminated because Dal represented the southern limit of the High Dam reservoir, Kerma sites would have been located with increasing frequency. Relatively few Kerma cemeteries were found along the Second Cataract itself. All in all the claim that the Kerma people should be identified with the enemy described with such vehemence by Senusret III in his Semna stela, is difficult to sustain.

Kerma itself cannot be left without a description of Reisner's most significant discovery there. In the extensive cemetery near the Eastern Defufa he excavated three large tumuli and they turned out to be the burials of what he described as the Egyptian governors of Kerma, one of them being a Prince of Assiut in Egypt named Hepzefa. No better description can be given than Reisner's own.

> The grave tumuli of the Egyptian governors were of a type unknown in Egypt. Imagine a circle 80 to 90 metres in diameter laid out on the hard desert surface, outlined by a wall of mud-brick only 10 centimetres high, and crossed from east to west by two long mud-brick walls forming a corridor 2 or 3 metres wide. From the outside of this corridor, cross-walls of mud-brick, built at intervals of 1 or 2 metres, ran out to the circumference. Beginning with a height of 10 centimetres at the circumference, these walls all rise in a curve to a height of 2 or 3 metres in the middle. All the spaces in the circle, except the corridor, were filled in with loose earth. Opening off the middle of the southern side of the corridor was a chamber roofed with a mud-brick vault. The tomb was thus ready for the burial. A great funerary feast was made at which over a thousand oxen were slaughtered and their skulls buried around the southern half of the circle outside. The body of the prince was then laid to rest in the vaulted chamber, with his offerings; and the wooden door was closed. The sacrificial victims, all local Nubians, either stupefied during the feast by a drug, or strangled, were brought in and laid out on the floor of the corridor—from two to three hundred men, women, and children. With these Nubians were placed a few pots and pans, occasionally a sword, and often their personal ornaments. Then the corridor was filled in with earth, forming a low, domed mound. The top was covered with a floor of mud-brick. A great quartzite pyramidion was set up on top, and I believe that a mud-brick chapel was built around the stone.

As Reisner himself says, nothing could have been more un-Egyptian in character than these burials. Among them were several royal statues and statuettes, and in Hepzefa's alleged tomb there came to light the lower half of a life-size statue of him and a complete statue of his wife, Sennuwy. Reisner did not carry out a petrological examination of the stone which could have shown whether the statues were made locally or imported from Egypt. The number of funerary objects, ranging from beakers of faience to a glazed quartz bed, was as varied as it was large; Reisner commented that the 130 copper daggers were more than had been found in the whole of Egypt in all ancient periods. He believed that Egyptian craftsmen made the objects even though most are un-Egyptian in character. Some, the alabaster pots for instance, were obviously imported from Egypt but the majority were of local design. The beds on which the bodies of the deceased had been laid were unique in having footboards, decorated with inlaid patterns of ivory.

Bed burials are as much a feature of Kerma graves as the distinctive funerary pottery which was probably the most delicate ever made in the Nile Valley; occasionally too, a second body, probably that of a slave, is laid in the grave with the owner. Mills found several such burials during the Survey. All the Kerma interments excavated by him were identical, the body lying crouched on its right side, head facing north. Often it was laid on a bed consisting of a simple wooden frame with rawhide springing while around the body were offerings in the form of pots and sacrificed animals.

Junker and Säve-Söderbergh, among others, believe that Kerma was probably the centre of Kushite power and that the graves found by Reisner could have been those of Kushite kings. Hepzefa himself had a magnificent tomb back in Egypt at Assiut and even if he died in Kerma, such was the fanatical distaste of the Egyptian for foreign burial that the likelihood is that his body would have been mummified and carried back to Egypt for burial in its proper place. This is the conclusion reached by the French scholar Jacques Vandier in his recent publication of a Hepzefa statue.

That Kerma was a civilisation of purely African origins is beyond doubt and it seems possible that the burial customs of 2000 BC were still being practised in pre-Islamic Sudan at the time of Norman William's conquest of Britain. The Arab scholar Abd-el-Aziz el Bakri writing in the eleventh century describes how when death comes to a king of the Sudan he is laid on a bed beneath a large wooden cupola. Placed near him are his jewelry, his arms and his eating and drinking vessels. Into the cupola are put food and drink together with some of his servants after which the door is closed and earth heaped upon the structure until it becomes a huge hill. After this a moat is dug around the hill and animals are slaughtered to the dead therein. The points of similarity in the foregoing account–bed burial without a coffin, personal funerary objects, the burying alive of servants–with Reisner's account of the Kerma tumuli is remarkable.

Kerma cemeteries were found and excavated by several of the expeditions in Nubia but the number of graves in them was always small, an exception being the large necropolis at Akasha already referred to. The most important Kerma cemetery was that discovered at Mirgissa because it showed the continuance of a Kerma presence in Nubia late into the Second Intermediate Period. The Scandinavians came across Kerma pottery, seals and ivories in C-Group burials and also in New Kingdom tombs dating well into the Eighteenth Dynasty but these could mean no more than, for example, an Englishman's widow burying with him a much treasured Ming vase; a fanciful thought which brings to mind an even more fanciful projection made by Professor Säve-Söderbergh. We were discussing over a breakfast break the tendency of some field archaeologists to draw the most sweeping conclusions from the flimsiest of evidence and he produced a delightful example based on the kerosene cooking stoves made in Sweden and used in every Arab household. Two thousand years in the future archaeologists digging in the ruins of a decimated world find in Middle Eastern townsites curious artefacts of unknown application with 'Primus' engraved on them. So numerous and widespread are these objects that inevitably the ancient users are labelled "Primus People". Other archaeologists digging in Sweden discover the provenance of these puzzling objects when unearthing a group of "workshops". Immediately a new study is born to determine the cultural relationship between the peoples of the Middle East and the tribes of Northern Europe in 2000 AD and the extent to which the one absorbed the other by mass movements across the Mediterranean!

The discovery of a Kerma site always excited the finders but, alas, as often as not it would be plundered or at best would reveal little more than was already known of this enigmatic people. Probably the Kerma culture embraced more than one tribe or social grouping, each exhibiting minor yet distinct variations in burial customs, funerary objects and pottery.

If Kerma is ruled out as the controversial enemy we are left with the C-Group people. Certainly they were occupying Nubia when the Middle Kingdom Pharaohs moved in; indeed excavation of the many C-Group cemeteries has shown that the C-Group appear in Nubia earlier than was hitherto believed, as far back as the Archaic Period. The excavations show moreover that in Lower Nubia (Wawat) C-Group were thick on the ground and a C-Group cemetery has been found inside Egypt itself some 30 miles downstream from Assuan. But south of Semna the sites become fewer until before Dal is reached they peter out. Of course there is the possibility that beyond the Dal Cataract where the cliffs of the Belly of Stone fall back to expose a wide alluvial plain, C-Group sites could re-appear. Obviously it is important to know the full extent of C-Group penetration to the south; whether it really stopped short of Dal only an archaeological survey can decide.

Very early in the campaign, the UNESCO archaeologists conducting the survey of Sudanese Nubia drew attention to the similarities in character and distribution of material from A-Group and C-Group sites. The proximity of A-Group and C-Group cemeteries and the mixture of the two types of sherds in habitation sites was observed repeatedly and led to the conclusion that they were two strands of the same population at different stages of cultural development. In Nubia the C-Group were sedentary cattle owners and to them we should probably attribute the thousands of carvings of cattle on the rocks of Nubia; they sometimes scratched outlines of long-horned cattle on their pots; frequently the cattle are buried around the grave superstructures; scratchings of cattle appear on the flat stone monoliths erected outside their earlier graves and it has been noted that right across the Sahara as far west as Mauretania there are tumuli with similar stone erections bearing carvings of cattle. Another curious coincidence arises from the many rock pictures of cattle in the Chad region of the Sahara which show the horns as being bent forwards and downwards artificially. Hans Nordström of the Sudan Survey, in excavating a C-Group cemetery at Faras, found ox-skulls with precisely the same artificial deformation and later in Khartoum he learnt that the Nilotic peoples of southern Sudan, the Dinkas and Shilluks, still deform their cattle in this way. Egyptian tomb paintings of the Old Kingdom Period around 2500 BC show cattle with horns deliberately distorted and the custom was still practised much later by the Meroitic people around 600 BC. Here then is a tradition as widespread as it is ancient. The C-Group could well have been descendants of cattle-breeders who roamed the Sahara from about 3000 BC and who drifted into the Nile Valley, driven by increasing desiccation of their customary grazing lands.

The graves where Nordström found his deformed cattle skulls were good examples of early C-Group burials. The body, clothed in a leather kilt, lay in a circular pit with a loose stone construction raised over it, in the shape of a drystone cylinder about one metre above ground level. In the sand outside this stonework the horned skulls were laid, usually facing south and buried on the north side were earthenware pots and dishes.

It was in graves of this type that the Scandinavians discovered several of the so-called 'button' seals which provided them with a firm date for the burials: towards the latter part of the Old Kingdom, in other words the Pyramid Age. The Scandinavian Joint Expedition was a model of organisation and enterprise. Presiding over its component groups from Denmark, Finland, Norway and Sweden was the man recognised as a leading authority on Nubian history, Professor T. Säve-Söderbergh of Uppsala University. At times the expedition totalled as many as twenty and thanks to their numbers and excellent co-ordination they were able to put several teams in the field simultaneously. By this means and through the introduction of simple–but for Nubian archaeology, revolutionary–innovations they were able to clear and record up to thirty graves daily. Rubber-tyred wheelbarrows proved much more effective in removing spoil than the woven palm-leaf baskets traditionally used by labourers and carried on their heads and ordinary spades more efficient than the traditional mattock. Another novel introduction was a remote controlled camera which, working from a tripod up to 40 feet high, largely eliminated the laborious task of measuring and surveying sites at ground level.

By the luck of the draw the Scandinavian concession turned out to be one of the richest in Nubia, yielding thousands of graves and sites ranging in date from prehistoric to Christian. C-Group cemeteries in particular were so numerous and well-spaced in the timespan of this culture that it enabled the Scandinavians to trace the development of the C-Group from its arrival in Nubia to its extinction more than a thousand years later. Debeira, on the east bank of the Nile north of Wadi Halfa, was within the Scandinavian concession and judging from the number of cemeteries located it seems to have been one of the most thickly populated parts of the Second Cataract region throughout Nubian history. Schoenbaeck, the deputy leader of the Joint Expedition told me that he reckoned there were at least a quarter of a million graves in the area. One should of course bear in mind that they spanned more than forty centuries. Still, for Nubia which was never a fertile land, it is a sizable number.

Most of the C-Group cemeteries cleared by the various expeditions along the Second Cataract were on the east bank. Only as they approached the Egyptian border along Halfa Reach did they find concentrations of C-Group on the west bank, usually small. Otherwise the west bank was a waterless, sandy desert, easy for the Egyptians of old to watch and patrol but difficult for a large force of men and animals to cross; like the camel caravans of our day they could never travel far from the river, their sole source of water. This could very well be the reason for all the forts being built, with one exception, on the west bank or on islands, thus using the Nile itself as an additional line of defence against rebellious peoples concentrated on the east bank. If put there for purely defensive purposes the forts were admirably placed to discourage revolt and nip in the bud any attempt to organise an invasion of Egypt. The 'execration' texts found by the French Mission at Mirgissa and since assembled and studied, show that the Egyptian army commanders were fully informed about the political structure of their enemies, the divisions of the enemy "principalities" and the names of the kings or chieftains, even names of members of their families. From time to time there would be sorties from the forts for a show of strength, as we would say today, probably during low Nile when river and rapids become crossable. At high Nile, corresponding to the months of summer, the swollen river would offer protection enough and the garrisons could shut themselves up inside their mud-brick strongholds in one of the hottest climates on earth. Cut off from the bountiful living of the Lower Nile Valley they must have been the most reluctant of heroes. The Egyptian was never happy away from his homeland, a characteristic that persists to this day.

Säve-Söderbergh has long believed in a connection between the Egyptian forts and the concentrations of C-Group people in areas round about; it would explain the location of the fort at Serra, the only stronghold on the east bank, which was only a few miles from Debeira East with its extensive C-Group cemeteries and which was itself surrounded by others. Säve-Söderbergh has no doubt that the C-Group were the people whose presence so alarmed the Middle Kingdom Egyptians. Other scholars have refused to consider the C-Group as Egypt's enemy on the grounds of their being contemporary with the Middle Kingdom military presence, existing as it were in the same area of space and time, and because they were a peaceable people. This assessment of the C-Group character is based on the assertion that no weapons appear in the graves, although this is not strictly true because in their final season the Scandinavians found weapons, admittedly not many but enough to show that the C-Group were familiar with their use. One could argue—and Säve-Söderbergh agrees on this—that weapons, particularly if made of metal, would be far too precious to waste on the dead, but would tend to be jealously conserved for handing down from one generation to the next.

The Nubians themselves, settled in a reach of the Nile that yielded little more than a marginal living, would have been less than human not to harbour animosity towards the northern intruders with their opulence and sophistication and, one suspects, arrogant ways. As a pastoral people their deepest source of resentment must have been the periodical confiscation of their cattle as tribute. Then there was the exploitation of their mineral wealth. It has long been known that in Egypt criminals and wrongdoers generally were put to work in the mines as punishment. But in far off Nubia local labour would be needed and for the Nubians there could be no escape from the labour of extracting the ore from the blistering rocks of their own land. All in all the Nubians had little cause to love the Egyptians and it would be only natural for their resentment to break out from time to time into open revolt against the unwelcome foreigners in their midst. Theirs was a situation not unfamiliar in recent colonial history.

Yet commerce is more profitable than war and it would be wrong to assume a state of constant warfare between the holders of the forts and the surrounding C-Group people over the span of about two hundred years. In Europe we have the example of the Hundred Years War. The mere fact of Mirgissa (Ikn) being established as a market indicates that the local people were not always hostile to the military occupiers of their territory but were willing to accept trading relations for much of the time; in fact there seems little doubt that the forts met the dual requirements of defence and commerce.

One has to admit, however, that the instinct of successive Pharaohs to see the southern peoples as potential invaders and to take appropriate defence measures was sound. The day was to come when a Kushite king with his army would sail down the Nile and take over the throne of the Pharaohs. But that was 1200 years after the C-Group people had dropped out of the historical record and the fortresses, long since unmanned, were no more than heaps of crumbling brick.

What happened, then, to the C-Group culture and why did it vanish from history? An answer has been found among the many cemeteries excavated. It was in Debeira East that in 1955 a large rock-cut tomb of the Eighteenth Dynasty was cleared by Sayed Thabit Hassan Thabit of the Sudan Antiquities Service. It had been made for one Djehuty-Hotep, Prince of Teh-Khet (Debeira East). Here was an Egyptian tomb conventional in every way, in its design, its wall paintings and in the pottery it contained. Incidentally several trees painted on its walls have not yet been identified. Moreover the names and titles shown in the tomb identified Djehuty-Hotep as an Egyptian grandee. In fact he was a Nubian. Seven years later in Debeira West across the river from his tomb, I stood on top of a hill watching with Professor Säve-Soderbergh a gang of men straining with ropes and beams at a large boulder buried in rubble. This hill was named Sidi Qurnein after some long-forgotten holy man. We refused to believe he was actually buried there but one never knew and a tricky moment arose when a snake wriggled out from under the stone enclosure. "The spirit of the holy man" muttered one of the labourers. There was a silence, then someone laughed and the moment passed. The men were standing in line and passing the many boulders down from the top of the hill to the bottom, singing with gusto a bawdy Bedawi song about the improbable adventures of a mythical girl; it seemed to me that they positively enjoyed handling heavy stones. Meanwhile, smothered in flying dust, the archaeologist assisted by the Egyptian *qufti* (foreman) was quietly marking the outlines of walls, surveying levels with his theodolite, noting the stratification, and photographing each stage of the work. I never saw a busier man or a more methodical one. I got into conversation with the aged guardian of the place who was worried that he would lose his job now that we had been so inconsiderate as to demonstrate the non-existence of the holy man and his tomb, more especially since his family had guarded it for five generations. He himself had worked as a servant for many years with several of the wealthiest of Alexandria's European families yet now he was content to end his days in a mud-brick house on the river's edge, tending his little plot of tobacco and keeping an occasional eye on the tomb that nobody ever visited.

Suddenly with a final heave the great stone lifted and toppled to reveal a shaft cut in the rock below. At its bottom was a passage 40 feet long littered with pots and vessels, leading to the burial chamber. The chamber was empty but among the vessels in the passage were several canopic jars bearing the name of the tomb's owner, Prince Amenemhet of Teh Khet. His name and titles were confirmed on a fine granite stela found lying in the tomb chapel further down the hill. Here was an extraordinary coincidence. Amenemhet was the brother of Djehuti Hotep buried across the river and to all intents and purposes he too was an Egyptian, if the design and contents of his tomb were to be believed. Those two Nubian brothers, living in the glittering days of Egypt's Eighteenth Dynasty as accepted members of the Egyptian administrative establishment, represent the end of the line for the C-Group people as a distinctive culture. In scores of humbler graves the pattern was repeated, to demonstrate clearly how as the centuries passed the graves and the objects in them became ever more Egyptian in character until the time arrived when cultural assimilation was complete. The Scandinavians had the good fortune to locate several C-Group houses in a fair state of preservation and the latest of them was built exactly like an Egyptian house of the same period; only the C-Group pottery inside the rooms testified to its Nubian origin.

Not far from Debeira, at Fadrus, a New Kingdom cemetery produced well over 600 tombs, many of them unrobbed. The river had deposited on the site a layer of packed gravel 40 centimetres thick so that the graves were effectively sealed from human eyes and it was only the Scandinavians' practice of walking in extended line across the ground and using sharp iron rods to prod below the surface, that revealed the cemetery. It yielded a rich haul of objects, many of museum standard, including gold mounted scarabs, and they were all of late Hyksos or early New Kingdom types. This cemetery was contemporary with the late C-Group tombs and it raised the question of whether the burials there were of true Egyptians or whether they were Egyptianised Nubians less conservative than certain of their neighbours who still preferred to be interred in the local, traditional manner.

In 1964 just over the Egyptian border and only fifteen miles or so north of Serra, I came across the Nubian Expedition of the Oriental Institute of the University of Chicago, headed by Dr Keith B. Seele. He took me to a large cemetery of New Kingdom type graves which had yielded objects of high artistic merit and, much more important, names which corresponded with those of well-known figures of the early Eighteenth Dynasty; Ahmose was one, after the founder of the Eighteenth Dynasty and Sensenabu, mother of Thutmose I, was another. Because of these and other indications Seele inclined to the belief that at the very beginning of the Eighteenth Dynasty Egypt had established an outpost here in Wawat important enough to attract senior officials from the Court at Thebes, 350 miles down-stream.

Examination of the skeletal material led him to think that many of the officials took Nubian wives—presumably C-Group women—and Sensenabu seems to have been one of them. Incidentally this necropolis had shown no surface traces and was in fact 'discovered' by a jeep which sank into a tomb while running across the open desert. In the same area, at Adandam, the Oriental Institute excavated several C-Group cemeteries all of the late period and therefore contemporary with the New Kingdom necropolis already described, and in one of the graves along with a highly polished axe-head of copper was the skeleton of a woman whose skull was unusually well-preserved. Her ugliness, emphasised by a set of protruding teeth, was so marked that she was irreverently dubbed by expedition members as the Belle of Adandam.

However, we are running ahead of history. Between the cultural assimilation of the C-Group of New Kingdom times and the earlier Thirteenth Dynasty there remain some two hundred years to be accounted for. We are now entering another of those periods in Egypt's history when the close-knit structure of her society seemed to fall apart. The record becomes so fragmentary, contradictory even, that it is impossible to give coherence to the course of events. A potent factor was the increasing infiltration into Lower Egypt of Palestinians, called Hyksos by the Egyptians, at a time when the dynamic Middle Kingdom Pharaohs had run their course. At some time towards the latter part of the Thirteenth Dynasty, or more probably in the confused period that immediately followed it, the Hyksos kings seized power and established Avaris in the Nile Delta as their capital. That the intruders made a determined effort to come to terms with Egypt is shown by their adoption of the Egyptian religion and Egyptian writing and customs, and Säve-Söderbergh suggests, through titulary and textual deduction, that a considerable section of the Egyptian population settled down to co-exist with the Asiatics. Evidence recently come to light makes it clear that the Hyksos hegemony never extended far south of the Nile Delta, and that generations of the Theban Princes of southern Egypt kept the intruders at bay until the day when one of their line, Kamose, declared against the Hyksos king, Awoserrē-Apopi and carried the war to the gates of Avaris itself. On the way down-stream he made a point of punishing his 'collaborator' countrymen: "I razed their towns and burned their places, they being made into red ruins forever on account of the damage which they did within this Egypt, and they had made themselves serve the Asiatics and had forsaken Egypt their mistress."

While Egypt was experiencing these stirring events, what was happening in Nubia? Kamose seems to have used Medjay-Nubian troops to punish some of those Egyptian collaborators; he speaks of the Nubians as being ". . . aloft upon our cabins to spy out the Setyu and to destroy their places". And this is odd because at the time a king of Kush was in alliance with the Hyksos king! Kamose records how his men intercepted a messenger carrying a letter from Avaris to Kush:

> Awoserrē, the son of Re, Apopi, greets my son the ruler of Kush [or, the son of the ruler of Kush]. Why have you risen without letting me know? Do you not see what Egypt has done against me? The ruler there, Kamose, given life, is attacking me on the ground. [And yet] I had not attacked him in the same way as everything he had done against you. He chooses these two lands to harass them, my land and yours, he has destroyed them. Come, journey downstream. Do not be afraid. Lo! he [Kamose] is here with me and there is nobody who will stand up against you in Egypt and, behold, I shall not give him [free] road until you arrive. Then we shall divide the towns of Egypt [between us] and our [two lands] shall thrive in joy.

Here was an offer that must have greatly tempted the Kushite King.

Kamose, naturally, took a very different view: "In the south there is a Nubian, in the north an Asiatic, and I am sitting between them."

The foregoing fascinating vignette of Egyptian history comes from a stela unearthed at Karnak only recently, in 1954. No discovery in the field of Egyptology in recent years has caused so much excitement among scholars, since it throws light on the critical happenings that led to the expulsion of the Hyksos and the founding of Egypt's Eighteenth Dynasty by Kamose's son Ahmose, and the emergence of the New Kingdom. Between this momentous event and the death of the last of the Twelfth Dynasty Pharaohs two hundred years had elapsed.

(*left*) Sarras: granite-pounder in Middle Kingdom gold processing 'workshop' excavated by A. J. Mills of the UNESCO/Sudan Government Archaeological Survey. He is demonstrating the method of crushing the quartz. (*above*) Duweishat: ancient Egyptian workings in Africa's richest gold mine north of the Equator.

(*below*) Semna West: dismantling the fort's Eighteenth-Dynasty temple under the direction of Professor Hinkel. The block is from the roof. The temple is buried in rubble to facilitate removal of the stones.

(*above*) Khartoum: the temple from Semna West, re-erected in the gardens of the New Museum. The movable 'hangar' protects it during the rainy season. (*left*) Semna East: one of the mysterious group of cairns contemporary with the fortresses, discovered by A. J. Mills in a remote valley of the Belly of Stone.

The Karnak stela reveals for the first time that Kush was independent of Egypt during the years of the Seventeenth Dynasty and was, indeed, at enmity with her northern neighbour but did not feel strong enough to launch an outright attack, despite the enticing invitation from Avaris. We know, in fact, that the king of Kush had Egyptian officials in his employ. One of them, Haunkhef, was an army officer and he relates on his funerary stela at Edfu in southern Egypt how, when after six years he retired and returned to Egypt, he brought with him 26 *deben* of gold (about 5 pounds in weight), in short a handsome bonus for services rendered. All this leads us to suppose that the Second Cataract forts were still manned in the Seventeenth Dynasty and Vercoutter's discovery at Mirgissa would seem to support this view. Furthermore it seems likely that the garrisons were Egyptianised Nubians or native Egyptians driven from Upper Egypt for condoning Hyksos rule, probably both. The absence of funerary stelae and offering tables in the Mirgissa necropolis would suggest the former. All the Mirgissa cemeteries were dated from the end of the Middle Kingdom and the Second Intermediate and Hyksos Periods, and most of the funerary objects in the graves were of Egyptian origin. To clarify the identity of the garrisons, some three hundred skulls were collected by the French Mission and taken to Paris for study by specialists but at the time of writing no results have emerged. Whoever the defenders were at this time their defences would seem to be turned to the north, with Egypt as the enemy and potential agressor: it is significant that the northern fortifications of Mirgissa were particularly strong. Could it be that the forts remained intact through most of the Second Intermediate Period, and finally it was an army from Egypt that stormed and burned them, only to rebuild and enlarge them a generation or so later when the annexation of Nubia was consolidated? This is pure supposition but it does seem to fit the facts as revealed in the recent excavations. It would be a nice irony if strongholds built by the Egyptians to protect their country from the Nubians should by a twist of fate be used by those same Nubians to protect their territory from the Egyptians. The wheel would have turned full circle.

Probably we shall never know the actual name of the C-Group people, for the absorption of Nubia their homeland closed a chapter of more than a thousand years of unbroken cultural development. With the Kerma people it could be otherwise, since the focal point of their culture remains undisturbed, awaiting only the archaeologists' spade to uncover its roots and connections. Unlike the Kerma people, the C-Group seems to have been a diffuse culture with no definite point of origin. A considerable collection of their funerary objects, some indications of their burial habits far from understood but which do admittedly provide pointers to their historic termination as a separate culture, and a few hundred skeletons removed to museums for examination, these represent the sum total of our knowledge of a people who were something more than a thorn in the side of mighty Egypt for well over a century.

When documentary evidence is confused or absent and much of the archaeological evidence essentially negative, any reconstruction of cultural history such as that attempted in this chapter can only be based largely on supposition and, inevitably, will be controversial. The excavations in Nubia have done little to clarify the ethnic and cultural relationship between the Kerma and C-Group peoples, despite the incontrovertible fact of their having co-existed in Nubia for at least five hundred years. It could even be said that the work done in Nubia during the 1960s has produced more problems than solutions in relation to these two African cultures.

CHAPTER IX

Kingdom of Kush

The rise of Egypt's Eighteenth Dynasty coincided with a re-grouping of the great nations of the ancient east, four of them more or less equal in power—Babylonia, the Minoan Kingdom of Crete, the Aryan Kingdom of the Mitanni and the Hittite Confederation. A fifth, Assyria, was only beginning to stir and the time would come when she would exercise a power greater than them all. But now in the sixteenth century BC Egypt was in the ascendant and the moment had come for her to control the destiny of nations, so that by the end of Thutmose III's reign the whole of the civilised east was subservient to the Kingdom on the Nile and the stage set for that glittering period of the ancient world which has come to be known as the Amarna Age when Akhenaton, the 'heretic' Pharaoh who founded the world's first monotheistic religion, reigned in the City of the Horizon with Nefertiti as his consort. The names and monuments of the Eighteenth Dynasty have stirred the imagination and the admiration of the world above all others in the Valley of the Nile, and for more than a century the temples of Karnak and the painted tombs of the Valley of Kings have been the magnet which has drawn visitors from every civilized land. The royal names have become legendary: Hatshepsut and Thutmose, Amenhotep and Akhenaton, and above all Tutankhamun, a minor Pharaoh whose sole claim to fame lies in the splendour of his funerary equipment. All were of the Eighteenth Dynasty when Pharaoh's Court was the centre of the world.

In that brilliant pageant of Empire what part did Nubia play? Very little, it must be said, apart from supplying the bulk of the gold essential to Egypt's facade of magnificence. Trade with Africa was still a cornerstone of Egypt's economy; more than ever did she need the produce of the south and manpower for her conquering armies, and of course gold. Some idea of the value of the ore mined in Nubia can be gleaned from the tribute of Wawat (Lower Nubia) and Kush (Upper Nubia) as recorded in the Annals of Thutmose III, the consolidator of the Egyptian Empire.

YEAR	WAWAT	KUSH
31	92 cattle, 1 harvest	
33	20 slaves, 104 cattle, 1 harvest	
34	254 deben of gold, 10 slaves and an unspecified number of cattle	300 deben of gold, 60 Negro slaves, 275 cattle, ivory and ebony
35	34 slaves, 94 cattle, 1 harvest	70 deben, 1 kidet of gold, an unspecified number of slaves and cattle, ivory and ebony, 1 harvest
38	2,844 deben of gold, 16 slaves, 77 cattle	100 deben, 6 kidet of gold, 36 Negro slaves, 306 cattle, ivory and ebony, 1 harvest
39	89 cattle, ivory and ebony	144 deben, 3 kidet of gold, 101 negro slaves and an unspecified number of cattle
41	3,144 deben, 3 kidet of gold, 114 cattle and an unspecified quantity of ivory	94 deben, 2 kidet of gold, 21 negro slaves and an unspecified number of cattle
42	2,374 deben, 1 kidet of gold, and 1 harvest	

Translated into modern terms, 31,000 ounces of gold were extracted from Wawat alone over a span of eight years.

The Semna barrier, no longer the southern frontier which by now had been established four hundred miles further up-river, once more saw the passage of caravans and fleets; the derelict fortresses of the Belly of Stone now re-built as trading posts again housed their quota of soldiers and officials with Buhen as the administrative centre; new temples arose, among them the Nineteenth Dynasty sanctuary of Rameses II at Abu Simbel. Nubia's short-lived independence had passed into memory and she was now a mere province of Egypt ruled by a Viceroy with absolute powers over the two administrations of Wawat and Kush. Thuwre, who was appointed by Amenhotep I, is the first Viceroy of whom we have detailed knowledge and he and his successors were to rule Nubia in unbroken line for the next five hundred years. Up and down the length of Nubia in temples and on rocks their names and titles were recorded for posterity and of their many titles the most prized was "King's Son of Kush". The Viceroy's main responsibility apart from governing was the collection of the annual tribute for Pharaoh's treasury which took the form of slaves, cattle, incense, semi-precious stones, animal skins, ivory and, of course, gold. Its value was immense and the Viceroy, consequently, must have been a man of unshakeable probity, indeed the earlier viceroys were appointed by the Pharaoh personally. Nevertheless for reasons seldom disclosed several of them fell from grace as we know from the erasure of their names and titles from the walls of tombs and temples. Nehi, who built the two stone temples at Semna, was one of these unfortunates, incurring the displeasure of the warrior king Thutmose III.

In the Theban necropolis, very near to the Valley of Kings, is the tomb of Amenhotep-Huy who was Viceroy of Kush under the short-lived Pharaoh Tutankhamun and the paintings on its walls give fascinating glimpses of the ceremonies attendant upon the appointment of a King's Son of Kush. We see Huy being handed the signet ring of office which empowers him to take decisions in the Pharaoh's name; there, too, is the splendidly appointed barge, complete with stalls for his chariot horses, which carries him to his headquarters at Buhen and on arrival his officials give him a respectful welcome agreeably heightened by gifts of gold and jewellery. Delivery of the annual tribute would be via the river in convoys of shipping or along the old Nubian Highway using caravans of pack-animals. One delivery of this kind is shown on the walls of the tomb in considerable detail and includes the usual long-horned cattle, various precious metals, bows and arrows, ivory and ebony, and a pair of giraffes. In one painting the tribute is being brought to the Viceroy by a Princess of Kush in person. Accompanied by a retinue of negroes she rides in a chariot under the shade of a ceremonial umbrella with two children bringing up the rear of the procession. The chieftains of Wawat and Kush are easily distinguished–the former wear their hair bound with a fillet holding two feathers while the latter carry only one feather in their hair, which is unbound.

The names of 25 of the Viceroys are recorded, one of the last being Panehesi who, towards the end of the Twentieth Dynasty, took it upon himself to intervene in the internal affairs of Egypt when with his Nubian troops he marched north to put down an insurrection. He made no attempt to seize the throne but returned to his post in Nubia. Over the centuries Nubia and Egypt seem to have been well served by the Viceroys. Their ability was matched by the trust placed in them by successive Royal masters and the titles they received are indicative of their status in the hierarchy:

"Fan-bearer on the King's Right" (the most coveted of civil honours), "First Royal Herald", "Overseer of the Treasury", "Steward of the Peasantry", "Overseer of the Countries of the Gold of Amun", "King's Messenger to Every Land", "Overseer of Masons", "Director of Works at Karnak", "King's Scribe", "Overseer of the Southern Countries", "King's Son of Kush", "Viceroy".

Returning to the archaeological record as revealed during the Campaign we find a hiatus that is difficult to explain; in effect the record in Nubia goes blank for the best part of a thousand years. The Eighteenth and Nineteenth Dynasty Pharaohs had continued to tax and exploit the native Nubians, some of whom had joined the administration to become completely Egyptianised. Sons of the chieftains, according to time-honoured Egyptian custom, had been raised and educated in Egypt to return to Nubia as "King's men". But towards the end of the Eighteenth Dynasty the number of burials in Nubia falls off sharply. In the whole region not more than a hundred Nineteenth Dynasty graves are known and less than ten from the Twentieth Dynasty. By 1100 BC Nubia had been abandoned by Nubians and Egyptians alike. Only a natural disaster could have brought about the total evacuation of a land that had been continuously husbanded by man for at least two thousand years. Professor W. Y. Adams of Kentucky University and formerly leader of the UNESCO team working on the Sudan Archaeological Survey in Nubia believes that a clue can be found in the observations of a geologist, Professor R. Fairbridge, who was attached to the Columbia University Expedition. Professor Fairbridge has drawn attention to a series of five distinct climatic changes in the Nile Valley over the last 25,000 years and the resulting oscillations in the pattern of Nile floodings over the same period. Between 3000 and 7000 years ago there began in the Upper Nile Valley a steady falling off in the monsoon and equatorial rains, and this decline corresponded with a slight increase in winter rains along the southern Mediterranean. In consequence Egypt enjoyed a fairly regular winter and summer rainfall, but in Nubia the monsoon rains of summer progressively diminished with a resulting increase in aridity and decrease in fertility. At some time during the New Kingdom period came a sharp fall in the volume of Nile floodings to levels approximating those of today. This change in the pattern of rainfall, believes Adams, is the key to the puzzle. No longer would it be possible to lift water for irrigation up the steep banks of the Nile by means of the traditional *shaduf,* a simple device consisting of a counterbalancd bucket on the end of a long pole swivelling on an upright post. This failure of technology to meet a changed situation, plus the diminution of the annual rainfall, brought about a decline in agriculture to a point where all productivity ceased. But by then no doubt the depopulation of Lower Nubia was complete, the Egyptians having returned to their homeland down-river while the native Nubians, an African people, would almost certainly have moved south to more fertile reaches of the Nile between the Third and Fourth Cataracts where they would find people of like race and traditions. For the first time in the history of the Nile Valley, Nubia ceased to function as the cultural corridor between inner Africa and the Mediterranean. For the next thousand years the focus of history insofar as it relates to Nubia moves south, to the reach of the Nile that lies between the Third and Sixth

Cataracts. Again we are entering another of those controversial areas of scholarship where the incompleteness of the archaeological record imposes a handicap on those who attempt to interpret it.

Downstream of the Fourth Cataract near the modern town of Kareima, a mass of rock stands high above the surrounding plain in splendid isolation. This is Gebel Barkal, known as the Holy Mount because of its fancied resemblance to the throne of Amun-Re. Both Thutmose III and IV of the Eighteenth Dynasty had built temples at the foot of the mountain and, during the Nineteenth Dynasty another temple to Amun arose which is described by Reisner who excavated it as second only to the great temple of Amun at Karnak (Thebes). Obviously the Egyptian priesthood had established itself deep inside Kush and no doubt was supported by many Egyptian officials, craftsmen, traders and scribes who had followed the priests and settled there. Probably, too, this Egyptian enclave was swelled by exiles from Thebes when the Twenty-Second (Libyan) Dynasty seized power in Egypt (*c.* 950 BC). Nubia was effectively cut off from Egypt and it was now that the Kingdom of Kush was established, and a remarkable line of kings introduced what has come to be known as the Napatan era, so-called after their capital city of Napata in the vicinity of Gebel Barkal. In Reisner's view the Napatans were Libyan invaders from the western oases; other Egyptologists see them as being of Theban origin springing perhaps from the established Egyptian priesthood at Barkal. Equally, and this view is gaining ground, the Napatans could have been Nubians of mixed Kerma and C-Group stock who, inspired by long familiarity with Egyptian religion and social organisation, developed a vigorous and prosperous state of their own choosing, Pharaonic in its outward observances but remaining essentially Nubian in character and culture.

The first two to three centuries of Napatan civilisation are hidden from us; written records are negligible and most of what is known of early Napata derives from Reisner's excavations of the Gebel Barkal temples and the nearby pyramid fields some fifty years ago. Temple inscriptions to the glorification of a king and his deeds are essentially of a propagandist nature and not necessarily historically accurate.

An outstanding example is Rameses II's celebrated account of the battle of Kadesh as inscribed on the walls of Abu Simbel temple. In it he claims a total victory over the Hittites, yet the Hittite version of the battle, as revealed by the archaeological record, describes Kadesh as a defeat for Rameses. Any attempt to reconstruct a period of history when the only evidence available is that drawn from temples, cemeteries and royal tombs must result in a lop-sided picture of the society of that time. The missing dimension, in the absence of written records, should come from the excavation of town or habitation sites, of large secular constructions such as magazines, palaces or fortresses, and works of civil engineering such as barrages, irrigation systems, and so on. The first two centuries of the Napatan civilisation are hidden from us largely because the whole region of Upper Nubia has yet to be archaeologically surveyed and studied. The site of Napata itself has not yet been located, let alone excavated. It seems we must await the construction of a High Dam at the Dal Cataract and another international salvage operation!

At Kuru near Gebel Barkal, is the cemetery of the early Napatan kings and queens. The first royal graves are simple round tumuli and they develop through the generations into mastaba tombs, to culminate with Piankhy's burial in a true masonry pyramid—a style which was to continue until the end of the royal Napatan line and was taken over by its successors at Meroë. Not a single name of the 16 predecessors of Piankhy was recovered from the Kura necropolis although one of them was presumably Kashta, Piankhy's father, who made an abortive attempt to control Egypt. It is with Piankhy that Kush firmly enters the historical record and the entry is dramatic.

The Napatan rulers supported a Pharaonic-style Court and established the Egyptian cult of Amun as the state religion. They styled themselves "King of Upper and Lower Egypt" and undoubtedly regarded their line as champions and custodians of all that was finest in Egyptian civilisation. So it was that when Piankhy set off downstream with his Nubian army bound for Egypt he saw himself not as an invader but a liberator come to free the Two Lands from the forces of barbarism that engulfed it. A parallel situation would be the

English Civil War when the Puritans felt it their duty to put an end to the loose and riotous behaviour of the Stuart Court. Egypt had again fallen on evil days. A long struggle between the state and the priesthood of Amun had culminated in the break-up of the ancient kingdom and from Thebes to the Delta petty rulers squabbled and fought over the carcass. How Piankhy restored order and established his line on the throne of the Pharaohs as the Twenty-fifth Dynasty is recorded in detail on the granite stela set up at Gebel Barkal in the Twenty-first year of his reign (731 BC). Last of the Egyptian princelings to submit was one Tefnakhte, who gave Piankhy a great deal of trouble but whom he treated with magnanimity; in fact Piankhy emerges from the Egyptian campaign as a man of admirable character. Having had himself crowned Pharaoh at Memphis he returned to Napata where he ended his days. Thus the despised Nubians became masters of their former conquerors. For 70 years Nubia was a world power. The Napatan Empire, known to the ancients as the Kingdom of Kush and Misr (Egypt), at its greatest extent stretched from the shores of the Mediterranean to the Central Sudan. The Napatans ruled with varying fortunes. They were able men, Taharqa in particular being an outstanding figure, and they might have restored Egypt to her former greatness had it not been for Assyria, now at her most aggressive and bent on subduing the ancient world. The Napatans were no match for the Assyrian soldiery and with the withdrawal of Tarharqa's son, Tanutamen, to Napata the Kushite Dynasty in Egypt ended.

During their constant journeyings between Napata and Egypt the Kushites passed through a Lower Nubia that was virtually uninhabited. Apart from inscriptions left by Taharqa at Faras and Buhen, and at Semna West where he may have erected a small temple, there is nothing in the archaeological record to show that the Napatans had ever passed along that stretch of the Nile Valley between the First and Dal Cataracts. In the Second Cataract region alone the archeological surveys and excavations of the 1960s disclosed over a thousand sites but not one of them was Napatan. On the other hand, at Sedeinga fifty miles up-river from Dal, links with the Napatan Kingdom have been found in a necropolis excavated in 1963-4 by the Italian Schiff-Giorgini Expedition. Among a small group of tombs with pyramid-type superstructures was one tomb more imposing than its neighbours. It had been robbed, but bones found scattered in the burial chamber and ante-room were reassembled into a complete skeleton, and among a number of inscribed blocks lying on the stairway leading to the burial chamber was a royal figure wearing a red crown, and the lower part of two cartouches bearing the name of Taharqa.

With the end of the Egyptian adventure the focus of Kushite power returned to the Sudan and there the kingdom founded by Piankhy's ancestors continued uninterrupted for the next thousand years. In the sixth century BC the administrative capital was shifted south to Meroë, between the Fifth and Sixth Cataracts, although some scholars make the move at least a century later. Napata, however, remained the religious centre of the kingdom and for centuries to come each king on his accession had to make the journey downstream to receive the acclamation of Amun at Gebel Barkal. The move to Meroë may have been provoked by the sack of Napata by Psamtik II of Egypt whose army of Carian and Greek mercenaries inflicted a crushing defeat on the Kushites in the year 591 BC. On the other hand it could have been forced on the Napatans by increasing desiccation of their lands through pressure of animal herds. Unlike Napata where fertile land is restricted to the river banks and where rainfall is low and uncertain, Meroë, up-river, lies in a belt of annual rainfall which together with its good soil makes it a region capable of providing pasture for large herds of animals and producing ample crops. The Island of Meroë, as it was called, lies in the triangle of land between the Nile and the river Atbara. Meroë town itself was well placed for trade on the caravan routes between Red Sea and Nile. Moreover, the hills nearby held an abundance of iron ore with a plentiful supply of wood for smelting the iron, and the skill of the Meroites as ironworkers was to make them pre-eminent in prosperity and influence. Altogether the move from Napata to Meroë conferred considerable benefits on Kushite economy and agriculture.

The last king to be buried at Napata, in the Nuri pyramid

field, was Nastasen (*c.*335–310 BC); he had lived at a time when Alexander the Great was incorporating Egypt into his empire. Thenceforward it was the pyramid cemeteries at Meroë which received the royal burials. Piankhy's successors number between 65 and 70 and span more than ten centuries, yet in all that time there are only three known dates and even these are approximate. The list of Kushite kings was compiled by Reisner using the evidence of the royal burials at Nuri and Barkal and at Meroë itself, all of which he excavated. The pyramids yielded the names of their owners but did not provide him with a chronology of the kings. All the pyramids were plundered in antiquity but a variety of objects had been overlooked by the robbers in each of them, enough to enable Reisner to make a comparison of types. This study, together with a close examination of the geographical situation of the burials in terms of the best and most commanding positions in the necropoli, was all that he had to go on–of direct evidence there was none–nevertheless Reisner with his keen deductive talent worked out a chronological list that fitted the few facts that were known. It was a *tour de force* and by and large his work has stood the test of time. However it was done 50 years ago and in the light of more recent discoveries and further studies, modifications to the original list have been made by Dr Dows-Dunham of the Boston Museum of Fine Arts and Professor Fritz Hintze of Humboldt University.

It appears then that the Meroitic culture was a direct continuation of the Napatan which itself was a cultural offspring of Egypt. Looked at from that point of view many Egyptologists see the period which followed the fall of the Kushite Twenty-fifth Dynasty as a millennium of slow, unrelieved disintegration; as the native Egyptian artists and artisans, scribes and priests die and the memory of their achievements wanes, the Egyptianised Kingdom of Kush becomes increasingly debased until the day comes when the Egyptian language itself is no longer understood and the hieroglyphic symbols are taken over to express the native, Meroitic, tongue. The forces of primitive Africa have triumphed and the Meroitic Empire, politically weakened and culturally degenerate, sinks to an inglorious close and final extinction in the fourth century of the Christian era.

It is a hypothesis that other scholars will have none of, Professor W. Y. Adams among them: "Our view . . . is consistently refracted through the eyes of Egyptologists, who are inclined to see in it [the Meroic culture of Nubia] little more than perversions of a classic tradition." Reisner, himself an Egyptologist, held to the classic view. Adams among others thinks it possible there may have been two kingdoms and two capitals, one at Napata the other at Meroë, during most of this long period. He agrees that the Meroitic culture is lineally descended from the Napatan and that Reisner's chronology could be substantially correct but he refuses to accept that Meroë is an extension of the cultural decline of Napata with its Pharaonic tradition. Rather, he sees Meroë as a strong and vigorous native culture stripping away the Egyptian veneer and replacing it with a homogeneous blend of native and imported traditions which include Egyptian and Graeco-Roman.

Among Meroë's achievements we must acknowledge the expansion of its cultural influence over areas of Africa including its re-occupation of Lower Nubia. The wave of temple building in the Meroitic era is another indication of cultural vigour and it is matched by the decorated pottery, as abundant and varied as it is beautiful. It ranks with the finest products of the potter's craft anywhere in the ancient world; if the quality and distribution of pottery is regarded as a pointer to the artistic level of a culture, then Meroë rates very highly indeed.

It is Adams who has reduced to a semblance of order the vast quantities of pottery retrieved from the many sites of Nubia and through his own excavations he has been able to classify it and establish at least the beginnings of a chronology of Meroitic pottery. Most other examples of Meroitic art recovered from the cemeteries, among them jewellery, are very fine indeed, and many show a wide variety of foreign influences, including Indian and Graeco-Roman. Evidence that literacy was more widespread than at any other period of Nubian history is provided by the Meroitic achievement of writing down the spoken language. While the script has been deciphered, the language itself remains a mystery in spite of the many inscriptions that have survived. Until it can be read many gaps in the history of this remarkable African civilisation will remain–in particular the state organisation and an appreciation of Meroitic religious observaces. Meroitic temples and tombs show that the official religion remained wedded to the Egyptian pantheon, notably to Amun of Thebes, although the Meroites did have their own native gods. Foremost among them was the Lion-god Apedemek while at Musawwaret-es-Sufra, a site on the Island of Meroë, elephants are so often represented on walls of temples and palaces that this animal, like the lion, must have been regarded as divine. Finally there is the Meroë of the ironworkers as revealed by the great mounds of slag lying near the ruins of the capital city together with the clay crucibles in which the metal was cast. The manufacture and export of iron implements and weapons must have developed into a cornerstone of the Meroitic economy and exerted a profound influence on surrounding African peoples.

This was the culture that arrived fully-fledged in the deserted reaches of Lower Nubia and the Second Cataract, probably in the century that preceded the beginning of the Christian era, and there it remained until the fourth century, vigorous and productive. The re-population of Nubia came about because of an invention in irrigation technology introduced into the Nile Valley at this time: the *saqia*. It is a device used to this day and is essentially a pair of huge wooden cog-wheels which when driven by a bullock lift an endless chain of water buckets from a pit that can extend to any depth. For the first time in the history of the Valley irrigation was made independent of the level of the Nile. *Saqia* pots are easily recognised by their fastening knobs and large numbers of them have been recovered from Meroitic sites in Lower Nubia and along the Second Cataract.

After a thousand years Nubia was back in the mainstream of history and it is now possible to pick up the interrupted thread of the archaeological narrative. Let me say at once that none of the discoveries made in Nubia have added anything significant to our knowledge of the Meroitic Empire. Just inside the Sudan border with Egypt is Faras. Pachoras, to give Faras its ancient name, was the capital of the Meroitic province of Lower Nubia and it was ruled by a viceroy. At Faras, shortly before the first World War, the late Professor F. Ll. Griffith excavated a Meroitic cemetery containing more than two thousand burials, and the wealth of material he recovered enabled him to envolve a typology and containing more than two thousand burials, and the wealth of buildings of an official nature and the remains of a small temple of Tutankhamun built by Huy, the Eighteenth Dynasty Viceroy of Kush. Surrounding a large mound which was the most prominent feature of the site was a wall of impressive height, its first 4 metres built of small sandstone blocks surmounted by another 8 metres of sun-dried brick; it was a Meroitic construction. The main town site was never located either by Griffith or by the Polish Expedition that obtained the concession to excavate Faras at the start of the Nubian Campaign. When I was taken to Faras by Hans Nordström to see the Meroitic bath recently excavated, I noticed to the east of it, denuded to desert level, a complex of buildings which appeared to cover a very large area. It was some distance from the great mound and well inland from the Nile and it occurred to me that this might well be the missing town site; I was horrified to learn later that it could not be excavated.

Indications at Faras had led to expectations that a Meroitic temple and probably a fortress would come to light and, since Faras, the only major Meroitic site in Sudanese Nubia, was so close to Egypt, there was always the possibility that it might produce the long-sought bilingual text, especially in view of its well-documented historical associations with Ptolemaic and Roman Egypt. Moreover Faras had been an important administrative centre in New Kingdom times and a number of inscribed blocks lying around the area made it certain that a Pharaonic temple lay concealed under the dunes. Unfortunately none of these hopes and expectations were realised. The Poles started with the clearance of the large mound and quickly uncovered a cathedral which proved to be of outstanding importance in the history of Christianity in Lower Nubia. The results of their activities will be described in the next chapter; here it is enough to say that nearly all their time in Nubia was absorbed by the cathedral with its associated tombs and buildings. Consequently clearance of the rest of the site, which covered an immense area, had to go by default. Now it is too late; Faras, 27 miles north of Wadi Halfa was the first site in Sudanese Nubia to go under water. As I have pointed out elsewhere, the Faras concession like that of Mirgissa should have been parcelled out among several expeditions. The Poles, like the French at Mirgissa, were faced with a dilemma which need never have arisen.

Having removed the frescoes they had exposed in the interior of the cathedral, they partly dismantled the building to recover some of the re-used stones in its walls. During four seasons of work the Poles recovered just under five hundred of these blocks, all Pharaonic and all decorated and inscribed. Most of them could be dated to Thutmose III, one to Tutankhamun, 17 to the Ramesside period and one to Taharqa of the ill-fated Twenth-fifth Dynasty. Meroitic remains were scanty, outstanding among them being a stone doorway and a beautifully sculptured window grille; presumably at one time a monumental edifice stood under the church where they were found. In a corridor under the northern end of the large mound which was part of the complex of Christian buildings the Poles were delighted to find a collection of Meroitic cups, jars and amphorae, all in perfect condition. Their excitement was somewhat dampened when they saw on them identification marks made by Griffith fifty years earlier. The first two seasons of the Archaeological Survey produced on the West Bank alone between Faras and Gemai, ten Meroitic cemeteries, two settlement sites, a pottery kiln and a 'bath house' fitted for hot and cold water, all in a distance of 40 miles.

In 1964, at Ballana just across the border from Faras, Dr Keith B. Seele decided to investigate a cemetery which, although found by Emery during the Second Survey of Lower Nubia during the 1930s, had not been touched by him because it appeared to have been heavily plundered. That he hadn't done so was Seele's good fortune because Emery had the reputation of clearing a site so thoroughly that nothing was left but the dust. It turned out to be an exceptionally rich Meroitic cemetery which yielded, to use Seele's own (*above*) Semna West (Kumma): inscriptions registering Nile flood levels during the Middle Kingdom occupation of the forts. Some 8 metres higher than in our day, they provided a clue to Vercoutter's discovery of the artificial barrage. (*below*) Kerma: the Western Defufa, one of two puzzling buildings excavated by Reisner 60 years ago. He believed them to be Egyptian fortified trading posts of Middle Kingdom date, an assumption now in question.

(*above*) Belly of Stone: Examples of the distinctive funerary pottery of the Kerma culture. Such beakers are among the most delicate and attractive ever made in the Nile Valley. (*below left*) Second Cataract: Kerma bed burial *c.* 1900 BC. The body faces north. Part of the bed is visible. Broken Kerma beakers lie above the skull of a 'slave' buried with the deceased. (*below right*) Serra East: C-Group cemetery *c.* 1600 BC showing characteristic superstructures. They were photographed from the remote-controlled camera tower used in surveying and measuring sites.

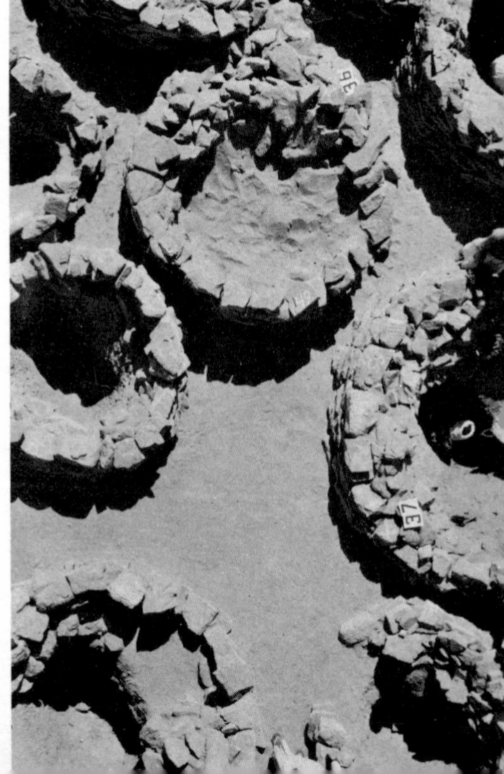

words, "very interesting and important pottery with a great many paintings on the pots not only fantastic but really quite exquisite." He took me aboard the river steamer which was the Expedition's headquarters to see them displayed. He had not exaggerated. There were more than two hundred pieces of ceramic and they were superb, even by Meroitic standards. Apart from highly original painted motifs, some of the vessels had the delicacy and translucence of china. He also showed me several pieces of glassware, some weapons and a number of interesting metal balls which he had not been able to identify. A Meroitic settlement, probably associated with the cemetery, was also cleared but produced no rewards.

In the same area the expedition of the American Research Centre had cleared a Meroitic cemetery which was remarkable for inscriptions made by its robbers and for the fact that five of the tombs had pyramid superstructures of the Meroë type.

Back on the Sudanese side of the border the Survey under Adams discovered and excavated two unusual Meroitic houses on the Island of Gamnarti in the Second Cataract. During excavation I visited the site several times and can still recall with pleasure the exceptionally beautiful situation of this islet set in the middle of a whole clutter of islands and backwaters. To reach it from the mainland involved an enjoyable half-hour of scrambling over rocks and dunes and through sweet-scented bushes and trees, wading across shallow pools and swift-running backwaters until finally came the crossing of a dangerous rapid on a cockleshell of a boat cobbled together out of flattened oildrums. At the end of each day the journey back was tiring but wholly enchanting in the warm glow of the setting sun. During the working day all was choking dust as the gang of 36 labourers, singing and chatting noisily, removed soil as fine as talcum powder to expose a collection of walls and doorways. Imagine a single house of 21 rooms arranged as flatlets, no one pair of rooms having any communication with the others; the larger room of each pair held the fireplace and cooking pots while the considerable quantity of utility vessels in the smaller room suggested its use as a storage place for food. The second house was smaller, containing only 11 rooms, but was as substantially built as the other. A closer inspection revealed that the houses started with a small nucleus of rooms and grew with the passing of time and Adams suggests that we may see in them the growth of a single extended family arising from the acquisition of additional wives. That the buildings had been flooded more than once and evacuated was shown by clear indications of three occupation levels. Perhaps it was the hasty departure of the inhabitants that caused them to leave behind so many domestic implements in bone and stone and enormous quantities of pottery. For me a never failing source of astonishment is the prodigious number of broken pots that an ancient town-site produces, but Gamnarti was in a class on its own. From those two buildings emerged no less than 20,000 sherds all of which had to be cleaned and classified. The Gamnarti houses were the first examples of Meroitic dwellings to be found in the Second Cataract region. A year or so later also on an island–Tila–deep in the Belly of Stone, James Knudstad of the Survey excavated a sizable and prosperous Meroitic community consisting of ten extremely large communal houses of anything up to fifty rooms each.

Another interesting Meroitic house found at Saras West by the Survey, was in a corner of an enormous enclosure of the same period; 2 metres thick in places, the stone wall enclosed an area 570 metres long and 50 to 100 metres wide. There were three gates all on the western side facing the desert. Its purpose is unknown. On top of the Rock of Abusir at the entrance to the Cataract, Adams showed me an example of the many stone huts standing on high points along the Cataract. The pottery found in them indicated that these watch towers dated from the Middle Kingdom and had been re-used in Meroitic times. Each contained the remains of a water jar and a smaller vessel, presumably for food. They suggest that the Meroites like their Egyptian predecessor two thousand years earlier, found it necessary to keep watch over movements in the surrounding desert. The view is superb but it must have been a lonely vigil up on those windy heights.

Some extraordinary Meroitic burials were found by the Franco-Argentine Expedition at Aksha. The bodies were in such good shape that not only skin but muscle and tissue were preserved. The unique feature, however, lay in the elaborate tatooing on two of the torsos; one had a necklace tatooed right round the neck and the other a design which was carried on the arms, down the chest and onto the thighs. The design resembles closely the scarifying still practised by the Nilotic peoples of Southern Sudan.

Meroitic sites were excavated by all the expeditions working in Sudanese Nubia during the 1960s, the Scandinavians in particular being fortunate in the quality of the objects recovered from the cemeteries in their concession. Usually the tombs had been plundered but many contained examples of the famous pottery jugs, cups and bowls, and sufficient objects in the form of toilet equipment and glass and bronze vessels of Egyptian Ptolemaic or Roman origin to show that Meroë had maintained relations with its northern neighbour. Throughout the first and second centuries AD Roman luxury goods continued to find their way to Meroë and eventually into the royal tombs but it was inevitable that Meroë should one day come into conflict with Rome and the catastrophe (from the Meroitic point of view) was precipitated by the Meroites themselves. In the year 30 BC Cleopatra died and Egypt became a Roman province. Within a year the Meroites had been "pressurised" into accepting that the northern part of Lower Nubia should become a protectorate of Rome while remaining a part of the Meroitic Empire in name. The Meroites bided their time for a favourable moment to retaliate. It came in the year 23 BC when Petronius was the Prefect of Egypt, newly appointed. Several classical writers have described the campaign which was conducted by the Meroitic Queen in person; Strabo refers to her as "... Candace, who was a ruler of the Aethiopians in my time, a masculine sort of woman, and blind in one eye." Candace, however, seems to have been a generic title for a queen; her actual name was probably Amanirenas. The account of Dio Cassius is the most succinct:

> About this time the Ethiopians, who dwell beyond Egypt, advanced as far as the city called Elephantine, with Candace as their leader, ravaging everything they encountered. At Elephantine, however, learning that Petronius, the governor of Egypt was approaching, they hastily retreated before he arrived, hoping to

> make good their escape. But being overtaken on the road, they were defeated and thus drew him after them into their own country. There, too, he fought successfully with them, and took Napata, their capital, among other cities. This place was razed to the ground, and a garrison left at another point; for Petronius finding himself unable either to advance further, on account of the sand and the heat, or advantageously to remain where he was with his entire army, withdrew, taking the greater part of it with him. Thereupon, the Ethiopians attacked the garrisons, but he again proceeded against them, rescued his own men, and compelled Candace to make terms with him.

These events may be connected with a well-known bronze head of the Emperor Augustus found in the course of excavations at Meroë, the royal city. The head was buried under the threshold of a building and was obviously regarded as an important trophy. The staring eyes of inlaid glass, are a reminder of Pliny's striking description of the Emperor: "Augustus had eyes like those of a horse, the eyeballs very white and of more than common size, and that is why he was offended if anyone gazed steadily at them."

Their defeat and the destruction of Napata, the holy city, must have been a sore blow for the Meroites in spite of the very favourable peace terms granted to the Meroitic ambassadors by Caesar when they sought him out on Samos. Their empire continued to flourish for at least another three centuries. Relations with Rome were re-established and Meroites living in the northern province were able to continue making the annual pilgrimage to the Shrine of Isis at Philae, which was now inside Roman territory. The end of Meroë as an independent state seems to have come around the beginning of the fourth century AD. The last king of Meroë reigned, according to Hinze, between AD 308 and 320.

The collapse of central authority in Meroë after so long a period of stability—it had, after all, enjoyed a thousand years of settled government—seems to have been brought about by the movement into the Meroitic heartland of a people called the Noba. It is still a matter of debate as to whether the Axumite army of King Aezanes defeated the Meroites or whether, when the Axumites arrived at the Island of Meroë around AD 350, they found it already occupied by an alien people.

A significant factor in Meroë's decline, as Kirwan points out, was probably the increasing isolation of the Meroitic heartland from Roman Egypt. The years following AD 25 were critical for Rome and a policy of strategic withdrawal culminated, as far as Meroë was concerned, with the withdrawal by Diocletian of the garrisons in Nubia, around AD 297. Kirwan goes on to draw attention to the last known inscription of a Meroitic king at Philae which dates from AD 265–266.

The ultimate fate of Meroë continues to elude the historian. What became of Meroë's royal family, and the extent to which the knowledge of her iron-working techniques was spread abroad by migration of her artisans, are questions which only study and, above all, archaeological exploration of western and central Sudan and the Sahara west of the Sixth Cataract, may provide the answers. One thing, however, can be stated with confidence. In Meroë, Africa gave birth to a civilisation whose organisational skill was equalled only by its inventiveness and durability. Meroitic culture in the north did not long survive the disappearance of the central power. Nevertheless, despite the mounting depredations of desert tribes no longer deterred by Roman power, it seems to have lingered into the fourth century, after which it melts into the twilight zone that separates the last flickerings of pagan belief from the upsurge of Christianity in Nubia.

CHAPTER X

The Christian Tide

Miss Amelia Edwards and her remarkable powers of observation have already been described in this book, and now she appears once more. Almost within sight of the Nile terraces that so stirred her imagination, her curiosity was again aroused.

> Some way beyond Kalat Adda, when the Abu Simbel range and the palm island have all but vanished in the distance and the lonely peak, called the Mountain of the Sun (Gebel esh-Shems), has been left far behind, we come upon a new wonder—namely, upon two groups of scattered tumuli, one on the eastern, one on the western bank. Not volcanic forms these; not even accidental forms, if one may venture to form an opinion from so far off. They are of various sizes; some little, some big; all perfectly round and smooth, and covered with a rich greenish-brown alluvial soil. How did they come there? Who made them? What did they contain? The Roman ruin close by—the 240,000 deserters who must have passed this way—the Egyptian and Ethiopian armies that might have fought many a battle on this open plain, suggest all kinds of possibilites, and fill one's head with visions of buried arms, and jewels, and cinerary urns. We are more than half-minded to stop the boat and land that very moment; but are content on second thoughts with promising ourselves that we will at least excavate one of the smaller hillocks on our way back.

And on the return journey from Wadi Halfa that is what they did:

> Selecting one of about eight feet high, we then set the sailors to work; and although it was impossible, with so few men and such insufficient tools, to cut straight through the centre of the mound, we at all events succeeded in digging down to a solid substratum of lumps of crude clay, evidently moulded by hand.
>
> Whether these formed only the foundation of the tumulus, or

concealed a grave excavated below the level of the desert, we had neither time nor means to ascertain. It was something, at all events, to have convinced ourselves that the moulds were artificial. On referring to Col. H. Vyse's *Voyage into Upper Egypt*, etc. I see that he also opened one of these tumuli, but "found no indication of an artificial construction." I can only conclude that he did not carry his excavation low enough. As it is difficult to suppose the tumuli made for nothing, I cannot help believing that they would repay a more systematic investigation.

"Who made them? What did they contain?" When one has seen the tumuli is becomes scarcely credible that 54 years were to pass before anyone took the trouble to find out whether these highly conspicuous mounds were artificial or natural. Several prominent Egyptologists had inspected Lower Nubia up to the Sudan frontier between 1907 and 1911 in connection with the First Archaeological Survey of Nubia. Yet in none of the resulting reports are the mounds as much as mentioned. It was left to W. B. Emery who, with L P. Kirwan, now Director of the Royal Geographic Society, conducted the Second Archaeological Survey to Lower Nubia, to investigate the mounds and make the most spectacular discovery in the archaeological history of Lower Nubia.

In 1927 a geological expedition had taken note of the mounds but pronounced them to be natural deposits of silt blown by the wind into circular hills. Fortunately Emery had not read the report at the time of his discovery. October in Nubia is stifling and Emery had climbed to the top of one of the "hills" to try to capture a whiff of breeze. Suddenly he was struck by the regularity of the crest on which he was sitting, it looked too round to be natural and Kirwan who had joined him agreed. A few days later they crossed the Nile to Qustol where there were other similar mounds and there they made their first trial dig. They were indeed burial mounds and from under them Emery and Kirwan removed the bodies and funerary equipment of the kings of the so-called X-Group people. Emery himself has given a vivid description of the discovery in his book *Egypt in Nubia* but I prefer the account he recorded for me one night at Buhen after supper. He was in a reminiscent mood—we had known one another since 1936 and had been talking over old times.

Here is what he told me, reproduced in full:

> We cut into, I remember, what we called Mound No. 2 at Qustol, that was our first effort. The first thing we discovered, only a few feet in the mound, was an iron axe-head in almost perfect preservation—it looked as though it had come straight from the blacksmith's anvil, a sort of blue colour; in fact it looked almost as though it were still warm. We were all astonished about this, in fact rather embarrassed because we weren't quite certain—at least I wasn't—whether the workmen were having a bit of fun with us and had planted the thing there. Anyway work continued and the next object to turn up in the debris of the mound was a contraption—a metal contraption—that looked, at first, rather like a pair of handcuffs. We were really very puzzled as to what it was. When my wife examined it and started cleaning it—back on the *dahabieh* that evening—she found at once that it was silver. Solid silver. Still we weren't certain what it was. However, next day we penetrated into the entrance of a tomb of one of the X-Group kings which was below the mound, and there the first thing we came across were the skeletons of sacrificed horses, and sacrificed camels, donkeys and so on, that had been placed outside the king's tomb for his use in the next world. Now these horses, many of them were covered with elaborate silver horse trappings—silver bridles and silver saddles; and this mysterious object which we'd found the day before was, in actual fact, a horse-bit made of solid silver. The horses themselves were, as I say, most elaborately dressed. Apart from the silver bits, silver saddles and trappings, they had horse collars with jewelled medallions around their necks. We then penetrated into the tombs themselves and there we found the kings, with their silver crowns on their heads, even the guards sacrificed, and finally we found the queens had been sacrificed also to accompany the king in his life in the next world. But the interesting part about the whole of this discovery of the X-Group tombs, which took us three whole seasons to completely excavate and yielded a mass of material that has now been on show in two galleries of the Cairo Museum for many years, is that it was an extraordinary mixture. I always speak of it as the last page in the history of ancient Egypt, because while Christianity in the fifth and sixth centuries was flourishing in Egypt itself and while, we might say, the Sutton Hoo treasure was being buried in England and Saxon England was flourishing, at that time there down in the far south were the remnants of ancient Egypt, with these X-Group kings—whoever they were—still considering themselves Pharaohs. Wearing silver jewelled crowns with the ancient Egyptian emblems, the ancient Egyptian crowns and the figures of the Goddess Isis on the saddles of their horses. All that mixed up with other objects that they'd obviously plundered from Egypt itself, objects with the crucifix and other Christian emblems on them. And again their weapons appeared to be all very African in character, their rather

shovel-headed spears similar to what you get far south with the Masai tribes at the present day.

Today the word 'sensational' has almost lost its meaning but it is the only word that fits Emery's discovery of Nubia's X-Group kings. Yet oddly enough the publicity it received was negligible. Indeed until quite recently many archaeologists had never heard of the discovery despite Emery's admirable publication of the excavations issued in 1938. Ballana up to the time of its disappearance under the new reservoir was, in Nubian terms, a flourishing little town supporting a sizable population with post office, school, hospital and other official buildings, and with large plantations of date palms, vegetables and animal fodder. This prosperity was a direct outcome of Emery's excavations in the '30s. Eighteen inches below the sand around the tombs they found alluvial soil and the remains of an extensive irrigation system. Back in Cairo Emery reported his discovery to the Ministry of Agriculture and very soon the ancient system had been cleared and was restored to cultivation simply by bringing water to it via pumps. Obviously in X-Group times the area had been thickly populated and because of the royal burials the capital city must have been in the vicinity. Emery searched for it and came to the conclusion that it had been destroyed during changes in the course of the Nile. The huge tumuli opened by Emery have now gone under water but when I last saw them they were still the most imposing feature of the surrounding plain.

Now we come to a vexed question: who were the X-Group people and how did they come to be in Nubia? "X-Group" is the name given by Reisner to one of the cultures he identified in 1907 and which flourished in Nubia between the third and sixth centuries after Christ. Some authorities, Emery among them, believe them to be the people referred to by the Romans as Blemmyes, a savage and warlike tribe who may have come from the eastern desert. Others identify the X-Group with a people known as the Nobatae who are believed to have migrated into Nubia from western Sudan or from the western desert. At this time Egypt was a province of Christian Rome administered from Byzantium, and Assuan was the southern frontier of the Roman Empire. South of

Assuan, Nubia, formerly an integral part of Egypt, was now hostile territory peopled by pagans who were a constant thorn in the side of Christian Rome. Their religion seems to have been a synthesis of deities, which impressed the Byzantine historian Procopius: "Now both these nations, the Blemmyes and the Nobatae, believe in all the gods in which the Greeks believed; and they also reverence Isis and Osiris, and not least of all, Priapus. But the Blemmyes are accustomed also to sacrifice human beings to the sun."

The Blemmyes above all were devotees of the goddess Isis and this was probably one of the reasons that brought them into conflict with Rome over a period of centuries. The centre of Isis worship was in Roman territory, on the island of Philae, which is in the First Cataract a few miles south of Assuan, or 'Syene' as the Romans called it. A common antagonism to Christianity seems to have united both Nobatae and Blemmyes at least until the fifth century, for they made life a misery to soldiers and travellers alike, the Blemmyes in particular raiding over the frontier, plundering, burning and killing. A traveller of the first half of the fifth century AD has left a record of conditions in Nubia at that time.

> And it came to pass one night, when both of us were sleeping in our place of abode, that the demons made a raid in the valley and they uttered cries in the language of the Blemmyes. And when I heard them I was terrified and I nudged my father saying "The Blemmyes are upon us."

In the year 453 the Emperor Marcianus had had enough of the depredations of Nobatae and Blemmyes and he instructed Maximinus, his Commander-in-Chief in Egypt, to destroy them. Maximinus defeated them, but it is a measure of the weakness of the Byzantines and the strength of their barbarian enemies that he was forced to accept terms humiliating to a Christian, nothing less than that both Blemmyes and Nobatae should be allowed free access to the temples of Philae and to borrow the statue of Isis from time to time to use as an oracle in their own land. In return they agreed to keep the peace for a hundred years. Suprisingly the truce, apart from occasional lapses, seems to have been honoured by both sides. But Philae, now an oasis of pagan worship in an increasingly Christian Nubia, became more and more a focus of conspiracy and political intrigue and around the year 540 shortly after the 100-year treaty ran out, the Emperor of Byzantium made an end of Philae as Procopius recorded:

> These temples in Philae were held by the barbarians even until my time but the Emperor Justinian decided to destroy them. Narseus the Persarmenian, who I have mentioned before as having passed over to the Romans, being chief of the soldiers in that region destroyed the temples, having received the order from the Emperor, and imprisoned the priests and sent the statues of the gods to Byzantium. So the last stronghold of the ancient gods was reduced and their worship passed into memory. But the temples remained in romantic ruin for posterity to wonder at.

Inevitably, Amelia Edwards was among the many travellers to fall under the spell of Philae:

> The approach by water is quite the most beautiful. Seen from the level of a small boat, the island, with its palms, its colonnades, its pylons, seems to rise out of the river like a mirage. Piled rocks frame it in on either side, and purple mountains close up the distance. As the boat glides nearer between glistening boulders, those sculptured towers rise higher and even higher against the sky. They show no sign of ruin or of age. All looks solid, stately, perfect. One forgets for the moment that anything is changed. If a sound of antique chanting were to be borne along the quiet air—if a procession of white-robed priests bearing aloft the veiled ark of the God, were to come sweeping round between the palms and the pylons—we should not think it strange.

Miss Edwards was fortunate. Many years have passed since it was possible to see Philae as she did. With the raising of the first Assuan Dam the island with its temples slipped under water and remained submerged for the greater part of the year. Fortunately, the foresight of the Egyptian authorities of the day in strengthening the buildings and their foundations enabled them to resist the annual rise and fall of the Nile although, of course, the colouring on walls and columns which so enhanced the beauty of the temples soon disappeared. Now, with the completion of the High Dam Philae is again threatened. The level of the lake in which Philae stands fluctuates daily causing changes in temperature of a rapidity that no ancient masonry could support. To save Philae UNESCO has launched another international campaign and the work of salvage has already begun. Unfortunately the sacred island itself cannot be saved so its temples are to be dismantled for re-erection on a neighbouring island which stands above the highest level of the lake. Nevertheless when the work is done the walls and columns will again be reflected in the stillness of the blue water as in the days when the goddess, annointed and perfumed, awaited the coming of her barbarian adorers.

The closing of Philae by the emperor Justinian sealed the fate of the Blemmyes. The Nobatae, their former associates, had in the meantime allied themselves with the Romans and it fell to Silko, king of the Nobatae, finally to break the power of the Blemmyes and drive them from the pages of history. Following the period of social upheaval in the Central Sudan which resulted in the break-up of the Meroitic Empire in the fourth century AD, it seems likely that some elements of the former Empire would have moved north into Nubia where as we have seen, a strong Meroitic culture had long been established. The newcomers, whether we call them Blemmyes or Nobatae or X-Group were probably a small, dominant group who established themselves at Ballana and Qustol. Certainly there is no convincing evidence of a wholesale replacement of population at this time and the generally accepted view, following the work done in the campaign, is that the Meroitic inhabitants of Nubia simply became X-Group, just as the X-Group later became Christian. There is continuity rather than replacement. The grave objects indicate that the newcomers were a people with little material culture of their own but who made haste to adopt arts and crafts already flourishing in Nubia. The contents of the royal tombs were a hodgepodge of Byzantine Christian, ancient Egyptian, Meroitic and African, a perplexing mixture of the elegant and the barbaric. One suspects they were the booty from many a raid on church and temple. Only when it comes to the disposal of the dead do we see the new arrivals imposing their traditions on the older population.

With the appearance of the X-Group culture the design of Nubian tombs now changes from the Meroitic style of burial to the tumulus type of superstructure. The funerary customs change too, in particular with the re-introduction of human sacrifice, at least for royal and noble burials. What does not change abruptly is village organisation and architecture, as Adams was able to demonstrate in his clearance of a settlement on the island of Meinarti near the Second Cataract. This village was continuously occupied for more than a thousand years, from the Meroitic period when it was founded, right through the X-Group period to the end of the Christian epoch. X-Group settlements were found elsewhere; in one season alone the Survey excavated five, all of considerable size, with clusters of small rectangular chambers of mud-brick reinforced occasionally with masonry. All five had continued to be inhabited into Christian times. Two X-Group pottery kilns were identical with kilns made in Christian times much later.

Apart from Ballana and Qustol, other X-Group concentrations in Lower Nubia were at Kalabsha (ancient Talmis) and Kasr Ibrim (Primis) where the Egypt Exploration Society under the direction of W. B. Emery found X-Group houses and excavated two large tumulus cemeteries. Most of the tombs had been plundered but over three hundred were recorded and a valuable collection of objects recovered. It was at Kasr Ibrim that Emery had the good fortune to find two magazines overlooked by the plunderers and they yielded a fine collection of objects including bronze vessels and lamps and beautiful glassware, of the same types as those he had unearthed at Ballana thirty years before. It was at the scene of Emery's earlier triumph that Dr Keith B. Seele tackled near the royal tumuli an X-Group cemetery of less pretentious graves. Nevertheless he recovered a number of horse burials complete with trappings and several camel burials, also with trappings. Here was another funerary custom alien to the Meroitic predecessors of the X-Group.

In Sudanese Nubia there were X-Group concentrations at Gemai and Argin, and south of Dal at Firka and Sai. In between were many smaller cemeteries and several settlements, most of which were excavated. Few expeditions were as lucky as Emery! X-Group tombs with their huge earthern supersturctures anything from 6 to 12 metres in diameter, simply invited the attentions of robbers, but occasionally the intruders must have been disturbed at their digging and left behind objects ranging from pottery and glass vessels to weapons of iron and pieces of textile and tooled leather for the archaeologists of the 1960s to find.

By chance I was present at the excavation of the strangest of all X-Group tombs, if indeed it was an X-Group tomb. One bright morning I was wandering among the islands and channels of the Second Cataract with an ornithologist attached to the Scandinavian Joint Expedition. He was pointing out with delight some of the strange birds of which there were many, when rounding a rock we came upon a group of his colleagues busy digging into the alluvium. Surrounding them were a dozen or so of the familiar tumuli all thoroughly plundered. I deserted my ornithologist friend to climb down into a tunnel that resembled nothing so much as the approach to an early subway station. The sandstone slabs of which it was constructed must have been carried to the site with considerable labour since the nearest sandstone was on the other side of a Nile rapid fully a mile away. This odd subway was cleared by the Scandinavians for some fifty metres in the direction of the Nile after which they had to abandon it because it vanished under water. It was a frustrating experience and it reminded me of the stone-lined subterranean passage found by Emery at Buhen fortress. With great labour he followed its course running parallel with the Nile for 150 metres when to his astonishment (for he had assumed it was intended to carry water) it turned away from the Nile and wandered off into the desert. At which point he, like Säve-Söderbergh in the depths of the Second Cataract, gave up.

A number of X-Group bodies came to light, sometimes rather too well preserved by the bone-dry sand of Nubia to be comfortably handled. I recall a somewhat ghoulish incident with the Scandinavians. I had accompanied one of them to bring back an X-Group "mummy"–it was in fact a body wrapped in what looked like brown linen. We placed it on a stretcher and lifted it out of the tomb with ropes, for all the world like gravediggers in reverse, after which we slid the stretcher into the back of the truck and started off for headquarters. Unfortunately, in that featureless desert we lost our way and ran into some rocky outcrops. Our passenger was being given such a rough ride that I had to join him in back and embrace him to keep him from falling apart.

The Sudan Survey found in a trench alongside an X-Group tumulus 34 neatly stacked baskets abandoned or forgotten by the labourers who had made the mound some 1500 years before. They were perfectly preserved and looked very much like the baskets one could buy in Wadi Halfa market. In a grave nearby were several pieces of bread.

This X-Group cemetery was on a plain consisting of a deep layer of greyish sand intermixed with shells, clearly the alluvial deposit of an ancient river. The deposit sloped upwards towards the surface and while digging another of the graves Nordström found below the top stratum of sand the footprints of adults, children and camels, following what appeared to be a path in the direction of the river which was at least a kilometre away. The footprints were about a metre below the surface and Nordström traced them down for about 6 metres to where they disappeared under an alluvial deposit below. The footprints being beneath the graves showed that they were made by people and animals who lived at the very beginning of the X-Group period or immediately before it.

Nobatae or Blemmyes? Or perhaps both? I doubt if we shall ever know. Across the millennia the Nubian stretch of the Nile gave birth to many cultures. Of them all the X-Group seems to have been among the most barbarous. It is strange that a people who, like those earlier Nubians at Kerma, could sacrifice the entire household of their kings by cutting their throats or by strangulation, should have emerged towards the very end of Nubia's long and often splendid history. Admittedly they held the stage for no more than a brief 200 years, but they were the last followers of the ancient gods and with their passing the lingering religious beliefs and traditions of Pharaonic Egypt flickered and died.

Long before Justinian closed the temples on Philae, Christians had been moving into Nubia from Egypt to escape the persecutions ordered by successive Roman emperors in the first centuries of Christianity. Only with the accession of Constantine in AD 313 when Christianity became the state religion, did life become tolerable for Christians along the extended frontiers of the Empire. Missionaries were able to move without hindrance and in Africa proselytising was both rapid and effective. Within a few years Abyssinia had embraced the new religion and it was a Christian army from Axum in Abyssinia that moved into Meroë following the break-up of the Meroitic Empire. From the fourth century on, therefore, pagan Nubia was sandwiched between two Christian powers to north and south, but it was from the north that official conversion to Christianity came, in the year 543. The conversion provided the Byzantine Court with a heaven-sent opportunity to indulge the kind of intrigue in which it delighted. Justinian and his Empress Theodora supported rival sects of the Christian faith, Justinian the Orthodox and Theodora the Monophysite, and she so contrived matters that her emissary Julian reached the Nubian Court before his Orthodox rival. How Theodora outwitted her royal husband is related by the medieval historian Bar-Hebraeus in his *Ecclesiastical Chronicle:*

> The Emperor sent a certain bishop to Nubia and with him went envoys and presents for the king of that country. Not to be outdone, Theodora sent Julian also, and gave him a letter to the Duke of Thebaid, wherein she said: "I and the Emperor have determined to send an envoy unto the nation of Nobades and behold I have sent Julian the priest on my own behalf, and the Emperor hath sent other men, together with objects of price. Do thou take good care that my envoy entereth first, and let him make smooth the way for those whom the Emperor hath sent."
>
> When the Duke of the Thebaid had read the letter of the Empress, he did as she commanded him, and he detained the ambassadors of the Emperor until Julian arrived. And Julian taught and baptised the king and the nobles. Thus were all the people of the Kushites converted to the orthodox faith and they became subjects of the throne of Alexandria. . . And Julian remained there for a period of two years. And it is related that from the third unto the tenth hour he stood and baptised in caves full of water, naked, and with a girdle about him, and the only part of his body which was out of the water was the upper part thereof.

By the seventh century the whole of the Nile Valley to well south of Khartoum had been converted to one or other of the Christian sects and three separate kingdoms had come into being: in the far south Alodia with its capital at Soba near where Khartoum stands today; Makuria north of Alodia

(*far left*) Debeira: dagger found in C-Group burial. (*near left*) Debeira: Egyptian dagger found in C-Group burial. (*below*) Karnak Temple: Tutankhamun. This Eighteenth-Dynasty Pharaoh appointed Viceroys to Kush (Nubia) to govern and collect tribute. Much of the gold found in his tomb must have come from Nubia.

(*above*) Meroë: a corner of the pyramid field located between the Fifth and Sixth Cataracts where many of the Meroitic Kings and Queens were buried. (*below*) Nagar: temple of the Meroitic lion-god, Apedemek. This god is not in the Egyptian pantheon, although the temple obviously derives from far-off Egypt.

with its capital at Old Dongola; and in the extreme north, Nobatia with Panchoras (Faras) as its captial. Later Makuria was to unite with Nobatia which by then had been reconverted from the Monophysite (Coptic) sect to the Orthodox Byzantine faith. Later again Christianity in Nubia was to turn back to the Monophysite belief, owing allegiance to the Coptic Patriarch of Alexandria. However, they never used the Coptic language in their liturgy but held fast to the earlier links with Byzantine tradition, so that Greek inscriptions, albeit in very bad Greek, were found in the churches as late as the thirteenth century. Towards the middle of the seventh century came a blow which to Christians of the time must have seemed mortal but which turned out in the long run to be a blessing in disguise. Abdullah Ibn Saad, Governor of Moslem Egypt, invaded Nubia. He records that he found it governed by a single king, ruling from Assuan to Soba and with this ruler he made a treaty by which Nubia agreed to pay Egypt an annual tribute of 400 slaves. In return Nubia was to receive a valuable gift of barley, wheat, lentils, cloth, horses and wine. This treaty not only saved Christianity in Nubia from early extinction but enabled it to flourish for centuries, despite the occasional military adventure by one side or the other. A political and economic agreement that remained in force for over six hundred years is a phenomenon inconveivable in our enlightened age!

The baptism of the X-Group kings may well have been the reason for the transfer of their capital from Ballana to neighbouring Faras, where the see of Bishops of Pachoras was established and where in 1961 the Polish Archaeological Mission directed by Professor K. Michalowski found the tombs of many of them, in and around the great mound which was so prominent a feature of the site. The first tomb to be excavated was that of Bishop Joannes who, according to the stela buried with him, died at the age of 82—his body was found in a domed mausoleum that also contained a bronze cross and staff while the wall bore a wonderfully preserved fresco of the Archangel Michael—a foretaste of what was to come. In a niche in the great cathedral buried under the mound was a list of 27 bishops and subsequently the portraits of many of them were uncovered on the cathedral walls. Here was a unique opportunity to compare identified skulls with actual portraits and this was done by an anthropologist from Warsaw University who confirmed that the portraits reflected with remarkable faithfulness the facial characteristics of the skulls. The first date of the list, AD 707, is attached to Paulus, but he was fifth in the line of bishops, which means that the diocese was established at least a century before his day. Last name on the list was that of one Jesus and the date was AD 1169. Jesus was, however, by no means the last bishop to be appointed in Nubia, as we know from a discovery made during the excavations at Ibrim carried out in 1963-4 by Professor J. M. Plumley of the Egypt Exploration Society. With astonishment the excavators saw before them in a tomb a body clad in the full episcopal robes of a dignatory of the Eastern Church. Among the folds were two scrolls which when examined proved to be 16 feet long. Written in Arabic and Coptic, the scrolls embodied a letter from the Patriarch in Alexandria confirming the consecration of a Bishop of Faras and Ibrim in the year AD 1372, and the testimonies of the four bishops who attended the enthronement at Ibrim.

On the summit of the mound at Faras was a Moslem citadel of mud-brick and this had first to be removed before the mound itself could be attacked. By a happy chance I was visiting the Polish Mission on the very day they started to clear the mound. Within minutes the top of a white plastered wall appeared and on it painted in colours as fresh as the day they were applied was the haloed head of a saint. The expression it bore was that of anxious arrival at an unexpected and unidentified railway station. That painting aroused tremendous excitement among all of us there, and with reason, for by the end of four seasons' work no less than a 160 frescoes had been uncovered of which about 80 were sufficiently well-preserved for public exhibition. One, the "Nativity", measured 4½ by 6½ metres and the "Three Young Men in the Furnace" 3½ by 3 metres. To stand in the centre of that ruinous cathedral was indeed a memorable experience; the dun-coloured walls were almost hidden by a brilliantly coloured picture gallery of biblical scenes and portraits.

The murals show most vividly how a school of Nubian art was able to flourish in the Nile Valley far from Byzantium, the source of its influence and inspiration. The earlier paintings used the alfresco technique whereby the paint is applied to plaster which is still wet. The other method, and the bulk of the Faras murals are done in this way, is to paint on to plaster already dry. The work of conservation undertaken at Faras can only be described as a miracle of expertise. First the fresco was sprayed with a protective coating and a layer of tissue paper applied with hot beeswax. Then came muslin fixed to the surface by more hot beeswax ironed on to it; if necessary several layers of muslin were so applied. When all was thoroughly dry the restorers separated the painted plaster layer from the friable mud brick wall behind by manipulating sharp knives of various shapes. This, the most delicate part of the operation, was not made easier by blinding clouds of fine black dust scraped from the wall by the knives. When finally disengaged each painting was attached to a prepared wooden framework and lifted from the wall after which all superfluous mud was removed from the back. The painting was then ready for transport to the museum to be consolidated and restored. The work of removal and restoration was under the supervision of Mr Jozef Gazy, a huge man with the fingers of a surgeon. Over the centuries the interior of the cathedral had been given three layers of plaster, each with its quota of murals. Thus picture was painted over picture and Gazy and his colleagues actually succeeded in separating one layer of painting from another, dissecting, in effect, plaster brittle with the passage of 1200 years. It was an operation that demanded a degree of skill and patience that commanded wide-eyed admiration from a layman.

A year later I watched Gazy working on the consolidation of the murals in the new museum at Khartoum. What he had already accomplished I would not have believed possible had I not seen the originals, salt-encrusted and clinging insecurely to walls of crumbling mud-brick. Each picture now gave the appearance of having been painted by the original artist not on plaster but on to a rigid lightweight material impervious to humidity and insect attack. The paint had been fixed to the new surface with a type of epoxy resin glue which has no chemical reaction of any kind. One could run a hand over the surfaces without any danger of damage to the paintings on them. Glowing with colour these paintings, many of them 1300 years old, were, Gazy assured me, good for centuries and capable moreover of being transported anywhere for exhibition; a 5-foot high mural, for example, could be carried by one man with ease. The Faras frescoes are a triumphant example of modern conservation techniques. Fifty-two of them were presented to Poland by the Sudan Government and the remainder will stay in the Sudan for exhibition in the Khartoum Museum.

Apart from the murals, the cathedral walls bore over 500 inscriptions and graffiti left by visitors over the centuries. Written in Greek, Coptic or Old Nubian, between them they represent a valuable source of study for scholars.

In the seventh century there were at Faras two ecclesiastical buildings which fell to ruin. To replace them, a Bishop Paulus seems to have conceived the idea of using the site of the ruined Meroitic temple for building a cathedral and this was done, incorporating many pharaonic blocks in the walls of the new building which was dedicated by Paulus at the beginning of the eighth century, in the reign of King Mercurios. By the tenth century various modifications had developed the church from a wooden-roofed structure to a basilica with cupolas. Following a partial collapse of the edifice there was further re-construction. During all this time, from the eighth to the twelfth centuries, paintings were being executed, often one above the other, constituting in all a priceless record of the development of ecclesiastical art in Nubia.

By the beginning of the thirteenth century the Cathedral and many of its associated buildings had already become partly buried in drift sand. Thus, it is to the usually destructive winds of Nubia that we owe the marvellous state of preservation of these murals so brilliantly coloured on a shining white background; moreover the faces of the human and divine figures are unmutilated, a happy chance due solely to the complete smothering of the cathedral before the time of the Moslem conquest. In the church of Abd-el-Qadr, the village described in Chapter III of this book, was a fresco, now removed, which shows the head and shoulders of what is presumed to be an Eparch of Lower Nubia and he is shown presenting a model of the church, as was the custom in medieval Europe. His elaborate robe is untouched but the head has been defaced. Incidentally an interesting survival from the pagan past was the head-dress he wore, which embodied what could be a representation of the horns of Amun. This is one of the very few portraits of a Christian ruler to survive. As for the undiscovered royal burials of Nobatia, no doubt they have shared the fate of Pachorus the capital city, and now lie at the bottom of the reservoir, so the relationship between Church and State in Nubia which the tombs might have clarified remains obscure. The diocese of Faras and Ibrim included dozens of churches. The surveys listed a 125 of them along the 300-mile length of the inundated area from Aswan to the Dal Cataract. They were mostly small buildings, measuring on average 15 metres long by 7 metres wide. Murals were a feature of Nubian churches but the abrasive winds and Moslem defacement had destroyed all but a few fragments of the paintings in most of them.

All the churches still standing were examined during the 1960s and many were excavated. In village life the church was at the very heart of the community, for scarcely an island of the Cataract lacked a church, with the dwellings of the villagers clustered round it and, nearby, a cemetery. It was a pattern repeated on both banks of the Nile, wherever the river had deposited a patch of alluvium.

That Christian Nubia enjoyed prosperity is clear from the great number of village sites and other signs of human activity of the period. There is reason to believe that the level of the Nile rose during early Christian times and this would naturally lead to more cultivation and an increase in population. At Faras for example, before it was smothered by dunes, there was a second channel of the Nile, in effect an overflow which at times of low Nile must have made available thousands of additional acres for cultivation. Faras was the richest and most extensive agricultural area of Nubia and this undoubtedly was the reason why it became an important administrative and religious centre in New Kingdom times and later, as Pachorus, the capital of Nobatia.

Christian remains accounted for fully half the antiquities of Nubia and the expeditions found themselves faced with the clearance of numerous Christian irrigation works and fortifications, towns and settlements, churches and above all cemeteries. One of the largest of the towns was at Debeira West, some ten miles south of Faras. It was excavated by Professor P. Shinnie on behalf of the University of Ghana. When I saw it the site had been opened up like a doll's house laid on its back and Shinnie took me on a tour of the extraordinary patchwork of mud brick construction that constituted a Nubian town of a thousand years ago. We scrambled along streets and through doorways, up staircases onto roofs which in some buildings were still in place and paused to examine the town latrine with its drainage system and large soak-away packed with thousands of sherds. The town, Shinnie estimated, covered about ten acres and it seems to have come into existence at the very beginning of the Christian era in the seventh century as an ecclesiastical establishment, possibly a monastery. The original building expanded as the years passed, other buildings were added, then came dwellings and, presumably, a market, until three centuries later the town had reached its maximum level of population and prosperity. It continued to be inhabited, though with dwindling numbers as Moslem pressure increased, until the end of Christianity in Nubia and even beyond, when presumably the townsfolk who remained were persuaded to embrace Islam. A dwelling dating from a late period of the town's history differed from the others in being built of stone. It was tiny, with only two rooms, but was neatly laid out with an interior staircase leading to the roof and a courtyard outside the front door, with a kitchen to one side and a latrine on the other–an ideal flatlet, as Shinnie remarked, for a bachelor of AD 1100. He told me somewhat wryly that the site had yielded around a quarter of a million sherds all of which had been examined of course.

Several other Christian villages were cleared during the campaign. One, Abkanarti, in the region of the rock-drawings and neolithic settlements found by Myers, was cleared by the

Spanish Archaeological Mission with Francisco Presedo Velo as field director. The site, which contained two churches, did not however come up to expectations since it was found that the buildings had been badly disturbed by farmers in search of *marog* (fertiliser). However, enough remained for the excavators to draw up a plan of the place and of its architectural development and they were able to date its foundation to the eighth century. Their most interesting find was a parchment written in Old Nubian. James Knudstad had better luck at Serra where he conducted field operations for the Oriental Institute of Chicago. Serra has already been described in the chapter on the Middle Kingdom fortresses. The Nubians of the later Christian period had grasped the defensive possibilities of the ancient citadel with its massive fortifications designed to protect it on three sides with the river itself protecting the fourth. At this time increasing enemy pressure, probably from the surrounding desert, was forcing the smaller Christian communities to abandon the river banks for islands which were more easily defended. Others tended to protect themselves by moving into larger concentrations and Serra East was one of these late Christian settlements. Sheltering inside the fort were 30 large houses still standing, and a church; three more churches stood on the perimeter of the fort. All these buildings were constructed of mud brick and all were dated by the pottery in them to between the twelfth and thirteenth centuries. The Christian occupation of the fort was it seems, brief, nevertheless because it was so easily defended Serra may have been one of the last Christian settlements north of the Second Cataract to hold out against the Moslems. The buildings were extraordinarily well-preserved, most of them standing to the second storey. Among passengers on the Nile steamers that used to ply between Egypt and Wadi Halfa, Serra East always drew excited comment. And indeed, the rectangular fort built on a slope to the river's edge, its interior filled with large buildings apparently untouched by time, was an impressive thing to see. To get at the Middle Kingdom levels the excavators had literally to dismantle the Christian structures brick by brick and this enabled Knudstad, himself an architect, to record complete details of their construction.

In the foundations of one of the buildings was a book of 13 parchment pages. This is an extremely valuable find because it is written in Old Nubian which as a written language seems to have come into use in the second half of the eighth century.

The lengths to which the Nubian Christians were driven in fortifying their communities was dramatically illustrated by Definarti in the Second Cataract. This little island shaped like a sugar-loaf, was crowned by a church which provided a fine look-out post up and down river and across the surrounding desert. Down from the church spread buildings and dwellings literally one on top of the other right to the water's edge, and linking the buildings a network of defensive walls turned the whole island into a positive cocoon.

Kasanarti was another island settlement. W. Y. Adams who excavated it for the Sudan Antiquities Service was able to determine that the first settlement on Kasanarti was Meroitic. At its maximum extent the Christian village consisted of 25 of what he termed "unit houses" made up of about 150 individual rooms. The "unit houses" consisted of square dwellings each with from four to eight small rooms and a single entrance. They were detached and in effect remained so even after the spaces between them had been filled by other "unit houses", because wherever two dwellings adjoined Adams found a double wall. One of the most interesting structures and also one of the last to be built on Kasanarti was a square building with a second storey and its interest lay in the lack of any kind of entrance on the ground floor, the rooms of which could be entered only through hatchways from the floor above which was closed originally by heavy stone slabs. This was a design Adams was to find repeated elsewhere in settlements of the Late Christian period and eventually he was able to satisfy himself that it was a type of dwelling developed by a hard-pressed population as a means of defence. A fuller description is given later on in the chapter. During the course of the Survey Mills was surprised to find in Christian settlements many perishable objects in an excellent state of preservation: such things as basketry, leather work and wooden objects all seemed to have escaped the attentions of the termites. He was struck by remarkable similarities in these homely objects of the twelfth or thirteenth centuries to those in use in Nubian houses of today.

The picture one gets of Christian Nubia at the end of the first millennium is one of prosperity and stability. The potters are turning out an abundance and variety of wares and many imports from abroad are in general use, such things as textiles, glassware and bronze. Village communities are everywhere; wherever there is soil suitable for cultivation water is brought to the spot by irrigation which was intensive, as the large numbers of *saqia* pots found indicates, probably more so than in our day. The people have a written language and presumably some kind of secular administration headed by the king, but this aspect of Nubian social life is obscure. The centre of activity is the Church, the motivating and cohesive force of this riverain society.

The Church laid no strictures on the consumption of wine, indeed it was given official sanction by the famous *baqt* treaty of Abdullah Ibn Saad (AD 641) under the terms of which Nubia would receive among other things 1300 *kanyr* of wine annually. Up and down the length of Nubia twelve constructions have been unearthed—one was found by Adams on the Island of Meinarti—all more or less identical in design and they have been described as wine presses, although there is some disagreement on this interpretation of their use. Certain features common to all, notably a lion-head spout, lead Adams to conclude that they dated from the third or fourth century AD and were probably Meroitic in origin. The climate and soil of Nubia are not really suitable for viticulture and it is tempting to associate the Meroitic wine growing experiment with the disturbed relations between the Meroites and Rome towards the end of the third century AD, a schism which may well have interrupted the traditional import of wine from Egypt. With the advent of Christianity wine again flowed in. The vessels used were amphorae made in Assuan, always a centre of pottery manufacture and diffusion throughout much of Nubian history. The Assuan factory has never been identified and Adams has come up with the intriguing notion that it may still be operating, although its products have not been on the Nubian market for the last four hundred years. At Mirgissa in the plain below the fort, Vercoutter dug out a large rectangular mud-brick building of Christian date which fitted into no recognisable pattern of Nubian architecture of the period: at Abd-el-Qadir, Adams and Nordström found another curious building, large and well constructed of stone, containing eight rooms with an enclosed courtyard and within and around it were thousands of fragments of imported wine amphorae together with drinking cups and bowls. Adams considers that this building and the one at Mirgissa were nothing less than taverns. Similar taverns were excavated by the Austrian Mission at Sayala.

It was in 1960 on my first visit to Nubia that I met Bill Adams, at work on his first major excavation in the Nile Valley. It was a pottery at Faras, within a stone's throw of the Egyptian frontier, and it turned out to be the best example of a pottery industry yet found in either Nubia or Egypt (see Figure 16). Not only was it possible to follow the methods of operating and firing the various types of kilns over the centuries but also, from the abundance of raw materials on the site, to work out the actual techniques employed by the potters. In abundance too, were examples of finished and partly finished vessels in all stages of manufacture. Unbroken pots and sherds unearthed on site after site showed that Faras had been the main centre of manufacture and distribution of pottery for Christian Nubia. The closure of the factory was brought about not by hostile action but by the potters' inability to cope with the encroaching desert sand, no longer held at bay by the overflow channel of the Nile which had silted up. I found it a moving experience to see how the workmen had been driven to abandon room after room as the sand flowed in.

The study of pottery is the very backbone of archaeology particularly in the study of non-literate societies. Pottery is one of the most versatile and durable of human crafts and it reflects faithfully any changes in cultural patterns. Consequently, when analysed and understood it is one of the most sensitive of dating tools. In the main these remarks apply to the great variety of wares made on the wheel for sale. Hand-made pottery for domestic use is by comparison

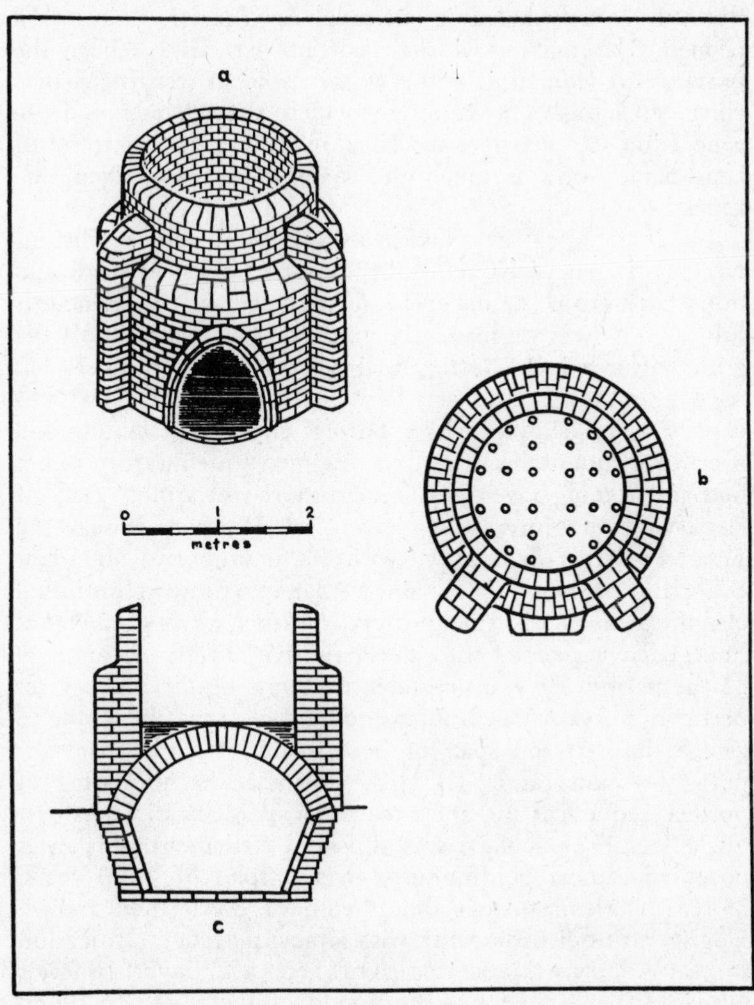

Fig. 16. Typical double-chamber cylindrical kiln (kiln 3 at Faras West) *a,* projection; *b,* plan; *c,* section

not only somewhat crude but much less susceptible to social change. The making of such pottery has always been the province of women; it is the women who in resisting change cling tenaciously to tradition which they hand on from generation to generation. Thus in Nubia the pattern of hand-made ware is much the same today as in Neolithic times.

Christian sites in Nubia always produced prodigious numbers of sherds. I remember how at Gamnarti we would bring back from the dig every night an average of ten baskets full. A boy was permanently employed on washing off the grime after which Nettie Adams would take over. It has always amused me to see how the archaeologist's wife is expected to shoulder the boring chore of sorting and discarding mountains of pottery fragments preparatory to her husband taking over the much more rewarding task of classifying the interesting 'left-overs'. However it was the Faras Potteries excavation with its unique and abundant collection of sherds that enabled Adams to draw up his initial classification of Christian pottery in Nubia, a work which has since been expanded into the definitive pottery chronology of the period. He can now identify some 65 different wares occurring in Christian Nubian sites and feels that he is able to give a date to the span of occupation of a site from the pottery found on it. Of great assistance in his dating of pottery sequences was the excavation of Meinarti, his largest 'dig' in Nubia. Meinarti was an island settlement which was occupied almost continuously over a span of 1100 years. Moreover Meinarti was that dream of every field archaeologist: an undisturbed site with almost perfect stratification so that Adams was able to peel off layer after layer, 18 levels in all. Starting at the top of the mound, 50 feet above the flood plain and where the topmost occupation dated from the Dervish wars at the end of the nineteenth century, he worked down successively through the many stages of Christian Nubia into the pagan period–represented by three X-Group levels contemporary with Byzantinium–until at the very bottom of the mound he reached the original Meroitic foundation, corresponding in time to Roman Egypt. The stratification revealed repeated destruction by floods in the early Christian levels, but quite suddenly in the eleventh century the high Niles apparently ceased and never again was the village destroyed by water. The village had also suffered from blown sand because on level seven, windows and doors had been blocked, walls buttressed or doubled and protective drift fences built. But the dunes defeated the villagers and eventually drove them to abandon their homes. When the inhabitants returned they found the sand had buried ever-thing to the rooftops so they built their new houses on the roofs of the old thus repeating the earlier architectural plan. Level five revealed another of those tantalising mysteries, this one akin to the riddle of the *Marie Celeste*. For no apparent reason the entire population moved out, not hurriedly as in an emergency, but at their leisure. That they had every intention of returning is clear since they left in the houses all their household goods and valuables; however something unforeseen happened because they never did come back and when the village was reoccupied the floors, now buried in sand, were left undisturbed and the newcomers simply covered the sand with a layer of mud plaster. So it came about that seven hundred years later Adams reaped an unprecedented haul of Christian domestic objects all in perfect condition. As each new level of habitation was exposed by the diggers, so the changes in cultural patterns could be read by comparing the architecture, the pottery and the artifacts of one level with the next. Thus Meinarti provided a near ideal situation for the study of the cultural development of a community over a long period of time, and the evidence of Meinarti is not that of abrupt social or cultural change but rather the normal evolutionary development of a single ethnic group. Unless Meinarti was unique among Nubian villages, which seems unlikely, then the modern inhabitants of Nubia may as Adams says: "legitimately regard themselves as the heirs of the first Meroites who reclaimed the region two thousand years ago".

The church at Meinarti was the only one excavated in Nubia that had remained in use from beginning to end of the Christian period, although destroyed and rebuilt several times. This building represented therefore, through its successive alterations, a microcosm of the entire history of Nubian church architecture.

Adams made the odd discovery that although Meinarti had been continuously inhabited from Roman times the first interments on the island dated only from the eleventh century; where the earlier inhabitants buried their dead remains a matter for conjecture.

Of all the Christian remains in Nubia by far the most numerous were cemeteries, a circumstance which reflects the high level of population in Christian times. Normally a cemetery could be linked to a settlement nearby although, as we have seen at Meinarti, it was not always so. Almost invariably the graves were simple pits suitable for extended burial; the low rectangular superstructures, wherever they existed, were usually of mud-brick with a small lamp box at the west end although occasionally a stone built superstructure would be found. Funerary objects were seldom, if ever, placed in the graves; still one never knew, so many Christian cemeteries received at least partial excavation. It was not a popular chore since the bone-dry sand of Nubia even after twelve hundred years or so had often preserved the corpses only too well. One young Englishman newly arrived for his first field dig was put to work on the clearance of a largish structure which turned out to be a mausoleum. The labourers started to remove from it 23 bodies—"in a disgusting state of preservation", but long before they had finished my young friend had taken himself off to vomit.

In the late fourteenth century Ibn Khaldum, the Arab historian, wrote of Nubia: "No trace of kingly authority remains in the country, and the people are now become bedouins, following the rains about as they do in Arabia." Yet he was referring to Upper Nubia and as we have seen from the discovery at Ibrim in Lower Nubia, a bishop was consecrated there as late at AD 1372. From this event one can deduce that Christians continued to live in isolated pockets along the Nubian stretch of the Nile for much longer than historians have hitherto accepted. It seems to bear out Adams' hypothesis that along the middle reach of the Nile in the region of Dongola, conversion to Islam was effected not from Egypt in the north, but by nomadic tribes crossing from Arabia in the east. According to this theory, although Dongola had been taken over by Islam by AD 1325, a substantial Christian population remained along the northern reaches of the river well beyond that date. It was to search for evidence of this "Terminal Phase" of Christianity, as he called it, that prompted Adams to excavate a site at Kulubnarti 80 miles south of Wadi Halfa. Deep in the Belly of Stone and as inaccessible as anywhere in Nubia, its isolation was complete and still may be, because when I saw it last in 1969 life for the local Nubians was "business as usual". They had refused to leave, arguing that because their villages were so near the southern end of the reservoir the Nile would never swallow them. It is to be hoped they are right since at Kulb ancient tradition and custom were more deeply rooted than almost anywhere else in Nubia.

Some half dozen sites were excavated at Kulb but the main objective was a large settlement of late Christian times on the island of Kulubnarti which could be described as a cluster of tall, well-preserved mud-brick and stone houses scattered over the top of a rocky knoll. My old friend Bill Adams, now Professor of Anthropology at Kentucky University, was leading an expedition sponsored by the University. The "unit houses" referred to earlier on in this chapter were very much in evidence at Kulubnarti, only they were better preserved than elsewhere in Nubia. I was able to clamber on to the roofs and walk through rooms of the upper stories with no danger of collapsing brickwork. It was in the upper storey that the occupants lived, the lower floor becoming in effect a cellar for storage of supplies or for concealment. The "cellar" was a labyrinth of tiny rooms which could be entered only through holes or hatches in the ceiling; there were no doorways into the cellar from ground level. Visitors could enter the houses only as I did, by climbing up a ladder from the street outside to a doorway in the upper storey. Each house had at least one "secret chamber" so effectively concealed as to give no sign of its existence. As the years went by the cellars became more and more labyrinthinc until they reached the point where a man could only pass between rooms by crawling on hands and knees, while some chambers were inaccessible. In the end the cellars became unusable for anything but the dumping of rubbish and that is exactly what the occupants did, filling them with ash and other refuse.

Probably the houses were so built for defensive reasons, not for protection from an organised enemy but rather against sporadic raids by nomads from the surrounding desert. Food and household goods could be concealed in the hidden rooms below while the occupants either abandoned the village temporarily, or pulled up the ladder, barred the door and waited for the danger to pass.

The most conspicuous building at Kulubnarti was what came to be known as the Castle. With its high walls and a tall tower at the south-east corner it was the most conspicuous landmark of that reach of the Nile. Originally it was a two-storey "unit house" but was successively enlarged and modified, always with defense in mind. An enclosed courtyard and tower were added and a small loopholed parapet built. A heavy deposit of manure showed that horses were kept in the courtyard at some period. The defensive nature of the building was revealed by the loopholing made when the original "unit house" was first modified. It took the form of narrow embrasures suitable for archery. Later these were blocked except for a round opening at the top, similar to openings built into the tower when that was constructed–the archer had been supplanted by the musketeer. Gunpowder had arrived in Nubia! This was known to have happened around AD 1520 at the time of the Ottoman conquest. According to local tradition the Castle was used as the residence of the local Ottoman *Kushef* (governor) and presumably as quarters for his armed retainers. This belief is supported by the discovery among refuse in the building of two scraps of letters written in Arabic and bearing the names "Hassan Daud Kashef" and "Ahmed Daud Kashef".

The Kulubnarti findings go to show that Christianity in Nubia lasted until the end of the fifteenth century, possibly even longer. For a thousand years the Christian way of life had moulded the Nubian character and modified old traditions, and the scene of its final extinction could well have been that rocky island in the heart of the Belly of Stone. Meanwhile, students of Christian Nubia are awaiting publication of the many documents of mediaeval and later date discovered at Kasr Ibrim by Professor Plumley. Written on a variety of materials in Old Nubian, Greek, Coptic, Arabic and (*right*) Khartoum: The Archangel Michael, a beautiful example of Nubian/Byzantine art from the Faras cathedral. The painting, like the others saved, is a miracle of restoration, having been lifted from mud-brick walls crumbling under the weight of twelve centuries. (*below*) Faras: one of the scores of fresco paintings covering the walls of the cathedral excavated by the Polish Mission, before removal.

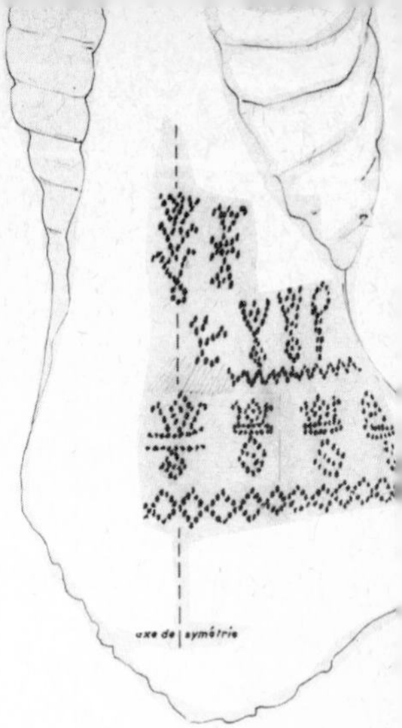

(*above left*): Aksha: elaborate tatooed designs on the torsos of two Meroitic bodies were a unique find by the French Expedition. Skin, muscle and tissue had been preserved. (*above right*) Aksha: explanatory drawing of the designs tattooed on the Meroitic bodies. (*below*) Gebel Adda: body of an X-Group female. After sixteen centuries or so X-Group bodies were often so well preserved that the hot sun quickly drove the excavators to re-inter them.

even Meroitic, they may eventually tell us more about the history of Christianity in Nubia, particularly in its later phases, than all the excavations put together.

With the monuments and remains of Islam in Nubia the Campaign was not concerned. Yet history continues to be written and in the four centuries of life remaining to Nubia many a battle was fought along this stretch of the Nile which for so long had been the cockpit of warring armies. The turn of our present century saw the final battle, against the Dervish followers of el Mahdi, and it was the railway built at that time by the Anglo-Egyptian forces for strategic reasons that gave Nubia its first glimpse of the technology that ultimately would be the agent of its destruction.

CHAPTER XI

Journey to the Heartlands

When I stepped off the train at new Wadi Halfa a sand storm had just blown itself out and the extreme clarity which is the after-effect of such storms was making a mockery of distance. For once I blessed the train for being late; we had dropped a brake rod and because of it the journey from Khartoum had taken 30 hours instead of the usual 23. As I have written elsewhere, exasperation is pointless in Nubia, everything works against the chafings of the impatient stranger. So I settled myself down to wait for something to happen. The Nubians around me, speaking in their usual measured tones, moved slowly or just stood motionless. Even the steam locomotive shunting around the desert seemed to be hissing "take it slowly, take it slowly". Certainly the Nubians had not changed but around me were many signs that new Wadi Halfa had. This was 1969 and since my previous visit three years before the rising reservoir had pushed the shanty town four miles further into the desert. But now it was here to stay and in time the shacks and lean-to's would grow into more substantial buildings. Already there was a railway station built of old sleepers and near it a police station and post office while a group of labourers were leisurely at work on the foundations of the building which would house the newly appointed administrative officer. Evidently Nubian tenacity had won the day and Wadi Halfa in Nubia was about to be re-placed on the map. Of old Wadi Halfa ten miles to the north, no trace remained, the Nile had swallowed it.

The new town is exactly opposite Mirgissa, which was my

first objective and I lost no time in hiring a felucca to take me there. Normally half an hour would have sufficed to cross the four miles of water but today the crossing took no less than six hours; it was my first and only experience of a windless day in Nubia. Like the Ancient Mariner we idled on a painted sea, drinking innumerable cups of coffee brewed with water scooped up from over the side. Ample time was given me to identify familiar landmarks but it was by no means easy. Buhen fort with its memories of Emery, now dead alas, had vanished, and engulfed too was the village of Abd-el-Qadr with its ruined church and the Hill of Sheikh Suleiman; but the shock came when I grasped that the knoll past which we were drifting was nothing less than the summit of the Rock of Abusir, the headland which once had reared its massive bulk above the entrance to the Second Cataract. That enchanting landscape of rocks and islands had gone, transformed into an unbroken expanse of water. Only the walls of Mirgissa fortress remained above the surface. The steep climb that had always left me breathless was no longer necessary and I stepped straight off the boat into what had been the Upper Fort. The vast sandy interior had been cleared since my previous visit and lay revealed as a veritable city. I wandered along street after street, each with its stone drainage system, and in and out of buildings many of them 3 metres high, until in the north-east corner I came to two rows of buttressed battlements. They were all of 5 metres high and many a time I had walked along their tops when they were level with the surrounding sand. The house where the French Mission had lived was scattered with the litter of an abandoned excavation, in sad contrast to the neat and orderly scene of former years, while outside lay dozens of pottery vessels brought there from the graves of the western cemetery and now left for sand and reservoir to bury. For three hours I wallowed in nostalgic memories of this, to me at least, the most moving of all Nubia's lost monuments. My last sight of Mirgissa as the wind filled the sail was a silhouette of broken towers black against a fiery sunset.

The Sudan Commissioner for Archaeology had very kindly placed at my disposal a driver and Land Rover to take me along the Nile from Wadi Halfa to the Fourth Cataract, a distance of 500 miles. The driver arrived next morning and within an hour we were off on the track which would lead me to the headquarters of the UNESCO team somewhere in the Belly of Stone. However, on the way I decided to make a detour for a last glimpse of Semna. The Belly of Stone is a lifeless wilderness so I was puzzled by a pillar of black smoke rising among the hills. Ten minutes later we came abreast of a broken-down truck and sitting in its shade were six Nubians cooking a meal over a burning rubber tyre which filled the valley with its stench; for two days and nights they had been waiting patiently for someone to rescue them and were not in the least worried by their predicament. For the next 15 miles we ground up a valley over sand and rock until cresting a rise, there below was the Nile. Broadened to the dimensions of a small lake it was of deep blue and garlanded with the green of plantations and palm groves, and on the far shore waves of golden dunes undulated to the horizon. After the Belly of Stone it was a revelation. With the raising of the water level the topography of Semna had of course changed but the change had enhanced its beauty. The lake was now dotted with palm-clad islands which once had been plantations; the gap through which the Nile had thrust its tumultous way was no more to be seen, while Kumma fort had again become an island. Standing on the hill over-looking that satisfying vista, it came to me that I was seeing Semna as a soldier of 4000 years ago must have seen it when the Pharaoh Senusret or one of his successors of the Twelfth Dynasty blocked the gap through which the river flowed and created a lake in extent much the same as today, with wavelets lapping the water-gate of the Semna South fortress.

Half an hour or so after leaving Semna we regained the bone-shaking track that follows the general line of the river to Dongola, about two hundred miles upstream; the group of Nubians still squatting by their smoking tyre grinned and waved as we passed. The Dongola track is cut at intervals by broad wadis which thread between granite outcrops overlaid with banks of sand to terminate at the Nile. Where wadis and river met were deposits of alluvium that supported hamlets and which usually contained ancient remains. Because so difficult of access these sites were probably the least visited by strangers of any along the entire length of the Nile. To reach them one had to zig-zag painfully back and forth across the 15 miles between river and Dongola track. One of these wadis led to the gold installations of Duweishat that I had explored three years before and on impulse I decided to follow it. The setting of Duweishat is theatrical; the spurs of the Belly of Stone terminate abruptly several hundred feet or so above the river which cascades violently over platforms of rock far below the track.

The processing plant, now partly under water, descended to the river in a series of steps. The ore crushing machines had been removed but the concrete beds remained to show where the machinery had stood. Here the quartz was crushed to a fine powder which was passed across sloping surfaces for washing and treating with mercury. Outside the plant an immense dump of quartz dust known as 'tailings' sparkled in the sunlight and this I had been told still contained gold amounting to decimal two per cent of its volume, which could be recovered by modern chemical methods of extraction. There before me on the bank of the Nile lay a comfortable fortune in gold but one that could never be realized. On a platform of rock above and behind the processing plant stood the deserted offices of the mining company, depressingly ugly buildings constructed of the greyish-brown local stone. Inside, scattered around the floors were dozens of papers, mostly pay sheets of the Nubians who had worked in the mine during the twelve years or so of its existence. One, I noticed, was dated 1957 and another 1960. Outside, the driver was picking over the debris that surrounded the buildings, bits of broken machinery, wheels and shafts, disembowelled engines—all the detritus of a recently deserted factory. The Belly of Stone is sombre enough but this abandoned industry with its heaps of rusting junk and empty buildings added a sinister touch which became more marked as we followed the road—the only metalled road in the whole of Nubia—to the mines back in the hills. Here the melancholy scene was repeated with boiler and engine houses containing expensive machinery too bulky to remove and ropeways leading up into the hills, buckets still suspended from them. I explored some of the many galleries both modern and ancient and in the latter noted how the mother rock was blackened by the heat of the fires used to crack and detach the quartz. One hill I walked across resembled an immense gruyere cheese; the Egyptians had driven shafts down from the surface wherever there were quartz outcrops, and these ran one into another following all the haphazard twists of the quartz veins so that the interior of the hill was a honeycomb of passages supported only by twisted pillars of friable rock. Seldom have I seen anything so dangerous, yet thirty odd centuries ago men had been forced to work in those galleries. Only the Nubian driver who had been happily loading the Land Rover with odds and ends of machinery, was sorry to leave Duweishat. Something like a million pounds had gone into this enterprise, the only profitable mine in the whole of the Sudan; the mine is well above the level of the reservoir and is far from worked out. Why then was it abandoned? Duweishat is an awful place, yet gold is gold and I am pretty sure that before very long the buckets will again rattle along the ropeways and the galleries echo to the scream of drills and the shouts of men.

Twenty miles on, the Dongola track turned west towards the river and when we reached it there below lay a relic of the Dervish Campaign. Sticking out of a sand dune were the rusty ribs of a gunboat. Some 60 feet of the starboard side was exposed with much of the iron plating still in place. The prow was wedged among huge black granite boulders, evidently the rocks on which the ship had foundered. One of the paddle wheels projected from the beach and nearby the boiler with its tubes exposed had an acacia tree growing up through the furnace box. The vessel lay in a stretch of the Nile as picturesque as anything the Cataract could show but I doubt whether the scene would have had much appeal to the soldiers and sailors aboard when the current seized their craft and flung it against the granite. She was named *Giza* and was one of a flotilla of gunboats pre-fabricated in England and put together at Wadi Halfa. They were intended to support the Anglo-Egyptian army advancing along the Nile bank and the role they played at the Battle of Ondurman, which saw the final defeat of the Dervishes, gave to the Campaign the name by which it is usually known: The River War. However,

Omdurman was 600 miles to the south and the boats had to be navigated safely through the perilous rapids of the Belly of Stone. The first of them the *Metemma* needed no less than 2000 men to drag her to smooth water by muscle power alone, an exercise of the kind all too familiar to the ancient forebears of the Egyptians present. One, the *Giza*, failed to get through and there at Tangour she lies, invisible by now at the bottom of the swollen Nile.

Fifteen miles beyond the wrecked gunboat the hills of the Belly of Stone fell back to disclose the broad alluvial plain of Akasha and my eye was caught by a cloud of dust hanging over an islet in the river; basket-laden figures were toiling up and down its flanks. Here at last was the UNESCO team engaged on the last leg of the Archaeological Survey of the Sudan Antiquities Service.

Anthony Mills, with James Knudstad and Lars Gezelius as assistants, were encamped in a Nubian house of the deserted village of Ukma. The knotty problem of catering was in the capable hands of Lesley Mills who, like all wives of field archaeologists, also washed and sorted the basketloads of potsherds brought in daily from the surrounding digs while keeping a watchful eye on her two small children forever rolling in the dirt. The Mills' children like those of Bill and Nettie Adams had spent most of their young lives in Nubia, having been practically born there and I have yet to see bonnier youngsters, despite the mud-dust, the heat and the flies, the spartan food and the Nile drinking water. The welcome I was given was enthusiastic, partly due I suspected, to the supply of fresh provisions I had brought for them from Khartoum. With them I spent ten enjoyable days examining surrounding sites and accompanying them to their various digs, well-wrapped against the sand hurled around by a chilling wind. Knudstad was working on the clearance of a group of Christian dwellings on the island I had seen on arrival; downstream Gezelius was tracing the denuded foundations of a Christian fort while Mills himself was among the sand dunes on the opposite bank testing the large Kerma cemetery already described. The Mission was now on the last leg of the Survey with only 12 miles of river remaining to be examined—between Ukma and Dal. The mass of data collected by the Survey is formidable but the results will not be assessed until the material can be sorted, coordinated and above all, written up and published in report form, a task for which the Sudan Antiquities Service is responsible. Only then will the results of ten years of archaeological exploration become available for Nubian scholarship.

Friday in Nubia is a day of rest and I spent the morning helping Knudstad rig a contraption consisting of a petrol tin fitted with a tap and suspended over a palm beam wedged in the mud wall, the theory being that you stood underneath the tin and turned on the tap which caused a trickle of water to descend on your spine. I could think of nothing more repellent—the night temperature at the time was falling to 9 degrees centigrade, the lowest ever recorded in Nubia. In the afternoon we paid a visit to Akasha village about five miles upstream. It was a largish place and was for a time Kitchener's headquarters during the River War. It even had a rest-house with the luxury of a cement floor and the only telephone in 200 miles. I had stayed in it three years before and was so fascinated by the antique telephone instrument that it was all I could do to resist winding the handle and asking the operator to put me through to Paris. It was a single-line 'phone which gives one an idea of its antiquity; the "return" line was the earth itself and I was amused to see how each morning as the sun rose the *ghaffir* of the rest-house solemnly poured a tin of water into the bone-dry sand where the return wire was buried.

Knudstad and I clambered up to the Kitchener fort which overlooked the village and afforded magnificent views of the river and the mountains bordering it. Several miles away were two watch towers and down in the plain a slender stone pyramid about ten feet high inscribed, as I knew, to the memory of the British officers and men who died in the Dervish Campaign. We could trace a spur of the railway embankment leading to a huddle of mud-brick, all that remained of a station, and behind it a row of ruined buildings so regimented in design that they could only have been military barracks. Standing there on the ridge we found it hard to accept that the broad plain below with its many buildings and relics of the past would progressively be transformed into a lake as the Nile rose ever higher in its bed. Knudstad and I were still pre-occupied with the River War when we got back to Ukma in time for the BBC's evening news bulletin. It announced the death of the last survivor of the 21st Lancers who had fought under Kitchener at Omdurman, the battle in which the young Winston Churchill so nearly lost his life.

An amusing example of the pitfalls that await the unwary archaeologist was provided in the Akasha plain where an area of several square miles was dotted with rectangular enclosures laid out on the desert surface; they were obviously graves but when dug invariably contained nothing. Since there were many they presented an archaeological puzzle and one could have predicted the emergence of learned speculations based on the origin of this unaccountable Akasha culture had not several elderly Nubians still living in Akasha been able to recall the curious pastime of a fellow villager who spent his lifetime laying out those pseudo-graves—more than 400 of them.

In Akasha itself was the headquarters of the Joint Expedition of the University of Geneva and the Blackmer Foundation. They were the last group of excavators to work in the threatened area of Sudanese Nubia and when I visited them they numbered five archaeologists. The leader of the expedition was absent, searching for a stretch of desert suitable for an aeroplane to land on. In that boulder-strewn plain I should have thought it impossible but evidently he succeeded because on the following day we heard the unaccustomed beat of an aero engine bringing Mr Blackmer himself on a brief tour of inspection. Before leaving Akasha I spent an enjoyable day with Bill Adams at Kulb near Dal, where on behalf of the University of Kentucky he was excavating a Late Christian site. As usual he was surrounded by a small mountain of sherds and it was there that he gave me the details of his work at Kulb which have been described in the previous chapter.

With reluctance I said goodbye to my UNESCO friends and an hour later was passing the Dal Cataract. From now on the Campaign was quite literally behind me and I was about to move into the heartlands of the Kerma and Napatan cultures. I was now entering a stretch of the Nile that has never been surveyed archaeologically; only large monuments above ground, mostly temples, have received the attention of excavators, in most cases many years ago. Baikie in his book *Egyptian Antiquities of the Nile Valley* published in 1932 remarks "... the antiquities here are almost inaccessible to the tourist and can only be reached by caravan and boat, and at considerable toil and expense". It is an observation that applied equally in 1969 except that the Land Rover has largely supplanted the camel caravan. Even so the journey of 500 miles took 10 days to cover. The region is rarely visited by Europeans and without Arabic a traveller would have difficulty in making his needs known. Not even my driver, himself a Nubian, knew English but it is remarkable what one's mind can do when driven, and within a day or so long forgotten Arabic phrases were dredged to the surface to my great relief. This region is full of reminders of the River War with its memories of General Gordon, of the Mahdi and of Kitchener; crumbling forts and barracks are spread along the embankment of the old railway pushed through to Dongola by Kitchener's engineers ahead of the advancing troops, and everywhere are the 'beehive' tombs of Dervish soldiers and the stone pyramid memorials of their Anglo-Egyptian adversaries. I was to pass through villages that were household words in Europe at the end of the nineteenth century but which seem now to belong to a past as remote as that of the surrounding antiquities. One such is Firka just south of the Dal Cataract where a famous battle was fought, and it was at Firka that L. P. Kirwan excavated an extensive X-Group cemetery; I could see the giant tumuli through the window of the house where I sat drinking coffee with the village *Omdeh* and listening to his schoolboy grandson's detailed account of a battle fought 60 years before he was born. The boy was a pupil at one of the large boarding schools established by the Sudan government for the education of children in the more remote corners of its sprawling territory. At Firka too, is a Dervish fort, the first I had come across. It was a mud brick affair built to follow the contours of a rocky massif and it was most picturesquely situated in a palm grove bordering the Nile. Its several towers were linked by undulating walls enclosing rooms built in a haphazard fashion at various levels, all very different from the stern, regular outlines of its Anglo-Egyptian equivalents. Clustered round the foot of the citadel were the houses of a deserted village where the Dervish soldiers and their families had lived. It was a pattern I was to see repeated many times over the next 10 days.

At the Dal Cataract the turbulent Nile of the Belly of Stone was transformed into a well-ordered river, rippling across concealed rocks through a landscape in marked contrast to the harsh beauty of the Second Cataract. Networks of irrigation channels fed by pumping engines carried the cultivation well back from the river; the palm groves were denser and the villages larger and less far apart. Across the Nile on the west bank, the granite outcrops had given place to desert that stretched in unbroken aridity right across Africa for 2000 miles to the Atlantic shore. The climate, too, had changed so that no longer were blankets needed at night, and this only a hundred miles from Semna with its evening temperatures of only 9 degrees centigrade. By a quirk of the weather the Second Cataract, half-way between Luxor and Dongola, both with winter temperatures in the 80s, habitually experienced winters cold enough for heavy pullovers by day and three blankets at night. There were changes too in village architecture. The dwellings, while remaining Lower Nubian in size and general outline, now displayed windows and doors with curved architraves; exterior decoration was quite different and exterior pillars such as one never saw in Lower Nubia were common.

Some miles beyond Firka with not a village in sight the track skirted a solitary cube of mud-brick; above the door in English was a sign "Post Office" and alongside it a bright red pillar box. Overhead passed the famous single-line telephone wire but I noticed it ignored the post office below. The pharaonic site of Amara came into view overlooking the west bank of the river. Partly excavated by Fairman in the late 1930s and 1940s it consisted of a temple put up originally by that most prolific of builders Rameses II and added to by several of his successors. Found in the temple was a list of the southern peoples conquered by the Egyptians and it contained nearly a hundred names. Here, too, were signs of a fortress of the period, and evidence of the town site associated with the temple. From where I stood on the east bank that collection of buildings half buried in sand was tantalizing indeed but, alas, a quarter of a mile of water whipped up by a rising sandstorm lay between us making a crossing of the river impossible. This same storm a few miles on produced another of the riddles that in Nubia I had long since come to regard as commonplace. The Land Rover had plunged into a morass of powdered sand at the bottom of a wadi when through the swirling dust of the storm I noticed something plastered against a thorn bush by the wind. As we passed within a few feet of it I saw to my astonishment a torn sheet of yellowing newspaper and blazoned across it in huge letters was a headline: ". . . UTLAND". I shouted to the driver to stop but he refused. It was as much as he could do to keep us moving in the powdery sand so I shall never know how a fragment of an English newspaper of fifty-odd years ago announcing the naval battle of Jutland–for that I am convinced is what it was–came to be blowing around the Nubian desert.

The river divides 35 miles upstream of Dal to form the large island of Sai which has been referred to many times in earlier chapters. Sai is about fifteen miles long and three miles across and, being extremely fertile, it supports a large population and always has done as the many ancient sites on it testify. For this reason it rates a motorised ferry, the most northerly in the Sudan, and between dawn and sunset it chugs back and forth across the Nile carrying an unending procession of carts, camels, donkeys and decrepit motor buses. Joining the mêlée of animals, carts and villagers we managed to cross without damage and I was able to examine the nearest of the antiquities, most of them unexcavated sites–several large cemeteries of various periods, a pharaonic temple partly cleared and extensive early Christian and Dervish remains. The French Mission had departed at the end of the season but I took a brief look at the area inside a large enclosure which Vercoutter had started to excavate.

We were approaching the east bank on our return crossing when I noticed a largish sailing vessel constructed, as were the Second Cataract boats, in the ancient Egyptian manner but this one had a curious erection amidships resembling a huge inverted tea chest; in it was a door giving on to a platform and on the platform an elderly Nubian was pedalling away at an antiquated sewing machine. My driver explained that he was a floating tailor who sailed up and down the Nile making and repairing garments as he went. Driving away from the ferry we passed within a few feet of four vultures feeding off the carcass of a goat. They barely bothered to move as we passed, merely spreading their enormous wings and staring with those horrible hooded eyes before returning to their interrupted meal. The sun had now set and a line of date palms bordering the river was silhouetted against the afterglow. It was a classic picture reproduced in countless coloured postcards and with those thoughts in mind I was startled to see that all the palms appeared to be on fire, each with a plume of smoke above its crown twisting and spiralling in the wind. The driver explained. The "smoke" consisted of midges which appear by the million with the onset of the hot season and make life miserable for men and animals alike for several weeks. Next morning I had my first encounter with these fiendish insects. Smaller than a pin head they attack in clouds and within seconds one's hair, nostrils and ears are so stuffed with them as to make breathing difficult. The Nubians, I noticed, wore veils of fine muslin completely covering head and shoulders and in my misery I hastened to follow their example. Half the villagers accompanied me to the local tailor and, squatting in a circle, listened attentively while the serious business of bargaining went on. Having come to an arrangement satisfactory to all parties the tailor pointed to his one eye. Could I advise him on how to go about getting another eye, and not one of those plastic affairs? He had heard that in Europe they made eyes that would really work. We all discussed the matter at length over many cups of syrupy tea until the work was done, after which with much handshaking and many expressions of goodwill in the Nubian manner, I handed over the two shillings and drove away suitably hooded and rather fancying myself as a veiled Touareg.

I camped that night in a deserted hut alongside the track but not to sleep for Nubia was again in a wild mood, but at dawn all trace of sand had gone and the air was crystal clear. I stared across the Nile and there like a mirage were the columns of a great temple glowing in the first rays of the rising sun. By chance I had camped opposite Solb which I had intended to ignore, yet so captivated was I by the beauty of the distant temple that I decided on impulse to change my plans and make a breakfast call on the Schiff-Giorgini Expedition. An hour later I was walking across the sand towards the Expedition's extremely comfortable and well-ordered quarters. Waiting to greet me was a lean-faced Frenchman of film star appearance. He expressed no surprise at the arrival of a, to him, complete stranger turning up from nowhere at seven o'clock in the morning. He introduced himself as having recently arrived to join the small team of archaeologists and would I care for a hole or two of golf before breakfast? The Sudan and its odd happenings have long since ceased to startle me, but this casual invitation made me doubt my senses. In that trackless desert it was tantamount to being invited in Piccadilly Circus to take a ride up Regent Street on a camel. He produced a clutch of balls and some clubs and within minutes we were driving off on the first hole of a three hole course he had laid out on the sand. As in a dream I followed him round; he confessed later to being a regular player at St Andrews. The incident was in keeping with the air of fantasy which seems to pervade Solb, where always they have the most astonishing discoveries to show one, discoveries which sometimes seem to have no logical explanation. On my previous visit Mr Robichon, the senior archaeologist, explained how their excavations in the temple area had revealed a series of constructions and deliberate destructions, all obviously part of an ordered development covering a span of thirty years—the duration of Amenhotep IIIs reign—and culminating in the great temple of classical design that stands there today. To an Egyptian priest of 34 centuries ago the development plan was doubtless of profound religious significance but to the twentieth-century mind it is utterly incomprehensible. What, I wondered, would Robichon produce this time? Signora Giorgini was her usual charming and chic self and after a breakfast of bacon and eggs and honey and white bread—an unheard of luxury in

Nubia—Robichon carried me off to inspect his latest discoveries. He did not disappoint me. Bordering the Nile at Solb is a massive structure of solid masonry and some two hundred yards upstream of it is what appears to be a stone breakwater; something similar can be seen two hundred yards downstream. These two "breakwaters" become visible only when the Nile is at its lowest ebb. Soundings made by Robichon showed that they were indeed breakwaters that extended almost to the opposite bank, at this point rather more than a quarter of a mile away. Beyond the bank is what I had assumed to be a branch of the Nile when I crossed it, dry now but doubtless transformed into a swiftly running river with the arrival of the annual flood from the highlands of Ethiopia. Robichon had satisfied himself that this channel was in fact an artificial canal, a hundred yards in width and three quarters of a mile long, and that it was dug to carry the main body of the Nile's flow while the engineers worked in the river bed to construct the two breakwaters (or barrages) and the massive stone quay between them: this quay turned out on excavation to be a water gate. Here at Solb was another example of Egyptian skill in water control similar in design to the barrages constructed by the Middle Kingdom military engineers in the Second Cataract some five centuries earlier. Between water gate and temple the builders excavated a basin no less than four hundred yards across and the purpose of the water gate was to introduce the Nile into this basin at times of flood. When the deposit of silt in the basin reached a certain depth the water gate was blocked permanently. When dry the entire surface of the basin was covered with a layer of broken pots amounting to hundreds of tons. This extraordinary sequence of events was clearly to be seen in the stratification. The basin now became, according to Robichon, a compound in which lions were kept—the lion was always associated with the person of the Pharaoh in tomb decorations—and out in the rocky desert to the west he had located several excavations which could easily have been traps for large animals, lions for instance. Furthermore, in the same area he showed me a rectangular enclosure about 2 kilometres long and 500 metres wide; posts had been driven into the hard gravel at regular intervals—the desiccated wood was still at the bottom of the holes—and seem to have been used to support fencing. What could have been inside? Other animals perhaps, kept in captivity for Amenhotep the Magnificent to hunt at his pleasure. We followed an ancient causeway running north from Solb for several miles to Sedenga where there is a small ruinous temple built by Amenhotep in honour of his beloved Queen Tiy, the mother of the ill-starred Akhenaton. It had been partly restored by members of the Expedition. Round about was the large Meroitic cemetary of pyramid tombs described in an earlier chapter, among them a sepulchre inscribed with the name of Taharqa. Back at the camp, Robichon took me into his workshop and removed from a glass jar an object of indeterminate shape and colour about the size of a tennis ball. It was one of several he had unearthed inside the "lion compound" fronting the temple and he believed them to be lion droppings; the stratification made them contemporary with the construction of the great temple. Would I take one to Khartoum and ask the zoologist in the university there to compare it with droppings of live lions in the zoo? So I said goodbye to those delightful people and set off across the Nile clutching in one hand a cigar pressed on me at the last moment and in the other an Eighteenth Dynasty lion *crotte*. Solb had indeed come up to expectations. Later, when in Khartoum the zoologist obliged, Robichon's "lion compound" hypothesis was vindicated.

After leaving Solb we entered as nasty a stretch of landscape as had ever come my way, worse even than the hinterland of the Belly of Stone. The track deteriorated till we were down to three miles an hour jarring over rocks in bottom gear, and seven interminable hours were needed to cover the 40 miles between Solb and Delgo where I intended to pass the night. Delgo is the administrative centre of a district and boasts an Executive Officer who looks after the affairs of 6000 farmers. He turned out to be one of the tallest Sudanese I have ever seen; he had been warned of my coming through the bush-telegraph and had prepared an immense and terrifyingly oily meal as a result of which I suffered sorely for the three following days. Next morning, having passed a somewhat disturbed night in an abandoned police station I

(*above left*) Ballana: selection of painted pottery from a Meroitic cemetery excavated by the Oriental Institute of Chicago Expedition. (*above right*) Belly of Stone: section of the railway built by Kitchener's engineers from Wadi Halfa to Dongola during the Anglo-Egyptian war against the dervishes. (*below*) Kulubnarti: the 'castle' in the townsite near the Dal Cataract excavated by Professor W. Adams. Dating from around the fifteenth century AD, Kulubnarti was probably the last stronghold of Christianity in Nubia.

(*above*) Kuru: interior of Piankhy's modest tomb, *c*. 660 BC. Greatest of the Napatan line, this African king conquered Egypt itself and there sat on the throne of the Pharaohs to found the Twenty-fifth Dynasty. (*below*) Solb: the Sudan's finest temple, built by the Pharaoh Amenhotep III of the Eighteenth Dynasty. Excavating it over many years, the Schiff-Giorgini Expedition has made remarkable discoveries.

was walking down through the date palms to pick up the *felucca* which was to take me across the river to the next on my list of antiquities, when my eye was caught by what appeared to be the prow of a metal boat half hidden among the bushes. I found three boats painted black and grey, solid constructions of riveted plates about twenty feet long, far too heavy and cumbersome for the Nubians to handle. Then it came to me that the boats were relics of the River War. In such good shape were those cutters that they might have come from the shipyard that very month, yet they had been lying undisturbed among the date palms for seventy years.

Many of Delgo's farmers live on the opposite bank where there is a large village surrounded by many acres of intensive cultivation watered by pumping engines. Dominating this pastoral scene is a great mound covered in fortifications from summit to base. Examination of the mound showed that no attempt at clearance had ever been made and that among the many buildings at least three occupations were represented: Early Christian, Islamic and Anglo-Egyptian; I also detected signs that led me to speculate that possibly a Meroitic or even pharaonic fortress once stood guard over the river at this point. From the top of the mound the temple I had come to visit was clearly visible. All that remains of it is a small shrine erected by the Pharaoh Akhenaten. It is one of several "Gem-Aten" temples built during his reign and it is the only one which has survived. The architecture was undistinguished if the three squat columns still standing are any guide and unworthy of that great blossoming of Egyptian art known as the Amarna Age. Still, any monument associated with Akhenaten has a special interest and here the massive substructure on which the Aten shrine stands was built by Akhenaten while he was still Amenhotep IV, that is to say before he embraced the new faith of Aten and changed his name accordingly. In addition to the temples—it appears that there were three at one time—there was a block of temple store rooms and a township of small houses and narrow streets, the whole being enclosed by buttressed walls each pierced by a gateway faced with stone; the area thus enclosed measures 270 metres by 200. All in all, this remotely placed temple was well worth the trouble taken in reaching it.

Assuredly Upper Nubia enjoyed considerable prosperity in New Kingdom times as is clearly demonstrated by the number of temples built between Faras and Gebel Barkal, ten in all.

Only 55 miles lay between me and the site I had waited many years to see—Kerma—but on the way I paused at the Tombos granite quarries to examine the celebrated inscription. Here at the head of the Third Cataract Thutmose I (*c.*1540 BC) announced that he had subdued troublesome Nubia as far as this point which henceforward would be the southern limit of his Empire. To safeguard this new frontier a fortress was built with the grandiloquent name of "None Faces Him [Thutmose I] Among-the-Nine-Bows-Together"; the fortress has not been found. The Tombos inscription is also famous for the curious description of the Euphrates river: "that inverted water which goes down-stream in going up-stream". To Thutmose and his army accustomed to the flow of their own Nile, the Euphrates flowing from north to south was a reversal of the natural order of things. It also proves that Thutmose I did not penetrate any further south since had he reached the Fourth Cataract he would have seen the Nile behaving in the same topsy-turvy manner, as I shall describe later in the chapter. Lying among the hewn stones of the quarry was an unfinished statue, more than life size and obviously representing an Egyptian Pharaoh; in the absence of an inscription it was impossible to identify it.

Kerma when I reached it turned out to be a fair-sized town with a large central square in which was a market and a scattering of battered motor-buses serving the many villages of Dongola Reach. I passed the night in a comfortable Government Rest House where I revelled in the luxury of my first bath in a week and next morning set out for the scene of Reisner's remarkable discoveries of fifty years before. What Reisner's published reports had not prepared me for was the size of the site which must cover several square miles. I was pleased to note that the whole area had been enclosed within a barbed-wire fence to discourage illicit diggers. For me Kerma was both evocative and tantalizing. Those two baffling constructions of solid mud brick, the Defufas, dominate the surrounding desert and on all sides are the mounds and depressions of an immense cemetery scattered with fragments of the most delicate and attractive pottery ever made along the Nile Valley. I located Reisner's "store-rooms", choked now with sand, and the gigantic funerary mounds of the Egyptian "Governors" where 300 men, women and children were buried alive to accompany the deceased to the Underworld. The sand had flowed over them yet I was able to trace the interior plan of these enigmatic tombs just as Reisner described them. I walked across denuded walls of buildings and brick platforms that no spade had ever touched, and as far as the eye could see were numberless graves apparently undisturbed. Here beneath my feet lay the lost pages of the history of the first African culture to emerge from the shadows, around 4000 years ago. To dig Kerma thoroughly is a task that will fill many years and cost a great deal of money, yet one day it must be done.

South of Kerma the character of the houses and villages changes rapidly and no longer is Nubian spoken. We had now moved out of Nubia into that stretch of the Nile known as Dongola Reach and soon were crossing a dried-up branch of the river onto the island of Argo. Like Sai it is intensely cultivated and supports a large population. Its interest lies in a Napatan temple which I knew to be under excavation by the University of Geneva. Unfortunately they had closed the dig only two days before. The most prominent features of the site are two colossal figures–lying prone; hewn in granite, they are of the finest Egyptian workmanship and presumably represent Napatan kings–I say presumably because I could find no trace of a cartouche on either of them. Back on the mainland we were soon bowling across a hard sandy plain unmarked by tracks of any kind until, topping a slight rise, there below were the foundations of a large Pharaonic temple buried in sand. Statues and Kerma pottery found here at Kawa in 1949 when Macadam excavated the site, show that the temple's original foundation may be as far back as the Middle Kingdom and Kerma. It seems to have been rebuilt during the New Kingdom by Amenhotep the Magnificent or his son Akhenaten, while another interesting discovery was a small temple erected by Tutankhamun. Taharqa built a temple here and Kawa retained its importance as a religious centre for both Napatan and Meroitic kings over the next thousand years. Kawa had a long and eventful history yet today it has merged into the desert with nothing to indicate the splendour of its past.

Dongola, when we reached it, turned out to be a bigger edition of Kerma with the same battered trucks, and tiny shops selling everything from bolts of cloth to tins of custard powder, and a large camel market. The Kerma resthouse had been pleasant enough but Dongola's was a haven of luxury boasting easy chairs with cretonne covers, taps that actually produced water and to cap everything, a carpet. Old Dongola, my next objective, was I assumed somewhere in the vicinity of new Dongola but next morning when we set off I learned that it was 40 miles away and on the other side of the Nile, so it was fully six hours before we entered the former capital of the medieval Christian Kingdom of Makuria. During the time of the Mahdieh the city was re-occupied by the Dervishes and many of their beehive tombs stand on the surrounding slopes. It was here that the Dongola branch of Kitchener's railway terminated and here, too, the Dervish army suffered a crushing defeat. The ruined buildings cover many acres and some still stand as high as the second storey, but the desert has taken over and sand flowing in through windows and doorways now fills most of the dwellings. The city is overlooked by a large masonry structure heavily fortified, which has the appearance of a citadel but is in fact a church, used later as a mosque. Abandoned cities have an irresistible attraction for me and I spent an agreeable afternoon wandering alone in that solitary place. I found, too, what I had come to see. When the Poles closed down their excavations at Faras, they moved south to Old Dongola to start on the clearance of a church of the early Christian period. It was lying in a hollow, only partly cleared, but already they had exposed 30 granite columns still upright, and a stone building of impressive size was beginning to emerge from the sand. The Poles had already left at the end of the season but I saw enough to hope that their good fortune in finding the Faras Cathedral and its frescoes will be repeated at Old Dongola.

Approaching the ferry which, hopefully, would carry us

back across the Nile I noticed with a shock three men wearing European dress, trousers that is—the first I had seen since leaving Mills and Kudstad at Akasha. There was a policeman in a smart khaki uniform so heavily starched that it crackled as he moved and an even more startling sight was an ordinary saloon car. Obviously I was re-entering 'civilisation!' From Dongola to the Fourth Cataract and Gebel Barkal is a journey of two days as the Land Rover rattles, and most of it is across a sandy plain littered with immense black boulders. Occasionally a village came in sight and one of these was notable for the fresh coat of light grey paint that covered every house. Houses along the river are either rendered with brown mud plaster or whitewashed; evidently a local entrepreneur had picked up a cheap consignment of grey paint. Even more remarkable was the outline of a crocodile moulded in plaster alongside the front door of every single house.

Beyond Debba, a scruffy little town where I spent the night in a rest house that faithfully reflected the status of the community, the track follows a long stretch of the river which is filled with relics of the 1885 Campaign. This was the column which made the unsuccessful attempt to relieve General Gordon besieged in Khartoum. Memorials and bivouacs, Dervish tombs and forts followed one another mile after mile, until in front of the radiator appeared the white buildings of a large town and on the bank opposite, a precipitous mass of rock standing in isolation. The end of my trek was in sight for this was Gebel Barkal, the Holy Mount of Amun; this was the land which nurtured the genius that produced the most enduring of all African civilisations, the Kingdom of Kush, and to see it at last was for me the realisation of an ambition of thirty years' standing.

Half an hour later we were in Merowe—not to be confused with ancient Meroë near the Sixth Cataract—quite the most attractive town I had yet encountered. Pleasant houses with deep balconies fronted streets lined with flowering trees and everywhere was the purple and scarlet of bougainvillia in full bloom. Equally attractive was the rest-house standing in a garden facing the Nile. Merowe is the administrative town of a province wherein live 70,000 people, all agriculturalists.

Even so, the town has no electric light supply and when I called in at the government offices "to make my number" I was fascinated to see suspended from the ceiling a genuine punka, the first I had ever come across. This large flap of wood and matting was swung back and forth to disturb the air in hot weather by an unfortunate menial pulling on a rope. The rope, I was relieved to note, was no longer in evidence.

Since the Nuri pyramid field is on the Merowe side of the river I decided to go there first. These are true pyramids although considerably smaller than their much older Egyptian counterparts. The largest, Taharqa's, is only 170 feet square at the base. Surrounding it are 14 largish pyramids and 5 smaller ones. None of the pyramid chapels has survived. The pyramids were robbed in antiquity but in all of them Reisner found many objects overlooked by the plunderers; Taharqa's pyramid, for example, yielded more than a thousand *ushabti* figures, two canopic jars and several gold ornaments. There is something rather endearing about these slender little pyramids; the effect is that of rows of church spires removed from their towers and left standing on the ground. In the afternoon we drove for miles into a rock-strewn desert as desolate as anything on earth until, suddenly, we plunged into a hollow carpeted with greenery. It was a perfect example of a desert oasis—a grove of tiny fields and date palms encircling a well filled with clear water. Alongside the well a splendid specimen of a *saqia* wheel showed how water was lifted into the network of irrigation channels leading to the fields beyond. Only three human figures were visible and one of them, a very old man, was sitting motionless staring into the eye of the evening sun. I wondered how he could do this until drawing closer I realised he was blind. Nearby, two little girls were twisting rope from palm fibre; one, aged 15 possibly, carried a baby on her arm, the other, no older than 12, was pregnant.

On a knoll about two hundred yards off stood a collection of stone ruins. It was the Gazali Monastery and it dated to what Bill Adams terms the Classical Christian Period. Although the roofs had long since vanished, the walls and architraves, columns and pavements were well preserved.

Seeking relief from the gusty wind I took shelter in the monastery privy, an elaborate affair consisting of a long stone bench with three neatly chamfered holes cut in it and an admirable drainage system, also of stone. The monks of early Christendom loved solitude and here at the Gazali Oasis they had chosen well.

Early next morning I was down at the river bank waiting impatiently for the ferry to Kareima and Gebel Barkal when suddenly it seemed I had taken leave of my senses—the Nile was flowing backwards. Hurriedly I consulted the map and the phenomenon was explained. Here, at the Fourth Cataract the river has made an enormous U-bend and is in effect running back on itself so that for a time the flow is from north to south. It was all very confusing and I now knew just how Thutmose I felt when he first saw the river Euphrates. The temples at Gebel Barkal, ruinous as they are, came up to expectations. Gebel Barkal itself is flat-topped and half a mile in length and in that otherwise featureless expanse of desert it might have fallen from the sky, so much is it an anachronism. Little wonder the Napatans saw it as the Seat of the Gods.

I clambered up a pile of fallen masonry and looked about me with some emotion. At the foot of this mountain deep inside Africa devout worshippers had paid homage to the ancient gods over a span of 15 centuries. Here for a thousand years every Kushite king, first Napatan and then Meroitic, had come to be crowned and sanctified under the blessing of Amun. I was standing outside a rock-cut temple which contained carvings in low relief as fine as any at Abu Simbel; it had been partly destroyed in antiquity and was rebuilt and destroyed again by falls of rock from the cliffs that towered above me to a height of 300 feet, after which the priests must have decided to appease the wrath of Amun by abandoning it. All the temples are below the rock face fronting the Nile and of the four still standing the temple of Amun is by far the most impressive. The Nineteenth Dynasty builders modelled it on Amun's celebrated temple at Karnak and, indeed, in its heyday this great Nubian temple could have yielded little in size and magnificence to its Egyptian counterpart. Inevitably the temple was further embellished by Rameses II and was added to by the great Napatan king,

Piankhy, who doubtless sought the approval of Amun here before setting out to conquer Egypt. Taharqa and many of his successors added their quota of building. The last restoration was made in Roman times after which the old gods were ousted by the new Christian faith and the hallowed courts and shrines were left to the hyenas and jackals.

In exploring the temples I noted with dismay how they were paying the penalty of excavation. They are built of a particularly soft sandstone and when Reisner cleared the site he exposed them to the abrasive desert winds so that fifty years later columns, walls and inscriptions are terribly weathered and, in places, crumbling to powder. I walked towards the river until after a quarter of a mile I turned to look back at the cliff behind the temples. It is so shaped as to suggest four colossal figures fronting an artificial facade and some authorities believe it to be the remains of a rock-cut temple—of even greater size than Abu Simbel. Others maintain that the "temple" is nothing more than a natural rock formation. However, cartouches of Taharqa are claimed to have been seen high up on the cliff on the head of one of the supposed figures. The four colossal statues of Rameses II fronting the Abu Simbel temple are 60 feet high, here at Gebel Barkal the alleged statues would be nearer 100 feet. It is a controversy that can be resolved only by examination of the cliff face and by excavation at its foot.

At the highest point of the knoll was a low heap of rubble scattered with sherds. It suggested nothing more than spoil from a nearby excavation yet this was the Mound of the Ancestor, the tomb of the un-named African who sired the line of kings that ruled Kush for a thousand years. Here at Kuru one can see the development of the simple round tumulus grave of the Ancestor through seven stages of funerary construction culminating in the true pyramid of Piankhy, a style of monument that continued to be used for royal burials until the end of the Meroitic Empire. Here were buried all the Kushite kings who ruled Egypt as the Twenty-fifth Dynasty—Piankhy, Shabaka, Shabataka and the ill-fated Tanutamun who was driven out of Egypt by the Assyrians. The only exception was Taharqa who chose Nuri across the Nile as his last resting place.

How different are these modest structures of the Napatan kings from the grandiose expressions of power manifested in the pyramids and rock-cut sepulchres of Egypt's native rulers! The superstructure of Piankhy's pyramid, like most of the tombs of Kuru, has been denuded almost to ground level but the funerary chamber and ante-room at the bottom of a flight of 30 stone steps are perfectly preserved, with beautifully executed paintings of the pantheon of Egyptian gods glowing with colour. Much as I admire the character of this Napatan king I find it difficult to reconcile the unpretentiousness of this tomb with the conqueror of mighty Egypt. Piankhy had been a great lover of horses and he records on the Gebel Barkal stela that describes the Egyptian Campaign how enraged he was to discover in an Egyptian town under siege by his army that the horses in the governor's stables had been kept short of fodder. So attached were these Twenty-fifth Dynasty sovereigns to their favourite horses that they arranged for the animals to accompany them to Amentet, to the realm of the dead. The horse cemetery at Kuru lies behind the group of queens' tombs and the graves have long since filled with sand, but when Reisner cleared the area he found 16 horse burials, 4 to each of the Twenty-fifth Dynasty kings. They were all buried standing, heads looking south, and were fully equipped with trappings, mostly of gilded silver. One is reminded of the sacrificed horses found by Emery outside the tombs of the X-Group kings at Ballana and Qustol.

Reisner's excavations of fifty years ago at Kuru, at Nuri and at Gebel Barkal, and the conclusions he drew from his finds were, as I have explained elsewhere in this book, outstanding achievements. Yet many questions were left unanswered. Where, for example, is the site of Napata, the capital city of Kush? It was the centre of a great empire for many centuries yet it has never been located. Napata, like Kerma, is one of the most neglected episodes in ancient history and, like Kerma, it cries out for archaeological re-examination, for this is the heartland of the second great civilisation of purely African origin to arise in the Nile Valley.

Back in Merowe I called in at the little museum where

several fragmented statues of Napatan kings found by Reisner at Gebel Barkal had been patiently reassembled and were on display. Most impressive among them is the black granite colossus of the great Taharqa standing all of 12 feet high and of the finest Egyptian workmanship. The smallest among them, and the size is perhaps significant, represents Tanutamun, last king of the Twenty-fifth Dynasty. A surprise was provided by the statue of Atlanersa who ruled in Napata from 658 to 643 BC; it bore a notice to the effect that a companion statue was lying unfurnished in the granite quarries at Tombos where I had seen it several days before. On the outskirts of Merowe I came across a temple built by Taharqa; it had been partly cleared years before and nearby the excavators had found indications which suggested that the site of the town of Napata might not be far away. From the seventh century BC I was brought back to the twentieth century AD by the inscriptions on two small stone pyramids standing alongside the temple. They are memorials and the inscriptions are engraved on marble plaques: "In memory of officers, NCOs and men of the British Army who died in 1885" and "Garrison 1885, detachment of Naval Brigade, detachment of Royal Engineers, troops of the 19th Hussars, 1st Battalion Royal Highlanders, Commandant Col. W. F. Butler, C.B." The second pyramid is a reminder of Britain's long association with the Sudan: "To the memory of General Sir Herbert William Jackson Pasha, MBE, C.B. For forty-eight years he served the Sudan and for over twenty years, from 1902 to 1922 was governor of Dongola Province. He died at Merowe on the 28th January, 1931. Beloved of all." It was in a thoughtful mood that I drove back to the rest-house to pack in readiness for my departure at dawn.

The day before at Kareima I had watched with pleasure one of the fine old Pacific-type locomotives of Sudan Railways, resplendent in royal blue livery, puffing to and fro among the buildings and I had been tempted to take the train back to Khartoum. But a month of unbroken dust and grime was enough and I decided instead to go by air. The Otter aircraft is a trim little machine carrying a dozen or so passengers and a pilot; it was expressly designed for work in the frozen north of Canada which is I suppose as good a reason as any why several of them should be flying around one of the hottest and driest territories on earth. As we circled over the town I looked down on the Holy Mount of Amun with the temples clustered at its foot, all golden in the sunshine of early morning. It was a most satisfying sight and a fitting end to a journey that had lasted ten years and had covered six hundred miles of that most evocative of rivers, the Nile.

CHAPTER XII

Salvage Archaeology

The uniqueness of Nubia lay not only in the profusion of its archaeological sites but in the compression of them into two narrow strips of alluvium bordering a single river. Nowhere else in the world would it have been possible to find remains of half a dozen cultures spanning 5000 years literally within a stone's throw or walking distance of each other. The mass of data extracted from that 300-mile reach of the Nile over 9 years of concentrated excavation would daunt the most avid of historians, and while much of what it reveals is new to us, the findings of the expeditions are likely to be of most value in filling gaps and throwing light into dark corners left by the two earlier salvage campaigns in Lower Nubia. The analysis and publication of so great a quantity of material is a formidable task, and one not made easier by the large number of expeditions involved and the several languages of publication, nevertheless it is possible to publish with despatch, as the pre-historians who worked in Nubia have demonstrated. Other expeditions, notably the French and Scandinavian, are likewise well ahead with publication of their excavations. Early publication is always desirable, although the history of archaeology is lettered with melancholy examples of digs left unpublished and, therefore, lost to scholarship. In salvage archaeology, which by its very nature is likely to involve several excavations simultaneously, early publication becomes essential if the work is to have any meaning.

Most of the material used in this book has been drawn from the preliminary reports of the various expeditions and from information recorded by myself in Nubia during the 9 years of the Campaign. While most of the final reports have yet to appear, enough has already emerged to enable conclusions to be drawn; some are based, admittedly, on reasonable hypotheses rather than firm archaeological evidence, nevertheless it might be useful here to summarise what has been achieved.

For the first time Nubia has revealed the depth of her pre-history and has provided proof positive of the existence of vigorous palaeolithic life on the pre-Nile plateau, and given us new knowledge of the environment that shaped it. Connections have been found, though tenuous, between the Nubian A-group and the culture centred far to the south known as Khartoum Neolithic. The first colonisation of Nubia by Egypt has been shown to have started several centuries earlier than the accepted date, and it seems that the early Egyptian kings by their depredations in Nubia succeeded in disrupting the flowering A-Group culture and driving it from the Valley, at least for a period of time. The C-Group culture in Nubia was known to have preceded that of Kerma but evidence has emerged to show that the Kerma culture persisted in Nubia well beyond the Middle Kingdom Period, into the Seventeenth or even Eighteenth Dynasties. The Twelfth Dynasty forts of the Second Cataract have yielded an imposing corpus of architectural data together with many unique elements associated with the military occupation of Nubia, but the motives attributed to the Egyptians for the introduction into Nubia of such extravagent installations is not entirely convincing. The excavators had hoped with good reason that papyrus despatches of the Middle Kingdom would come to light, and indeed many thousands of the clay sealings that the Egyptians used to secure the papyrus rolls were unearthed, but the actual despatches remained elusive. So the identity of the African enemy so feared by Egypt is still not established although the consensus favours the C-Group. We do know however that the forts served as trading posts in between hostilities and one of them, Mirgissa, has been identified as Egypt's main entrepot in Nubia. There is evidence, too, that during the Middle Kingdom, the Nile was artificially dammed and a system of flood control along the Second Cataract introduced. The C-Group culture has been shown to have lasted longer than was hitherto believed and to have terminated not abruptly but by process of integration with that of Egypt, which by 1600 BC had incorporated Nubia into the Empire. A curious lacuna remains: the Napatan Dynasty of Kush, which originated at Gebel Barkal near the Fourth Cataract and which ruled Egypt for seventy years yet surprisingly left in Nubia neither settlements nor burials. In fact, for the last millennium BC Nubia was an archaeological blank, which can only imply a land empty of people over that span of time. The cause was probably a drastic fall in the level of the Nile's annual flood. Human habitation re-appears in the first Century AD with the Meroites who had at their disposal a new and efficient tool for irrigation: the *saqia*. Their successors, the X-Group culture, were fairly thin on the ground along the hundred miles between the Dal Cataract and the Egyptian frontier, the X-Group "explosions" being located across the Egyptian border at Ballana and Qustol and at Kasr Ibrim, and at Firka in the Sudan, a few miles south of the Dal Cataract. The true explosion of population was in the Christian Period, as was overwhelmingly demonstrated by the scores of churches, settlements and cemeteries. This was the period that produced the most spectacular of the many finds made in Sudanese Nubia: the cathedral at Faras with its splendid frescoes of the Byzantine school.

The foregoing summary seen as a chronological progression gives the impression of a succession of disconnected episodes in human affairs and, indeed, this has long been the accepted interpretation of Nubian history. It stems from Reisner's discoveries and the conclusions drawn from them at the beginning of the First Archaeological Survey in 1907, and it appeared to be confirmed by Emery's findings of the Second Survey in the 1930s. Reisner's use of the term "group" itself indicates the acceptance of separate and distinctive cultures. However, the UNESCO Campaign, by filling many blanks in the story, seems rather to reveal in Nubian history a sense of continuity over the millennia, a picture of on-going life and a more or less unbroken cultural development. A vigorous culture from outside the Valley occasionally superimposes itself on the indigenous population to form an elitist governing class, until eventually it is itself absorbed or superceded. At various periods there would also be the gradual movement of peoples into Nubia from the south or from the surrounding deserts.

The indications in Nubia and the conclusions to be drawn from them are very much in line with modern views of population shifts in ancient times. Any marked change in a cultural pattern used to be interpreted as a mass exodus of one population to be replaced by another of different origin, but modern excavation techniques applied to material drawn from settlements as well as cemeteries point not to discontinuity but to continuous occupation or re-occupation of the same sites. Meinarti Island with its 1200 years of unbroken occupation was an excellent example. Adams finds it hard not to believe that in Nubia the people of any one "culture" felt a strong sense of identity with their predecessors. There seems, therefore, little doubt that as far as the mass of the people of Nubia was concerned, the Meroites were ancestral to the X-Group who in turn fathered those who rejected paganism and became Christian. And if we go further back in time, we find marked cultural affinities between C-Group and A-Group while the A-Group in turn seem to have had cultural links with their neolithic predecessors.

Before 1960 it is doubtful whether one student of ancient history in ten had any knowledge of or interest in Nubia. If considered at all, it tended to be seen as a cultural backwater with little in it worthy of serious scholarship. It is an attitude that has been radically changed by the discoveries of the many expeditions who worked in the area in the 1960s. Nubia, and I refer now to Sudanese Nubia, is likely to become a subject for serious study in its own right, but it will be oriented to Africa rather than the Mediterranean. Most of the excavations of earlier years were conducted by Egyptologists seeking for evidence of Egypt's activities in Nubia, and the attitude they tended to adopt is well illustrated by Reisner's own view of Nubia:

> "Wretched Nubia" . . . was then at first a part of Egypt. After the First Dynasty it was only an appendage of the greater country, and its history is hardly more than an account of its use or neglect

> by Egypt. . . Its very race appears to be a product of its poverty and isolation—a negroid Egyptian mixture fused together on a desert river bank too far away and too poor to attract a stronger and a better race.

That interpretation of Nubia's place in the history of the Nile Valley is no longer acceptable. Nubia was part of the corridor which linked the Mediterranean with inner Africa. Egypt was an intruder, a foreign element; the indigenous cultures were all African in origin: A-Group, C-Group, Napatan, Meroitic and X-Group and it therefore follows that the discoveries made in the 1960s will become meaningful only when they are traced back to their centres of origin. That section of Nubia to go under the waters of the reservoir was little more than a rather poor frontier area on the fringes of the great cultural impulses, all of which had their centres of origin up river. And it is there that we should follow them in an archaeological march up the Nile to the Third Cataract, and beyond to the Fourth, Fifth and Sixth Cataracts. Here, in the middle reach of the Nile, we may expect to find the really significant Kerma, Napatan and Meroitic settlements. Moreover we should move south along the Wadi-el-Milk into Central Sudan, and westward across the Sahara to Chad and the lands bordering the Atlantic. Other exploration in the direction of the Red Sea would search for the old trade routes to Arabia, India and the Far East. Here is a pattern of exploration that could establish links between the ancient and diversified cultures of Africa, links not now apparent. Some of those African peoples of the Middle Nile Valley have left evidence enough to demonstrate their far from negligible achievements in the arts of civilisation; their influence on surrounding cultures must have been considerable and it is important to trace by archaeological exploration the paths and extent of its diffusion.

The Nubian Campaign may not have given many solutions to long debated problems, yet it has opened a door through which new vistas can be glimpsed. For the historian in search of Africa's lost history the Sudan offers exciting possibilities; for the field archaeologist it offers positive advantages, because here he will find virgin territory. It has long been the complaint of archaeologists digging in Egypt and elsewhere in the Middle East that virtually every worthwhile site has been worked over before by professional or illegal diggers—usually both. Consequently the stratification that every field archaeologist seeks is often so disturbed as to be useless. Not so in the Sudan. Neglected by all but a handful of devoted scholars, unattractive to international tourism because of the heat and difficulties in internal travel, this vast sprawling country is unspoiled as far as field archaeology is concerned. The Sudan is rich in sites that have never been touched—the Second Cataract region was an example. Those sites that were excavated have been dug once, and then only partially cleared—Kerma and Napata are good examples. In the Sudan the field archaeologist can approach a new dig confident in the knowledge that all the evidence is still *in situ,* moreover he will not be subject to the pressures of salvage archaeology that he may well find elsewhere. An excellent example of archaeological conditions in the Sudan is provided by the excavations carried out at Solb by the Schiff-Giorgini Mission. For nine years they excavated and recorded a single temple built by the Eighteenth Dynasty Pharaoh Amenhotep III, in honour of Amun-Ré. Located in a sandy desert 110 miles up-stream from Semna, Solb was in scale and magnificence, comparable with the great temples of Thebes. Although much of the masonry above ground had been removed for building stone, the foundations had never been disturbed or the temple overbuilt; thus for probably the only time in the history of Egyptology was it possible to follow a great Egyptian temple through the many stages of its growth and thereby to learn something of the abstruse religious ritual associated with its construction.

Here is the unhurried, thoughtful, approach to excavation that salvage archaeology cannot provide. Nevertheless with society set on a course of urban expansion and maximum exploitation of natural resources, salvage archaeology is not only here to stay but is bound to increase as more and more sites come under threat of destruction. Undoubtedly salvage archaeology has helped to revitalise archaeology *per se* by obliging the excavator to sample everything he excavates and thus extract the full record, rather than restricting himself to those elements that happen to fall within his special field of interest. Still, to quote Professor Adams: "It will indeed be an evil day for archaeology if it becomes entirely salvage and we have no more option to pick and choose and follow problems as we would like."

Archaeology itself is changing. It is embracing ever more and varied disciplines and seeks to use increasingly refined techniques as they become available through scientific discovery. Nowadays we hear much of the "new archaeology" which uses devices such as statistical analysis and mathematical models; its adherents see man as part of an ecosystem and seek to explain the behaviour of our forefathers in terms of the environment that shaped their attitudes and responses. Thus to a modern archaeologist the value of an artefact lies in the relationship it has to the circumstances of its time, insofar as he can ascertain them. Should the bowl or article of adornment have intrinsic beauty so much the better, but that is a secondary consideration; it becomes a clue, just one of the many, to the social organisation and cultural patterns, institutions and external relations of earlier civilisations, and at other levels, of communities and individual men and women. This is an approach that favours salvage archaeology, which is just as well in the present climate of exploitation for material gain. As man flexes his technological muscles we can expect to see salvage operations on a wider scale than that of Nubia, embracing possibly the territories of several countries. Inevitably UNESCO will become involved because it is the only organisation in existence with the prestige, the size and the diplomatic experience to organise archaeology on an intergovernmental level. Moreover the Nubian Campaign has given the Organisation considerable expertise in what was, after all, a totally new field of international cooperation.

The campaign in Nubia was an invaluable proving ground and from it many conclusions can be drawn for future application—or avoidance. The salvaging of the temples, in particular Abu Simbel, was a magnificent effort, and full credit for organising and carrying through that side of the Campaign must to to UNESCO. The Nubian experience was shared and supported by many nations and thus was a complete vindication of the "heritage of mankind" concept which UNESCO has canvassed over the years and which sought to establish world responsibility for the preservation of great monuments of the past, irrespective of where they happened to be located. The result has been the involvement of UNESCO in other large conservation programmes, notably the preservation of Venice and Isfahan, cities of surpassing beauty which are now threatened by industrial development. Other campaigns recently promoted are for the saving of the Philae temples in Egypt and the conservation of Hannibal's city of Carthage in Tunisia. All these are conservation programmes which have heavy financial implications and are therefore amenable to administrative procedures. Salvage archaeology is a very different matter. Here we are not concerned with the protection of cultural treasures but are seeking to extract from the ground knowledge of the past before it is lost forever. For the field archaeologists real difficulties arose during the campaign, problems which were never tackled, simply because the machinery to do so did not exist. Very properly the Nubian Executive Committee concentrated its efforts on the major task of temple conservation, so that the special needs and problems of the archaeological aspect of the campaign were not fully appreciated, and this gave rise to criticism from leaders of expeditions who would have liked to see a more logical coordination and distribution of field operations. UNESCO can hardly be blamed for its failure to meet this need because it was not geared to the handling of archaeological problems, not to mention archaeologists, who are not the easiest of people to satisfy. Archaeology is really a generic term for a group of loosely related disciplines which do not always see eye to eye or work in harmony. An experienced field archaeologist stationed at headquarters in Paris from the outset would have been a useful buffer between scholars and administrators. Eventually one was appointed—Louis Christophe, who was transferred from Cairo to supervise the Nubian Unit.

In salvage archaeology, where funds and expertise are likely to be in short supply, a means must be devised to ensure that conservation and excavation each get a fair proportion of what is available. The first and most important step would be to persuade the many institutions concerned with archaeology in its broadest sense to establish an international association of archaeologists who would be willing to cooperate in salvage operations. To this Association would be affiliated the Antiquities Departments of individual countries, or their equivalents. Something of the kind was done immediately after the Second World War when one of the first tasks laid upon the embryonic UNESCO was the creation of the International Council of Scientific Unions, which played a major role in re-activating world science after five years of stagnation. A similar association of archaeological bodies would be of great benefit to archaeology *per se* which, while regarding itself as a science, is almost alone in the many-faceted world of science in having no professional association of its own. An international body of the kind suggested could work with UNESCO in close partnership, and one can envisage "task forces" of archaeologists or civil engineers moving into a threatened area when the call for help comes. There they would conduct a rapid survey and from it would come recommendations for the resources, human and material, needed to deal with the emergency. A system of this nature has been in existence for some years in UNESCO's Division of Earth Sciences; around the world small groups of scientists and engineers stand ready to take off for the scene of an earthquake or flood disaster when alerted from Paris.

Among field expeditions tied to a deadline there could be more effective ways of organising, operating and reporting their activities. Experience in Nubia suggests that much could be done to streamline work in the field, particularly in the time-consuming chore of recording excavations. This is a subject for research which initially could be based on the pooling of ideas from among scholars of many countries with expertise in field archaeology. Salvage archaeology is likely to have a strong appeal for young people and "crash" courses for them could be organised to help relieve pressure on the professionals. Fellowships could be granted to those youngsters intending to make archaeology their life's work while others could be attached to the task forces to acquire practical training in the special needs of salvage archaeology.

In short, every effort should be made to enlist the enthusiasm of youth and bring to bear the idealism and vitality of young people on this growing cultural problem of our time.

The foregoing are only a few of the possibilities open to us. Individual countries can do much but in the long run the major responsibility is with the international community, in particular with the industrialised countries. They have a moral obligation to recognise the difficulties of the less-developed nations whose meagre resources are needed for the pressing problems of present and future and can be ill-spared for preserving the record of their past, no matter how glorious.

Between the launching of the Nubian Campaign by UNESCO's Director General and the departure of the last expedition from that ill-fated land lie ten years of international endeavour such as the world has rarely witnessed. Nubia offered unusual possibilities to archaeology and those possibilities were amply fulfilled; it demanded of those who were there the meticulous care that modern archaeological methods impose on field work, yet at the same time all were driven in their efforts by an unaccustomed urgency forced upon them by the impending destruction of the scene of their labours.

For those who sense such things, Nubia could cast a spell as hard to resist as it was difficult to pin down. There was the contrast between the Nile boiling through its Cataracts and the immobility of the deserts that enfolded it; there was the Nubian presence, calm and unhurried, in a pattern of living hallowed by practices as old as the river itself; there were the ancient settlements and places of worship, the fortresses and the graves, all indistinguishable in terms of time from the villages of our day, so that past and present, like life and death in Nubia, seemed never far apart. It was a disturbing magic because it induced a kind of topsy-turveydom, a feeling that this was the real world and that other world outside had no more substance than a half-remembered dream. Scattered around our problem-ridden planet are a few hundred men and women who had the good fortune to experience the unique flavour of Nubia in its closing years. I count myself favoured to have been among them.

Chronological Table

Events printed in italic type relate directly to a specific ruler

PREHISTORIC

Dates BC (approx.)	*Principal Events*
pre-50,000	Palaeolithic hunters roaming Nubian plateau for savanna type animals seemingly in abundance. Moderate climate with rainfall.
45,000	Mesolithic Age in Nubia.
25,000–4000	Upper and Final Stone Ages in Nubia.
25,000	Formation of Nile bed in Nubia.
13,000	Grindstones in use in Nubia.
7,500	Africa's earliest dated rock drawing at Abka in Second Cataract.
4,500	Nubian Ceramic Age.
3,200	Emergence of neolithic A-Group Culture in Nubia.

ARCHAIC PERIOD

Dynasties I & II

Dates BC (approx.)	Rulers	Principal Events
3000–2850 *1st Dynasty*	Narmer (Menes?) Aha	*Unification of Upper and Lower Egypt.* Founding of Memphis as capital city.
	Djer	*Military Expedition to Nubia*
	Wadjy (Zet) Udimu (Den) Adj-yib (Enizib) (Name in doubt) Kaa	Royal burials at Saqqara (Memphis). Emergence of A-Group people in Nubia.
2850–2700 *2nd Dynasty*	Nine kings	Stone masonry introduced in burial chambers. Further military expeditions to Nubia.

OLD KINGDOM

Dynasties III–VI

Dates BC (approx.)	Rulers	Principal Events
2700–2600 *3rd Dynasty*	Sa-nekht	*First widespread use of stone for building and sculpture.*
	Neter-khet (Zozer)	*Step Pyramid at Saqqara (first stone pyramid).*
	Sekhem-khet Kha-ba Neb-ka Huni	
2600–2500 *4th Dynasty*	Sneferu	*Marauding Expedition to Nubia* *Pyramid at Meydum.*
	Khufu (Cheops)	*Great Pyramid at Giza*
	Didufre (Rededef)	Egyptian Copper smelting town at Buhen
	Khafra (Chephren)	*Sphinx and Pyramid at Giza.*
	Menkaure (Mycerinus)	
	Shepseskaf	Trading voyages to Lebanon. Full flowering of Old Kingdom-civilisation; highest peak of art–and literature.

Continued

2500–2340 *5th Dynasty*	Userkaf Sahure Neferirkare Shepseskare Neferefre Neuserre Menkauhor Asosi (Isesy) Unis	Magnificent sculpture in wood and stone. Expeditions to Punt (Somaliland?)
2340–2180 *6th Dynasty*	Teti Userkare Pepi I Merenre	Princes of Elephantine. Trading and military expeditions south, up the Nile. Expeditions to Punt and Lebanon.
	Pepi II	*Longest reign in history, 90-odd years.*

FIRST INTERMEDIATE PERIOD

Dynasties VII–X

2180–2050 *7th Dynasty to 10th Dynasty*		Cattle breeding C-Group people appear in Nubia. Disintegration of Kingdom into warring city states; period of social and religious disillusion. End of A-Group people.

MIDDLE KINGDOM

Dynasties XI–XIII

2134–1990 *11th Dynasty*	Several kings reigning concurrently with kings of 10th Dynasty, the last two being:	
	Mentu-hotep I	*Reunification of Egypt.*
	Mentu-hotep II	Egyptian movement in Nubia. Large irrigation schemes, particularly in Fayum. Campaigns into Kush.
1990–1785 *12th Dynasty*	Amenemhet I	*Building of Second Cataract fortresses.*
	Senusret I (Sesostris)	
	Amenemhet II	Egyptian trading post at Kerma, above Third Cataract.
	Senusret II	

Continued

	Senusret III	Southern frontier fixed at Semna. *Possible damming of*
	Amenemhet III	*Nile at Semna and flood control of Second Cataract.*
	Amenemhet IV	Rise of Babylon to supremacy in Mesopotamia.
	Sebeknofru (Queen)	Trade between Egypt and Syria and Aegean. Gold mines in Kush exploited

SECOND INTERMEDIATE PERIOD

Dynasties XIII–XVII

1785–1570 *13th Dynasty to 17th Dynasty*	Large number of petty rulers ending with	Disintegration of central authority, resulting in easy conquest of Egypt by the Hyksos-an Asiatic people. Second Cataract Forts still manned.
	Kamose	*Nubian kinglet at Buhen.* Second Cataract Forts stormed and burned.

NEW KINGDOM (EMPIRE PERIOD)

Dynasties XVIII–XX

1570–1310 *18th Dynasty*	Ahmose Amenhotep I Thutmose I Thutmose II Hatshepsut (Queen)	*Expulsion of Hyksos from Egypt.* Nubian gold, slaves and African commodities now key-pin of Egyptian economy. Nubian soldiers in Egyptian Army.
	Thutmose III	Southern frontier fixed at Fourth Cataract.
	Amenhotep II Thutmose IV Amenhotep III	Second Cataract Forts rebuilt. Nubia (Kush) now an Egyptian province under a Viceroy. C-group people of Nubia culturally absorbed by Egypt. Introduction of new bronze weapons, horse and chariot. Capital at Thebes. Rise to power of Theban god Amun.

Continued

		Peak of Egyptian wealth and power with most of ancient world under Egyptian domination. Consequent mixing of Egyptian and Asian cultures culminating in glories of the Amarna Age.
	Amenhotep IV (Akhenaten)	*Feud of Akhenaten with Amun priesthood and introduction of monotheistic Aten worship, preaching "Living in Truth" and brotherhood of man. Moves capital from Thebes to City of Horizon (Amarna).* *Asiatic vassal-states in revolt.*
	Smenkhkere	Rise of Hittite Confederation. Destruction of Minoan (Cretan) civilisation.
	Tutankhamun	*Abandons Aten, and restores official worship of Amun and returns to Thebes.*
	Ay	Diminishing influence of Egypt in Asia. Nubia remains stable.
	Horemheb	*Attempt to restore dwindling empire.*
1310–1184 *19th Dynasty*	Rameses I	Hittites challenged in Syria.
	Seti I	
	Rameses II	*Battle of Kadesh in Syria.* *Uneasy truce with Hittites culminating in treaty and later marriage of Pharaoh with Hittite Princess.* *Capital moved from Thebes to Delta (Pi-Rameses).* *Great building activity including Abu Simbel and other temples in Nubia.* *Legend of Rameses the "Great" established by end of 67-year reign.*
	Merenptah	Fall of Troy.
	Seti II	
	Amenmesse	
	Siptah	

Continued

	3 minor kings and Tausre (Queen)	
1184–1080 *20th Dynasty*	Set-nakht Rameses III–XI	Decline in prestige of kingship. Eclipse of the Hittite Confederation. Loss of dependent states in Asia. Repulse of Libyans and "Sea-peoples". Royal tomb robberies at Thebes. Napatan line of kings established at Gebel Barkal near Fourth Cataract and Temple to Amun built. Archaeological record in Nubia goes blank.

THE LATE PERIOD

Dynasties XXI–XXXI

1080–940 *21st Dynasty*	Seven kings	Kings in Delta and at Thebes. Dorian invasion of Greece.
940–730 *22nd Dynasty* *23rd Dynasty*	Twelve kings of Libyan origin including Sheshonq and Osorkon	Kush independent. Temple at Jerusalem sacked.
730–715 *24th Dynasty*	Two kings	Deterioration of Egyptian religion and government provokes intervention of Kush. Growth of Assyrian power.
730–663 *25th Dynasty*	Piankhy	*Kushite kings in Napata move into Egypt to re-establish lost Egyptian virtues and revive religious beliefs.* *Piankhy proclaimed King of Upper and Lower Egypt.*
	Shabaka Shebitku Taharqa	Capital at Napata (in Kush) Thebes and Tanis. Invasion of Egypt by Assyrians (671)

Continued

		Sack of Thebes and expulsion of Kushites by Ashurbanipal (663)
	Tanutamun	*Kushites finally withdraw south to Napata.*
663–525 *26th Dynasty*	Psamtik I Necho	Independence from Assyria. Trade with Greece.
	Psamtik II	*Greek mercenaries on military expedition into Kush.*
	Apries Amasis Psamtik III	Kushite capital transferred south from Napata to Meroë. Destruction of Jerusalem and end of Kingdom of Judah.
525–404 *27th Dynasty* *(Persians)*	Cambyses	*Conquest of Egypt.* *Abortive Expedition to Kush (Meroë).*
	Darius I Xerxes Artaxerxes Darius II	Rise of Greek resistance to Persia. Meroitic Empire. Influence spreads in Africa through iron-working.
404–341 *28th Dynasty to* *30th Dynasty*	Ephemeral native rulers, the last being Nectanebo II	Liberation from Persia with Greek aid.
341–332 *31st Dynasty* *(Persians)*		Second Persian conquest of Egypt.
	THE GRAECO-ROMAN PERIOD	
332–323 *32nd Dynasty*	Alexander the Great Philip Arrchidaios Alexander II	*Founding of Alexandria as capital city.*
305–30 *33rd Dynasty*	Ptolemy Soter—one of Alexander's generals—founds Ptolemaic line of 15 rulers ending with death of Cleopatra	Alexandria becomes centre of learning. Great library founded there and Pharos built. Eratosthenes uses the well at Elephantine successfully to measure dimensions of the earth.

Continued

		Rival priesthoods of Khnum at Elephantine and Isis at Philae claim Dodekaschoinos (80-mile stretch of Lower Nubia).
c.100		*Introduction of Saqia wheel which restores life to Nubia.*
Rome in Egypt 30 BC–AD 641	Octavian (Agustus Caesar) conquers Egypt. Thereafter Emperors govern from Rome then from Byzantium	Kushite attacks on frontier end in defeat of Candace and destruction of Napata. Blemmyes and Nobatae in conflict with Rome in Lower Nubia.

Date AD	*Principal Events*
3rd–6th centuries	X-Group culture in Nubia. Tombs of X-Group kings at Ballana and Qustol. Break-up of Meroitic Empire. Silko defeats Blemmyes.
c. 540	Temples of Isis finally closed by Emperor Justinian and Nubia converted to Christianity.
641	Egypt submits to Arabs and Islam but Nubia remains Christian.
c. 700	Three Christian kingdoms established along Nile between modern Khartoum and Assuan with Pachoras (Faras) as Capital of Nobatia (the northernmost). Cathedral at Pachoras dedicated. Nubian population increases and prospers. Much building of churches.
1372	Bishop enthroned at Ibrim, but Christianity under great pressure from Islam, lingering on in pockets of the Second Cataract until beginning of sixteenth century.

Bibliography

Adams, William Y., "Post pharaonic Nubia in the light of archaeology" (*Journal of Egyptian Archaeology*, Oxford University Press, Vol. 50, 1964)

— "Organizational Problems in International Salvage Archaeology" (*Anthropological Quarterly*, Vol. 41, No. 3, July 1968, U.S.A.)

— "Settlement Pattern in Microcosm: The changing aspect of a Nubian village during Twelve Centuries" (*Settlement Archaeology*, ed. K. C. Chang, Palo Alto, Calif. National Press Books 1968)

— "Invasion, Diffusion, Evolution?" (*Antiquity*, Vol. XLII, 1968)

— "The University of Kentucky Excavations at Kulubnarti 1969" (Erschienen 1970 Im Verlag Aurel Bongers Recklinghausen)

— "The Evolution of Christian Nubian Pottery" (Erschienen 1970 Im Verlag Aurel Bongers Reclkinghausen)

— "Architectural Evolution of the Nubian Church, 500–1400 AD" (*Journal of the American Research Centre in Egypt*, Vol. IV 1965)

— "The Christian Potteries at Faras" (*Kush*, Vol. IX, 1961)

— "Pottery Kiln Excavations" (*Kush*, Vol. X, 1962)

— "An Introductory Classification of Christian Nubian Pottery" (*Kush*, Vol. X, 1962)

— "An Introductory Classification of Meroitic Pottery" (*Kush*, Vol. XII, 1964)

— "Sudan Antiquities Service Excavations in Nubia: Fourth Season 1962-63" (*Kush*, Vol. XII, 1964)

— "Sudan Antiquities Service Excavations at Meinarti 1963-64" (*Kush*, Vol. XIII, 1965)

— "The Vintage of Nubia" (*Kush*, Vol. XIV, 1966)

Adams, W. Y. and Allen, P. E. T., "The Aerial Survey" (*Kush*, Journal of the Sudan Antiquities Service, Vol. IX, 1961)

Adams, W. Y. and Nordström, H. A., "Archaeological Survey on West Bank of Nile, Third Season, 1961-62 (*Kush*, Vol. XI, 1963)

Aldred, Cyril, *Egypt to the End of the Old Kingdom* (Thames & Hudson, London, 1965)

Almagro, M., Presedo, F., Pellicer, M., "Preliminary Report of Spanish Excavations in the Sudan, 1961-62 (*Kush*, Vol. XI, 1963)

Amelagos, S. J., Ewing, G. H., Greene, D. L. and Greene, K. K., "Report of Physical Anthropology Section, University of Colorado Nubian Expedition" (*Kush,* Vol. XIII, 1965)

Antiquity, Vol. XLV, No. 180, December 1971, Editorial in

Arkell, A. J., *A History of the Sudan to 1831* (University of London, Athlone Press, 1961)

– "An Egyptian Invasion of the Sudan in 591 BC" (*Kush,* Vol. III, 1955)

Badawy, Alexander, "Askut: A Middle Kingdom Fortress in Nubia" (*Archaeology,* Vol. 18, No. 2, June 1965)

– "Preliminary Report of University of California Expedition at Askut, October 1962–January 1963" (*Kush,* Vol. XII, 1964)

Baikie, James, *The Amarna Age* (A. & C. Black, London, 1926)

– *Egyptian Antiquities in the Nile Valley* (Methuen 1932)

Bakr, Mohammed, "Relationship between C-Group, Kerma, Napatan and Meroitic Cultures (*Kush,* Vol. XIII, 1965)

Blanco y Caro, R and Presedo Velo, F., "Spanish Archaeological Mission to Argin–First Preliminary Report" (*Kush,* Vol. X, 1962)

Breasted, James Henry, *A History of Egypt* (Hodder & Stoughton, 1945, originally published by Charles Scribner's Sons, N.Y. 1905)

Caminos, R. A. "Surveying Semna Gharbi" (*Kush,* Vol. XII, 1964)

The Army in Ancient Egypt (Centre of Documentation and Studies on Ancient Egypt, Cairo)

Černý, Jaroslav, *Ancient Egyptian Religion* (Hutchinsons University Library, 1952)

Christophe, Louis "Sanctuaires Nubiens Disparus" (*Nubie*–Tome X des *Cahiers d'Histoire Egyptienne*)

Davis, Hester A. "Is there a Future for the Past?" (*Archaeology*–Archaeological Institute of America, October 1971, Vol. 24, No. 4)

Dows Dunham "The Harvard-Boston Archaeological Expedition in the Sudan" (*Kush,* Vol. III, 1955)

Edwards, Amelia B. *A Thousand Miles up the Nile* (George Routledge & Sons Ltd. 1891)

Edwards, I. E. S., *The Pyramids of Egypt* (Max Parrish 1961)

Emery, W. B., *Archaic Egypt* (Pelican Books 1961)

– *Egypt in Nubia* (Hutchinson, 1965)

– "A Preliminary Report on Excavations at Buhen" (*Kush,* Vol. VII, 1959)

– "Preliminary Report on the Excavations of the Egypt Exploration Society at Buhen 1958-59" (*Kush,* Vol. VIII, 1960)

– "Preliminary Report on Excavations of the Egypt Exploration Society at Buhen 1959-60" (*Kush,* Vol. IX, 1961)

– "Egypt Exploration Society: Preliminary Report on Excavations at Buhen 1960-61" (*Kush,* Vol. X, 1962)

– "Egypt Exploration Society: Preliminary Report at Buhen 1962" (*Kush,* Vol. XI, 1963)

– "Egypt Exploration Society: Preliminary Report on Work at Buhen 1962-63" (*Kush,* Vol. XII, 1964)

– Reports of the work of the Egypt Exploration Society (*Antiquity*, Vol. XXXVIII, No. 149, Vol. XXXIX, No. 153, Vol. XL, No. 158, Vol. XLI, No. 162)

Emery W. B. and Kirwan, L. P., *The Excavations and Survey between Wadi es Sebua and Adindan 1929-31* Vols. 1 and 2 (Service des Antiquités de l'Egypte, Cairo 1935)

– *The Royal Tombs of Ballana and Qustal 1929-1934* Vols. 1 and 2 (Service des Antiquités de l'Egypte, Cairo 1938)

Erman, A., *The Literature of the Ancient Egyptians.* Translated by Blackman (London 1927)

Fairbridge, R. W., "Nile Sedimentation above Wadi Halfa during last 20,000 years" (*Kush*, Vol. XI, 1963)

Gardiner, Sir Alan, *Egypt of the Pharaohs* (Oxford University Press 1961)

Griffith, F. Ll., "Oxford Excavations in Nubia" (*Liverpool Annals of Archaeology and Anthropology*, 1921-23, 1928)

Habachi, Labib, "The Administration of Nubia during the New Kingdom, with special reference to discoveries made during the last few years"

– "The First Two Viceroys of Kush and Their Family" (*Kush*, Vol. VII, 1959)

Hawkes, Jacquetta and Woolley, Sir Leonard, *Prehistory and the Beginnings of Civilisation* (UNESCO/George Allen & Unwin, 1963)

Hewes, G. W., "Gezira Dabarosa: Report of the University of Colorado Nubian Expedition 1962-63 Season" (*Kush*, Vol. XII, 1964)

– "Prehistoric Investigations of West Bank in the Batn el Hagar by University of Colorado Expedition" (*Kush*, Vol. XIV, 1966)

Hinkel, F., Report on Dismantling and Removal of Endangered Monuments in Sudanese Nubia 1962-63 (*Kush*, Vol. XII, 1964)

– Progress Report on Dismantling and Removal of Endangered Monuments in Sudanese Nubia from August 1963 to August 1964 (*Kush*, Vol. XIII, 1965)

Hintze F., Preliminary Note on Epigraphic Expedition to Sudanese Nubia 1963 (*Kush*, Vol. XII, 1964)

– Preliminary Note on Epigraphic Expedition to Sudanese Nubia 1964 (*Kush*, Vol. XIII, 1965)

Hughes, G. R., Serra East: University of Chicago Excavations 1961-62: A Preliminary Report (*Kush*, Vol. XI, 1963)

Irwin, H. T. and Wheat, J. B., Report of the Palaeolithic Section, University of Colorado Nubian Expedition (*Kush*, Vol. XIII 1965)

Keating, Rex, *Nubian Twilight* (Rupert Hart-Davis, 1962)

– "Digging for History" (*UNESCO Courier*, November 1962)

– "Return to the Land of Kush" (*UNESCO Courier*, December 1964)

– UNESCO Features, No. 549, April 11, 1969

Kerkegi, Max, "Les Nubiens au Caire" (*Nubie*—Tome X des *Cahiers d'Histoire Egyptienne*)

Kirwan, L. P., "Comments on Origins—History of the Nobatae of Procopius" (*Kush,* Vol. VI, 1958)

Knudstad, J., "Serra East and Dorginarti" (*Kush,* Vol. XIV, 1966)

Kronenberg, A. and W., Preliminary Report on Anthropological Field Work 1961-62 in Sudanese Nubia (*Kush,* Vol. XI, 1963)

— Preliminary Report on Anthropological Field-Work in Sudanese Nubia 1962-63 (*Kush,* Vol. XII, 1964)

— Preliminary Report on Anthropological Field Work in Sudanese Nubia, 1964 (*Kush*, Vol. XIII, 1965)

Lawrence, A. W., "Ancient Egyptian Fortifications" (*Journal of Egyptian Archaeology,* Vol. 51, 1965)

Meinardus, Otto F. A., "The Christian Kingdoms of Nubia" (*Nubie*—Tome X des *Cahiers d'Histoire Egyptienne*)

Michalowski, Casimir, "New Discoveries at Faras in Nubia" (*Archaeology,* June 1962, Vol. 15, No. 2)

— "Polish Excavations at Faras 1961" (*Kush,* Vol. X, 1962)

— "Polish Excavations at Faras—Second Season 1961-62" (*Kush,* Vol. XI, 1963)

— "Polish Excavations at Faras 1962-63" (*Kush,* Vol. XII, 1964)

— "Polish Excavations at Faras—Fourth Season 1963-64" (*Kush,* Vol. XIII, 1965)

— "Polish Excavations at Old Dongola: First Season, Nov.-Dec. 1964" (*Kush,* Vol. XIV, 1966)

Mills, A. J., Reconnaissance Survey from Gemai to Dal—Preliminary Report for 1963-64 (*Kush,* Vol. XIII, 1965)

Mills, A. J. and Nordström, H. A., Archaeological Survey from Gemai to Dal. Preliminary Report of Season 1964-65 (*Kush,* Vol. XIV, 1966)

Mus'ad Mustafa, M., "Islam in Mediaeval Nubia" (*Nubie*—Tome X des *Cahiers d'Histoire Egyptienne*)

Myers, O. H. "Abka re-excavated" (*Kush,* Vol. VI, 1958)

Nordström, H. A., Excavations and Survey in Faras, Argin and Dabarosa (*Kush,* Vol. X, 1962)

— A-Group and C-Group in Upper Nubia (*Kush,* Vol. XIV, 1966)

Reisner, G. A., "Clay Sealings of Dynasty XIII from Uronarti Fort" (*Kush,* Vol. III 1955)

— "The Egyptian Forts from Halfa to Semna" (*Kush,* Vol. VIII, 1960)

— *Excavations at Kerma* (Harvard African Studies, Vols. V & VI, Cambridge, Mass. 1923)

Rosenvasser, A., Preliminary Report on Excavations at Aksha by Franco-Argentine Expedition 1962-63 (*Kush,* Vol. XII, 1964)

Ruby, J. W., Preliminary Report of University of California Expedition to Dabnarti 1963 (*Kush,* Vol. XII, 1964)

Säve-Söderbergh, Torgny, *Pharaohs and Mortals* (Robert Hale, 1963, first published in Sweden)

— *"A Buhen Stela from the Second Intermediate Period" (Journal of Egyptian Archaeology,* London, 1949)

– "Preliminary Report of Scandinavian Joint Expedition" (*Kush*, Vol. X, 1962)

– "Preliminary Report of Scandinavian Joint Expedition; investigations between Faras and Gemai" (*Kush*, Vol. XI, 1963)

– "Tomb of Prince of Teh-Khet, Amenemhet", (*Kush*, Vol. XI, 1963)

– "Preliminary Report of Scandinavian Joint Expedition: Investigations between Faras and Gemai" (*Kush*, Vol. XII, 1964) (*Kush*, Vol. XII, 1964)

Schiff-Giorgini, M., "Soleb Campaigns 1961-63" (*Kush*, Vol. XII, 1964)

– "First Campaign of Excavations at Sedeinga, 1963-64 (*Kush*, Vol. XIII, 1965)

– Sedeinga, 1964-65 (*Kush*, Vol. XIV, 1966)

Shinnie, P. L. "Meroë, a Civilisation of the Sudan" (Thames & Hudson, 1967)

– "The Fall of Meroë (*Kush*, Vol. III, 1955)

– "University of Ghana Excavations at Debeira West (*Kush*, Vol. XI, 1963)

– "University of Ghana Excavation at Debeira West 1963 (*Kush*, Vol. XII, 1964)

– "University of Ghana Excavations at Debeira West, 1964 (*Kush*, Vol. XIII, 1965)

Shorter, Alan W., *The Egyptian Gods*, (Kegan, Paul, Trench, Trubner & Co. Ltd., 1937)

Smith, H. F. C., "Transfer of Capital of Kush from Napata to Meroë" (*Kush*, Vol. III, 1955)

Smith, H. S., "The Nubian B-Group" (*Kush*, Vol. XIV, 1966)

– "Report on Excavations of Egypt Exploration Society at Kor, 1965" (*Kush*, Vol. XIV, 1966)

Solecki, R. S., "Preliminary Statement of Prehistorical Investigations of Columbia University Nubian Expedition in Sudan 1961-62" (*Kush*, Vol. XI, 1963)

Stordy, John, "Journey into a New Life" (*Freedom from Hunger News*, FAO, Sept/Oct. 1964)

UNESCO "A Common Trust: The Preservation of the Ancient Monuments of Nubia"

Numerous reports and Recommendations of the Executive Committee of the International Campaign to save the monuments of Nubia

Vercoutter, Jean "La Nubie Soudanaise et le Nouveau Barrage d'Assouan" (*Etudes Archéologiques*, Paris 1963)

– "La Nubie au sud d'Abou Simbel" (*Journal des Savants*, juillet-sept. 1963)

– "Ancient Egyptian Influence in the Sudan (*Sudan Notes & Records*, Vol. XL, 1959)

– "La Stèle de Mirgissa et la Localisation d'Iken" (*La Société Française d'Egyptologie*—Tome 16)

– "Desert Highway Built for Ships" (*UNESCO Courier*, December 1964)

— "Excavations at Sai, 1955-57" (*Kush,* Vol. III, 1955)

— "The Gold of Kush" (*Kush,* Vol. VII, 1959)

— "Preliminary Report on Excavations at Aksha by the Franco-Argentine Archaeological Expedition" (*Kush*, Vol. X, 1962)

— "Excavations at Aksha Sept 1961-Jan 1962" (*Kush,* Vol. XI, 1963)

— "Excavations at Mirgissa, October—December 1962" (*Kush*, Vol. XII, 1964)

— "Excavations at Mirgissa, October 1963—March 1964" (*Kush,* Vol. XIII, 1965)

— "Semna South Fort and the Records of Nile Levels at Kumma" (*Kush,* Vol. XIV, 1966)

Vercoutter, Jean and Adams, W. Y., "Why Excavate in Sudanese Nubia?"

Verwers, G. J., "Archaeological Survey from Faras to Dabarosa" (*Kush,* Vol. X, 1962)

Vycichl, W., "The Burial of the Sudanese Kings" (*Kush,* Vol. VII, 1959)

Weigall, Arthur *The Glory of the Pharaohs* (Thornton Butterworth Ltd. London, 1923)

— *A Guide to the Antiquities of Upper Egypt* (Methuen 1910)

Wendorf, F., *The Pre-History of Nubia.* Papers assembled and edited by F. Wendorf. 2 vols. (Fort Burguin Research Centre and Southern Methodist University Press, Dallas, 1968)

Wendorf, F., Daugherty, R. D., Wechter, J., "Museum of New Mexico/Columbia University Nubian Expedition: 1962-63 Field Programme" (*Kush,* Vol. XII, 1964)

Wendorf, F., Shiner, J. L., Marks, A. E., de Heinzelin, J. and Chmielewski, W., "Combined Prehistoric Expedition: Summary of 1963-64 Field Season" (*Kush,* Vol. XIII, 1965)

Wendorf, F., Shiner, J. L., Marks, A. E., de Heinzelin, J., Chmielewski, W. and Schild, R., "1965 Field Season of Southern Methodist University" (*Kush,* Vol. XIV, 1966)

Wheeler, Noel F., "Diary of the Excavation of Mirgissa Fort" (*Kush,* Vol. IX, 1961)

Zernov, Nicholas *Eastern Christendom* (Weidenfeld & Nicholson, 1961)

Numerous interviews and observations recorded by the author in Nubia and elsewhere.

Index

Keating, Rex.

Nubian rescue / Rex Keating. -- London : R. Hale ; New York : Hawthorn Books, 1975.

xviii, 269 p., [12] leaves of plates : ill. ; 23 cm GB***

Bibliography: p. 252-257.
Includes index.
ISBN 0-8015-5469-1 (Hawthorn) : £3.80

1. Nubia--Antiquities. 2. Nubia--History I. Title

DT135.N8K39 1975 939'.78 75-321144
MARC

Library of Congress 75